Ask Me Why I Hurt

ASK ME WHY I HURT

The Kids Nobody Wants and the Doctor Who Heals Them

RANDY CHRISTENSEN, MD
WITH RENE DENFELD

BROADWAY PAPERBACKS | New York

Copyright © 2011 by Randy Christensen

Published in the United States by Broadway Books,
an imprint of the Crown Publishing Group,
a division of Random House, Inc., New York.
www.crownpublishing.com

BROADWAY BOOKS and the Broadway Books colophon
are trademarks of Random House, Inc.

Originally published in hardcover in the United States by
Broadway Books, an imprint of the Crown Publishing Group,
a division of Random House, Inc., New York, in 2011.

Library of Congress Cataloging-in-Publication Data
Christensen, Randy, Dr.
   Ask me why I hurt : the kids nobody wants and the
doctor who heals them / Randy Christensen with Rene
Denfeld.—1st ed.
      p.   cm.
   1. Homeless children—Medical care—Arizona.
2. Homeless children—Arizona. I. Denfeld, Rene.
II. Title.
   HV4506.A6C47 2011
   362.7—dc22
   [B]   2010039947

ISBN 978-0-307-71901-0
eISBN 978-0-307-71902-7

Printed in the United States of America

Book design by Cindy LaBreacht
Cover design by Dan Rembert
Cover photography by Troy Aossey

10   9   8   7   6   5   4

First Paperback Edition

TO OUR MOTHERS

JANE ROGERS ELLIS
11/10/1942 – 2/18/1984

MARIA CARMEN CHRISTENSEN
6/6/1944 – 12/16/2009

Randy & Amy Christensen

FOR MY CHILDREN

Luppi Milov, Tony, and Markel.
Because no child should go without a family.

Rene Denfeld

CONTENTS

A NOTE FROM THE AUTHOR

Dear Reader,

For many years now I have wanted to tell the stories in this book, *needed* to tell them. But having done so with similar stories in the past, I know the potential consequences. Years ago I introduced a reporter to a young street kid. She was eighteen years old and happily consented to an interview. Her story hit the papers and she was immediately and violently persecuted by some on the street. To this day I am still unsure what grave secret she disclosed. But to some people she knew, her disclosures mattered. I committed myself then to ensuring that such a situation would never arise again.

The stories here are true. The successes and the tragedies are all true. If anything I worry that I have not shed enough light on those dark places where we are all afraid to tread. In order to protect the kids involved, I have changed identifying characteristics such as their names, physical attributes, and identifying diagnoses. These children have already lost so much—the last thing I want is for them to lose their privacy as well. Instead I hope that this book will bring attention to their plight and in some way help to give them a chance at the good life they deserve.

—*Randy Christensen*

Ask Me Why I Hurt

1

CRISIS

When I first saw him, I could tell he was sick. His face was pale. The look in his eyes was vacant and confused. He held the side of the van wall, looking as if he were on the verge of collapse. His short brown hair was sweat stained. His wide mouth was rimmed in white, and his broad forehead was beaded with sweat.

He was wearing khaki trousers and a blue shirt that had the name of a tool company on the front. His arms were tanned; his face was broad with sun-bleached eyebrows and blue eyes. If I'd walked past him on the street, I would never have known he was homeless. He looked like your typical teenage boy, with an athletic build and a friendly smile, the kind of boy who could have been an all-star athlete or a gifted student or the editor of the school newspaper, if only he hadn't been sick and homeless. But he was homeless. And the day he came to the van, one late afternoon on a day blistering with heat, he was ready to die.

"Randy." It was my nurse-practitioner, Jan Putnam.

I had been in one of the van exam rooms, stocking supplies, and at the alarm in her voice I stuck my head out. I could tell immediately he was very ill.

I took three long steps to grab him. He fell limply against my shirt. My heart lurched, and I felt galvanized into action.

"Jan, let's get him in the back room. We need vitals right away." But she was already pulling out the equipment. She could always anticipate my thoughts.

The van was a mobile medical unit, as close to a real hospital as possible, if a hospital can be crammed into a Winnebago. The exam room was only feet away, down a tiny hallway. Everything was sparkling clean. I laid him down. He moaned, the paper cover on the exam table crackling under him. The white lights above were bright.

He looked defenseless in his blue shirt, baggy tan pants, and tennis shoes. It seemed like a lot of clothes to be wearing in an Arizona heat wave that was topping 108 degrees. "Tell me how you are feeling," I said, pulling on gloves.

"Sick, dude." He opened his bleary blue eyes at me. "Man, I'm tired. I've been sleeping now for . . . days." His voice trailed off. His skin was flushed, and I could feel the heat coming off him. It was probably from the sun. There was an underlying sweet smell of sickness on him. Sweat rolled down his cheeks, the tops of which were stained bright by fever.

"Sleeping where?" Jan asked, bustling around the exam room.

"Uh, under some bushes. Not far." He closed his eyes as if dizzy. "I can't even remember how I got here. Guess I walked." He made a small choking cough. "Dizzy."

"Just hang tight," I said soothingly. "We're going to take your vitals."

I started with his temperature. It was a 101—elevated. Maybe it's heatstroke, I thought. I took his heart rate. It was 112, also only slightly elevated. His blood pressure was next. It was perfectly normal, 110/75.

Confused, I removed the cuff. These were the vitals of a healthy person. This boy was presenting as extremely ill, yet his vitals were almost normal. I leaned over to look into his eyes. The pupils were dilated, outlined with a clear sky blue. His breathing was labored.

His chest rose and fell with effort. What was wrong with him? A hundred thoughts ran through my mind. Maybe it was drugs. Maybe it was the flu. Maybe it was food poisoning. Maybe it was an allergic reaction. No, that didn't fit.

Back at Phoenix Children's, the hospital where I worked, there would have been other doctors and nurses and lines of equipment for tests. We would have tackled this boy's sickness with all the power of an army. I'd have asked his parents everything I needed to know: How long has he been sick? Has he had any other symptoms? What has he eaten lately? Is there a chance he could be on drugs? Does he have any medical conditions?

But I wasn't in the hospital. I was in a mobile medical unit surrounded by empty lots in the middle of a rough area on the outskirts of town. The only things out here were sandy wastes, boarded-up houses, homeless kids, and the criminals who preyed on them. I was out here in a medical van with a patient I knew nothing about: no history, no known allergies, nothing.

He muttered something. His cheeks were starting to sink. I was watching him decline in front of me in a matter of seconds. His eyes flashed at me. I had seen this look before. It signaled profound distress, crisis. A wave of panic passed through me, and my mind raced. My experience as a doctor told me something was terribly wrong, even if his vital signs were not that abnormal.

I looked over at Jan. She was my BMX-riding, fiery red-haired nurse-practitioner who tolerated no cussing, no guff, and certainly no back talk. We had only just started our operation with the van, but already the homeless kids we treated loved her. She was watching the boy with concern and attention.

It came to me. "Let's do an orthostatic."

An orthostatic is a different kind of blood pressure test. Because young bodies are so strong, often they can mask the worst illnesses. Their blood vessels are elastic and will adapt and hide even bad infections. A child in the midst of shock can have perfectly normal vitals, which, in medical terms, is called compensated shock. It is something usually encountered only by pediatricians.

The problem is it can last until it is too late. By the time the victim crashes he or she is close to dying. By moving the boy from lying down to sitting up and then to standing up, I could break through his body's coping mechanisms.

I let him rest a moment. Then Jan helped me lift him to a sitting position. Up close he smelled of unwashed clothes, sweat, and hair that needed a shampoo. His carefully maintained appearance melted away up close, and it was clear now that he was homeless. To me it was the vulnerable smell of despair. He leaned against me in his weakness. When his head rolled against my arms, he felt like a large child in my arms. I helped him to a standing position. He wobbled on his feet.

Then I took his blood pressure again.

It had plummeted within moments.

"Oh, my," I said.

I took his pulse.

It had suddenly climbed to 150. I could almost see his heart racing in his chest.

"He's in shock. It's sepsis," I said quietly.

My voice was low, but I could hear the stress. The storm was taking place, and I was in the middle of it. Jan knew what those numbers meant. They were the vitals of a patient in severe crisis, a patient whose system was crashing. I could have just as easily said, "He's dying."

"Why?" Jan asked softly. The traces of silver in her red hair caught the light.

"Bacteremia, I'm guessing," I said. A huge blood infection.

I grabbed the stethoscope hanging around my neck and listened to his lungs. I had broken into a sudden sweat, and it was only the years of ingrained training that helped me stay calm. There it was, over the lung fields: a faint crackling like Rice Krispies. I held his wrist. His heart rate was climbing by the second. His body was done compensating. He was crashing. The boy who had weakly stepped into my van just minutes before was now moments from collapse and coma. If I didn't do something soon, he would die.

"I'm guessing a pneumonia," I said to Jan under my breath, "turned into a massive bacterial infection. The bacteria have spread, and they're in his blood now, all over." The blood vessels were leaking, like tiny hoses with holes in them. The leakage was making it impossible for his heart to take oxygen and nutrients to the rest of the body. He was going down rapidly, and what was I going to do? The boy's eyes, blind with confusion, looked up at me. His face was now covered with huge beads of sweat. I could see his heart pound in his chest. "Get the IV started," I heard myself saying. "Get some fluid in him. Vitamin R, quick."

"Large-bore?"

"Yes. Saline at the same time."

Jan was flying around the room. We both were in full emergency mode. The boy was losing fluid internally so rapidly that his veins had sunk deep inside his body. In seconds Jan had expertly located a vein, and the IV was up, delivering the strong antibiotic Rocephin into his system, along with saline. His body seemed to drink the fluids up. The next few minutes passed in a panic: I shouting orders, holding his wrist, talking to him; Jan on the phone to a hospital. The saline and antibiotic slipped into his body, and his cheeks slowly turned pink. His eyes opened and cleared, and his heart slowed. The antibiotics were fighting the front end of what might end up being a long war. But he was past the point of crisis.

Suddenly it was over. Maybe ten minutes had passed since Jan had called my name. The ambulance came screaming out to our deserted area and unloaded a stretcher. The boy was gone, on his way to the hospital.

I took a deep, shuddering breath. My hands were shaking. I held them out in front of my face. The daylight outside told me it had been a matter of minutes, not hours, since the boy had climbed our steps but it seemed like forever. The familiar metallic taste of stress was in my mouth. During an emergency I didn't feel things too closely. I couldn't afford to. But then afterward it all hit me. My skin tingled, and my heart lurched in my chest. Bottled-up adrenaline hit me like a wave. My skin was alive with nerves, and my stomach tightened. I felt as if I had been in a car accident. Oh, my God, I thought, that was close.

"That was close," I heard myself repeat out loud, as if from a faraway distance.

Jan looked dazed. "No kidding."

◻◻◻◻◻◻

It wasn't until that evening, when we shut down the mobile unit, that Jan and I talked about what had happened. My adrenaline was still running wild. There was the dark relief of knowing I had dodged a bullet, the skin-pricked elation and disbelief that come after ushering someone safely past the point of death. I kept thinking that boy had been so close to death he'd been touching it. But instead of reassuring me, the thought unsettled me. What if I hadn't reacted the same way? What if I had still been too late? He might be dying in the hospital right now. When seconds count, you examine each one critically. I kept replaying the events in my head. I felt uncertain. Did I get it right? Should I have done anything else? Maybe I should call the hospital and ask if I was right.

I paced the empty van, talking a mile a minute. The feelings came rushing out, and I talked in the way that doctors do when a crisis is past.

"Can you believe it, Jan? He was seconds away."

"Yes," she said softly.

"He could have *died*."

Jan touched my arm. "Are you OK?"

I wiped the sweat from my brow. "Yeah, I'm OK. I guess I just keep thinking, What if he hadn't come in at all? What if he had stayed under those bushes for just another hour or two?" Jan nodded along with me. "Or what if we'd had that flat tire today and not yesterday? What if we had parked somewhere else? Or if he'd shown up after we left? It was pure luck he didn't die."

"It was lucky that we were here," she said. Her eyes were caring.

"I guess it really just hit me how alone we are out here."

"Well, he was alone too," said Jan.

That stopped me. It was true. I had been thinking earlier how if I had been at the children's hospital, the boy would have come in with his parents to answer questions. They would have been able to tell us his medical history, his shot records, any allergies or surgeries or if he'd had a cough the past few weeks. What I hadn't thought about was how those parents were also there to hold hands and comfort and take care of their children when it was all over. When this boy finally left the hospital, he would return to no one. He had come to our van alone, and if he recovered, he would do so alone. Out here on the streets, the homeless children came with nothing at all.

☐☐☐☐☐☐

I was almost thirty-four when I started the mobile medical unit that became known around Arizona as Big Blue. I was a small-town boy, transplanted to Tucson, Arizona, where I played in the dry washes behind my family's modest house. Inside, the swamp cooler constantly blew cold, wet air. I was a goofy-looking boy with a bad stutter who talked so much about wanting to be a doctor my schoolmates started to sarcastically call me Doctor or, even less nicely, Mr. Quack. But as much as I dreamed I really didn't think it would happen. No one in my family was a doctor. Neither of my parents had a college degree, though I believed my dad had to be the smartest guy around. Both he and my mom expected me to do well in school, but exactly what my future was I wasn't sure. As a teenager I worked after school at the Golf n' Stuff, a miniature golf course and amusement park. After work my friend Danny and I would stop by the closest Eegee, to drink the fresh fruit slushies and eat footlongs. Somehow, when I talked with my best friend in that hard yellow booth, my childhood fancy of being a doctor started seeming as if it could become real. One day I told Danny about a flyer I had seen posted at our high school. The local hospital was offering a special program for teenagers to learn about the medical profession. Danny encouraged me to apply, and I did. Suddenly I was going from the Golf n' Stuff to the corridors of the hospital.

It was several years later, in medical school, that I first saw a mobile medical unit. This "hospital on wheels" amazed me. I was in a combined program at Tufts, where I was getting a doctorate in medicine and a master's degree in public health. In one of my classes I learned about the Bridge Over Troubled Waters program, which had a special van that took health care to the homeless. I was immediately intrigued. I rode the Boston subway out to Harvard Square, where the van was parked, just to look at it. It was small and looked worn, but the homeless lined up outside looked eager for help. I was struck by the concept. How perfect, I thought. With a hospital on wheels, I could take health care to any child who needed it.

I was graduated from Tufts University in 1995 and began a combined program in internal medicine and pediatrics at both Good Samaritan Hospital and the Phoenix Children's Hospital. Over the next few years I saw many homeless adults and children. As part of the residency we were assigned to a weekly medical clinic where we would practice "real world" medicine. For my pediatric clinic I chose the Thomas J. Pappas School, a school in a decrepit area of downtown Phoenix for children whose families were homeless, living in shelters, cheap motels, and cars or on the streets. The school allowed them to get not only educations but also social services. It had a clinic, staffed by local pediatricians like me, that opened once per week. For the first time I got to practice medicine in the community I wanted to help.

After graduation, I was hired on at the Phoenix Children's Hospital as a faculty physician. I got married, bought a house, and fell into a busy life with a lot of work, extended family, and friends. With a full-time demanding schedule and the continuing work of the Pappas school clinic, my dream of the medical van seemed out of reach.

But in 1999 all that changed. Phoenix Children's had teamed

up with a program called HomeBase Youth Services, an agency serving homeless youth in the Phoenix area. It had a drop-in center and a separate long-term shelter. The *Arizona Republic* newspaper ran an article drawing attention to homeless kids needing medical attention The article got the attention of the hospital administration, and soon the idea of a mobile medical unit was proposed. A grant was written and funded. Dr. Irwin Redlener of the Children's Health Fund came to town to give a talk. He and singer Paul Simon had founded the Children's Health Fund to help bring health care to America's most vulnerable children. When he heard about the idea of a mobile medical unit to serve homeless kids in Arizona, he eagerly got on board and offered to help.

As soon as I heard about the plan, I ran into the office of my boss at the hospital, Jeff Weiss. I wanted to run the van, I told him. I *needed* to run the van. But he wasn't so convinced. I was young, he said. I had barely started my career as a doctor. It was the kind of position that called for a doctor with tons of experience who possessed more than a little street smarts. Besides, funding was iffy. There probably wouldn't be enough money for a director for the van, he warned me. But I insisted. Finally, after weeks of my constant lobbying, he relented. I suspect he thought I'd never give up. There was still no money for my position, but I was confident it would all work out.

When I called my wife, Amy, to tell her I had been offered the position, my childhood stutter had returned, as it often did when I was excited. I had to take a few deep breaths and avoid the problem words that sometimes tripped me. Finally I got it out. "I got the job," I said.

It felt more like a question than a statement because I needed Amy's support. I felt the world stop until she answered.

"Go for it," she said. So I said yes, with neither a moment's hesitation nor the faintest idea of what I was getting into.

"OK, what do we do next?" I asked the folks who had gathered to help plan the launch of Phoenix's newest mobile medical unit. It was our first meeting. I was bubbling over with enthusiasm and so excited I could barely sit still. Silence greeted my question. Embarrassed, we all looked around the table. How *did* one start a mobile medical unit?

"Are there any books on the subject?" someone asked after a long pause.

Someone else opened up a laptop to do a search. More silence. "Apparently not."

"Well, one thing is clear," a colleague said. "We have no idea what we are doing . . . yet."

"We can at least start with a name," I said.

"How about something after Jim Crews?" a HomeBase staff member asked. Jim Crews was the CEO of Good Samaritan Hospital and a big supporter of the van. "Something like the Crews'n Healthmobile."

"Perfect," I said.

It turned out that making a hospital on wheels was incredibly complicated and expensive. The first step—getting an RV to remodel—was probably the easiest. Jim Crews arranged for the donation of a 1991 Winnebago. When the van arrived, I ran out behind the hospital to take a look. It was an old Winnebago, sure enough, but to me it was beautiful. The hard part was going to be turning it into a functioning hospital. Months of meetings were spent finding out the regulations on everything from which oxygen tanks we could use to what medical equipment would fit. We wanted a van that could offer high-quality hospital-level medical care, which meant having the right equipment that met hospital-level standards. The Children's Health Fund donated thousands of dollars, the Phoenix Children's Hospital and HomeBase chipped in, and the Flinn Foundation contributed huge amounts in a seed grant. The donations and grants were a godsend, yet the costs were staggering.

But finally the van was finished. We celebrated with verbal

champagne, telling one another, "Well done," instead of the real stuff because not only were we completely out of money, but we'd gone way over budget.

One of my first duties as the still-unpaid director had been to hire a nurse-practitioner. Jan Putnam was the first person I interviewed, and as soon as we were done talking, I knew she was the person for the job. She was trained in emergency care and was an excellent nurse-practitioner. More important, she had experience with at-risk populations. It was hard to believe this peppy lady was fifty. She had the zip of a woman half her age. Jan took to the job immediately. She was already looking over the budget in painstaking detail. It was the sort of job I detested, but fortunately Jan was good at it.

The day we announced the van was done Jan came to my hospital office. I was supposed to be answering e-mails, but in truth I was floating on a cloud of daydreams, seeing myself at the wheel of our van for our first day out, which was slated in a week.

"What's up?" I asked her, dubiously eyeing the stack of papers in her freckled arms.

She walked in and unceremoniously dropped the papers on my desk. "This is the budget," she said. There was a friendly smile on her sunny face, but her eyes were sober.

"OK," I said, looking at the papers as if they were distasteful. I didn't reach for them.

She flipped a few pages. "We've gone way over, but you already know that." I nodded. In my faith, I was sure we would make ends meet. Somehow.

"And we didn't budget any money for medications." She crossed her freckled arms. "The van has no medications."

I jerked abruptly to life. "Medications?" I felt cold water dash down my spine. In my daydreams I froze at the wheel.

"I know it probably came up in meetings," she said forgivingly. "I'm sure people figured most of our patients will have state insurance. But I'm not so sure they will, or will be able to get it. Even if they can, do we really want to give some homeless child a scrip for a lifesaving med and tell him to go find a pharmacy to fill it? How is that supposed to work? We need to have at least a basic supply of meds for uninsured people and for emergencies."

"Jeez." My mind went into calculator mode. I knew it was extremely expensive to stock medications. Just a month's supply of some psychotropics can cost close to a thousand dollars, and that was one month for one patient. A full stock of everything from antibiotics to asthma meds for the unit was going to be astronomical.

"It's an understandable mistake," Jan said soothingly. She was right. Most of the patients at the children's hospital had private or state Medicaid insurance. Even if they were poor, their meds were covered. But it was very possible that most homeless kids would not be insured, and I wasn't familiar with how to get them eligible for the state medical insurance. I needed to research these procedures. One more thing to do.

"As understandable as it is," I replied, "we don't have a dollar left for it."

"I know," she said compassionately. "But we can figure it out, Randy."

I was very depressed when I went home to Amy that night. Her dad was in town, visiting from California, and we all had planned to go out to his favorite hamburger joint for dinner. I was quiet as we ordered. Amy asked for her usual cheeseburger and added tons of fixings. Absently I made mine plain. Just salt and ketchup were enough for me. I was thinking that there was no way I would ask any of our donors for more money. Already they had given far more than they had planned.

"You're quiet tonight," Amy whispered to me.

I didn't want to spill such embarrassing news in front of her father. He would think I was incompetent. But he asked about how the van was proceeding, so finally I confessed the problem. We talked about it as the waitress brought our sodas.

"I can't believe I overlooked something so essential," I said.

Amy's father listened. He was a shrewd businessman. He began peppering me with questions. For the first time I found my plans for the van closely questioned. It had been easy to talk in ideals.

It was much harder to explain exactly *how* the van would work. How long had we budgeted our money to last? What exactly were our goals, and how would we determine if we were effective? How many kids did we plan to see? How would we track our successes and our failures? The more questions he asked, the more I felt I didn't have any real answers. I started to flounder and heard my stutter come back.

The waitress brought our burgers. "Why not take all that money and just put one homeless kid through college?" Amy's dad asked, picking up a fry and dipping it in ketchup. "Might be more effective."

"We want to reach a lot of kids," I said.

"Hmm. Seems like stocking this medication unit would have been a big part of your thinking then."

"I guess we just assumed they would have insurance," I said, feeling I was struggling to explain myself. I felt defensive. The last thing I wanted was for my wife's father to think I was a fool, and it sure seemed I was doing a good job of it. It occurred to me we could have used someone like Amy's dad on our planning committee. He would have pierced right through my pie-in-the-sky thinking. I berated myself for not having been more prepared. We needed someone like him.

"Eat your burger," he said, pointing to my plate.

A few days later my father-in-law called me at work. He had talked to Amy's brother and sister about their late mother, who had left a trust. He had asked them if some of the funds could be used for medications. Both Amy's brother and sister said yes, though they were saying good-bye to some of their inheritance. "We all agreed it would have made their mother happy to help homeless kids," he said. It was a huge gift, and I was overwhelmed by gratefulness. This was an inheritance that Amy's brother and sister could have kept. Instead they were giving it away. When I told Amy that night, she just hugged me and said she wasn't surprised. She was low-key about it, but I knew that was her family's way. "You seem much happier and more relaxed," she said.

"A huge obstacle was just overcome," I said. I hugged her back and thought that now Amy was even more a part of the van, and so was her family.

Once we had the meds all ordered, we had a party at the Dial Tower to celebrate and to thank our financial supporters. We parked the remodeled van in front of the building. It was gleaming with new blue paint and our new Crews'n Healthmobile logo across the front. The back of the van held a dedication to Amy's mother. When her father saw it, he got tears in his eyes. It was March in Phoenix, perfect light jacket weather. All the supporters were there. A local chef made soup, which we served in blue bowls, to illustrate how homeless kids need more than soup kitchens to get by. Amy had brought cases of beer and wine from Costco, along with water and soda and iced tea. We didn't want our supporters to have to spend any more money. I sweated through a speech in a blue suit I had bought for the occasion. I had never organized such an event, let alone been the subject of such attention. Jan navigated the crowd, a dazzling smile on her face.

I felt a tremendous sense of pride as I led tours of the van. Everything was ready. The meds were stocked. The oxygen tanks were on the walls, along with a defibrillator machine. There was a big examining table in the back room and smaller tables along the sides. The walls were painted a crisp hospital white. Tubes for blood draws were lined up on sparkling counters. There were two fridges, one for lab work and the other for vaccines. There was the reassuring smell of antiseptic. In my mind I could already hear the hum of the centrifuge machines. I was elated. Taking health care to homeless children seemed like my life's calling. I must have told myself that a hundred times that night. I felt a surge of happiness, of anxiety, and, more than anything, of conviction.

▯▯◡▯▯

The van was finally ready to go. I woke up before dawn that Monday, having tossed and turned all night from nerves and excitement. I was usually such a sound sleeper. These nerves were new to me. I put on my new work uniform: cargo pants, loafers, and one of the new bright yellow shirts we had made for the few of us working in the van. There would be Jan and I and sometimes a volunteer or two. Our Crews logo was proudly displayed across the front of the shirt. I briefly thought about putting on a tie. As a pediatrician I had a collection of Disney ties that I had worn to work at the children's hospital. But that seemed like a bad idea. The last thing homeless teenagers would appreciate seeing was a reminder of their own lost childhoods. With my stethoscope around my neck, I was ready to go.

I had always worn cargo-style pants to work because the pockets are perfect for medical codebooks. These are informational books doctors are always carrying around, and mine were extremely important to me. They can list everything from what kind of antibiotic should be given to kill a specific bacterium to the symptoms of obscure illnesses. I also had the keys for the new van in one pocket, the keys for the office in another. As helpful as the codebooks were, I worried that my obsession with them bordered on obsessive-compulsive disorder. There had been times I had gotten all the way to the hospital before realizing I had forgotten one. I had turned around and driven back home, calling in frantically to say I would be late. I worried at times that this OCD behavior was a sign of stress, but as much as I tried, I could not control the ritual.

Codebooks in the right pockets, I kissed Amy's sweet sleepy face—she was getting out of bed for her own job as a pediatrician in a family clinic—and drove to the HomeBase drop-in center, where the van was parked. A can of Diet Coke sloshed in my stomach. I had been too nervous to eat anything more substantial. HomeBase had kindly offered to let us use some of the space in the drop-in center for our offices outside the van. The building was old. The second floor was not fit for habitation, and we had only a small corner of the first-floor building to ourselves. We were not complaining. We needed someplace to store files and make calls. Our offices were small, with walls painted a dull, heavy blue. The desks were old green metal army desks, and the office chairs were a mismatch of swap meet finds. The carpet was ancient, and there was an unpleasant smell about the place. The roof had leaked over time, causing the ceiling on the condemned floor above us to buckle with damage. I suspected there might be mold problems. We planned to spend as little time in the offices as possible and as much on the van.

The van itself was parked behind a tall wire fence, gleaming in the dawnlight. Jan was there waiting. She too was wearing one of our new yellow shirts and looked to me to be the picture of unstoppable health and energy.

"I'll drive," she announced, bouncing into the huge driver's seat.

"Sure," I said, and handed her the keys.

She gave me a wink. "Leave the driving to the pro."

I smiled. As a boy I had driven hay trucks on my grandparents' farm. But it had been years since I had driven such a huge rig and was relieved she was doing it.

On the dashboard were some of our first brochures. They had been Jan's idea. We had printed up a bunch of them dirt cheap on paper that we had folded ourselves. In one crazy blitz we had left them in libraries, bus stops, and churches. We had a lofty mission statement that was quite a mouthful, pledging to provide "homeless, runaway and thrown away and at-risk youth" with comprehensive medical services. The inside of the brochure promised we would be appearing at sites from Mill Avenue in Tempe to local parks to downtown Phoenix. Social workers in particular needed to be able to find us. I took a deep breath. My new life was starting.

▱▱▱▱▱

That first day we drove to Tempe, one of the largest college cities in the country. It was reputed to have a shocking number of homeless kids. There were over five thousand homeless kids in Maricopa County alone, which included Tempe. These kids lived on the streets and in shelters. The largest percentage came from backgrounds of poverty, neglect, and sexual abuse. Many had parents with drug and alcohol addictions, and still others had untreated mental health issues or substance abuse problems themselves. Some had left bad homes, while others had no homes to go to: their parents were in jail or had turned them out. We had asked the HomeBase outreach workers to pass the word that we would be arriving, but we weren't expecting to see too many kids the first few weeks.

Jan pulled into an empty lot and parked. I jumped out of my seat ready to set everything up. But when we lowered the jacks, there was a horrible hissing and grinding sound. I jumped out in a panic and ran to the front of the van to examine four hydraulic jacks, designed to raise and lower the twenty-six-thousand-pound van. Instead of lowering properly, the front right one had stopped midway. Hydraulic fluid was jetting in a thick, oily stream. Already it had made a huge puddle over the gravel. Oh, no, not now, I thought. The van was sitting on a slant. Everything on the van, from the medical equipment to the refrigerators, was designed to work on a level surface. We couldn't see patients on a lopsided floor.

Jan hopped out through the narrow door behind me. "I'll take care of it," I told her. I crawled under the van, squirming. Fluid was still squirting out of the jack. Maybe I can pull it down in place myself, I thought. I put both hands on the metal. Hydraulic fluid poured down over my arms. As hard as I pulled, nothing moved. The thing was frozen. I crawled back out, my cargo pants ruined with dust and grease. The front of my yellow shirt was smeared with oil. I wiped my hands on my pants and began punching numbers madly into my phone. I was calling the mechanic who had helped us renovate the Winnebago.

Then I stopped. In the midst of my consternation, which had completely absorbed my attention, I looked up absentmindedly and beheld a sight that took my breath away. Homeless kids had materialized, seemingly out of nowhere, and were lined up next to the door of the van. Their silent faces confronted me. I had dealt with the occasional homeless teenager before but had never seen a line of them, and their physical reality was a shock. I could see road dust on their clothes. Some had packs across their backs. Others were empty-handed. One girl had a wide cherub's face. When she turned to look at me, I could see an infected sore on her cheek. I had yet to set out lawn chairs for seating or to organize anything, for that matter.

"Are you the doctor?" the girl with the cherub's face asked.

"Yes." My voice stuttered. I smoothed it out. "I'm Dr. Christensen."

She had blond hair held back with a dirty pale blue rubber band. She was short and barely came to my chest. The infected sore on her cheek looked bad. Her sneakers were busted out, the laces coated in grime. Jan had opened the door again and, standing on the gravel, was trying to pull down the steps. She was yanking with all her strength. At first the steps didn't work either. Nothing was going as planned. Once Jan finally got them down, the kids crowded up into the van.

"Excuse me," I told the girl. I went to wash hydraulic fluid off my hands in the tiny sink. Jan was handing out intake forms to the kids crowding around. My phone was ringing in my pocket with a call from the mechanic, and I didn't have time to answer it. I led the girl to an examination room. "Wait here," I said, signaling at the exam table, and went back up front to get an intake form. Jan was raising her voice, trying to organize the kids into some sort of queue. The floor *was* slanted. I couldn't find a pen, and the kids around Jan were getting loud with frustration.

"Jan, where are the clipboards?"

"I don't know. I didn't think to order any. Did you?"

I returned to the room and handed the girl a form. I took my pen out of my pocket, reminding myself to make sure I got it back.

"I don't get this," she said, looking down at the form she was supposed to fill out.

"What's the problem?" I asked, raising my voice to be heard. The noise out front was getting loud.

Someone knocked on the door. "Is Johnny in there?" the person shouted. "Hey, Johnny!"

My cheeks colored with frustration and embarrassment. This was not a professional environment.

The girl was pointing to the form, to where it asked for her immunization history. "I don't know about shots," she said. "I don't think I ever got any."

Of course, I thought. A homeless kid won't be carrying around an immunization record. I tried to say something, but the loud knocking came again. *"Johnny!"*

I looked down to see hydraulic fluid embedded in the pores of my forearms. I opened the door, flinching at all the noise outside. "Johnny's not here," I said more brusquely than I wanted.

The boy outside smiled sheepishly. "OK, dude. Chill out," he said, and wandered back up front.

I closed the door, feeling more and more frantic by the moment. I examined the infected sore on the girl's cheek. "How did you get this?" I asked.

"I think it was a spider," she said. "We've been sleeping in this abandoned house."

She lifted the bottom of her filthy shirt and showed me another infected bite on her belly. I looked at the angry sore. The edges were raised and swollen. I didn't think they were black widow bites; those caused stomach pains but didn't leave the kind of marks she had. I wasn't sure what these bites were. I realized I had a lot to learn about different kinds of insect and animal bites. The one on her belly concerned me. It was close to the lymph nodes in the groin. Her general health seemed pretty run-down too. Her immune system was not fighting back.

"These bites are pretty infected, and the infection is spreading," I told her. "You're going to need some oral antibiotics. I need to examine you. Then I'll see you in a week, see how you are doing."

"You mean you're coming back?" She looked disbelieving.

"We'll be coming to this location once a week—"

More pounding on the door distracted me. "Let me find some

cream," I said. I rushed through a wall of kids in the hall, all asking if it was their turn, to ask Jan where the antibiotic cream was kept. The front of the van was cacophony. Kids were talking and shouting and asking questions. Paper forms began drifting to the floor. I stuck my head down the steps and saw a group of kids outside, running around the van. Some were playing hacky sack in the gravel. Others looked as if they were giving up and started to leave.

"Hey, don't leave," I called.

I raced back with the cream. The girl was standing up, ready to go. "Don't leave yet," I said. I hadn't given her a full exam yet. I hadn't asked her why she was homeless. I hadn't even suggested a place for her to stay. I didn't even *know* if there was a shelter in Tempe for homeless kids. Maybe there weren't any. After a year of preparation, I thought, I am completely unprepared. The day was taking on the nightmarish hue of doom. We didn't have the right medicine for this or the right order form for that. I felt it would take me hours to get to the bottom of this one girl's medical situation, and there were a dozen more like her right outside my door, all with just as many needs. I felt panicky. I wanted to go back and start all over again. Only this time I would have clipboards and pens and an even floor.

"Randy." Jan knocked on the door. She was holding a urine sample. It was the color of thick yellow soup. If I had been in my right mind, I would have looked at it and worried about a case of severe dehydration. Instead I just felt a sharp frustration.

"Not now!" I snapped at her, and felt horrible. I sounded exactly like the kind of doctor I couldn't stand. As I turned back to go to the girl, my hands were trembling with nerves, and the smell of hydraulic fluid rose to greet me.

॰॰॰॰॰

We drove in silence back to the loading dock that night. I felt shell-shocked. I was deeply dismayed at how badly the day had gone. I kept thinking, What on earth made me think I could do this? I had known the extent of the problem. I knew there were thousands of homeless kids ranged across the country. It was the severity of their needs that had made me want to help them. But reality is different from numbers. Numbers are never real. These kids were real, and I felt I had barely helped any of them.

I didn't want to admit it, but I had thought my job would be easier. I knew it was only the first day, but I had pictured myself having the time to make meaningful connections with the kids. I really thought I would be dealing with their situation in a straight-forward manner. They would step on my van homeless, I would attend to their medical needs, and somehow this would help them get off the streets. I didn't know exactly how I had come up with this naive idea. I had just assumed that once I gave them medical care they would be happy and healthy and somehow transition into rewarding lives. It would be fulfilling, and I would feel good about myself. What I had not envisioned was being soaked in hydraulic fluid, the nurse-practitioner I respected radiating disappointment next to me, and a tsunami of doubt flooding my heart.

I looked out the passenger window. I tried to imagine myself doing this for ten years. Ten years of kids with infected bites and dirty clothes and distrustful eyes and immunization histories that were one long question mark. Ten years of teenagers who came to me with a list of problems that unfolded in layers, problems that spanned their lives and would not be solved in one visit, or even ten visits, or maybe even ever. Ten years of dealing with intractable problems that probably went back for generations. Could I deal with that? Could I deal with the prospect of kids whom I never helped?

We stopped by the children's hospital. It was late. I stepped out of the van weary. Jan followed. She was dragging a huge bag filled with the dirty gowns from the day. She looked uncharacteristically bushed. "I'll get those," I told her. Jan gratefully relinquished the bag. My first day ended with my lugging a bag of dirty gowns into an almost empty hospital, hoping to find someone to help me get them laundered. I had to smile at myself. I might have been the first doctor in the history of the hospital to finish his day by washing gowns.

It was again past eleven when I got home. I wondered how long my wife would put up with this. Luckily as a doctor she was used to crazy long hours, but still. "How did it go?" Amy asked, yawning. She was fresh out of the shower and sitting at the kitchen island, an empty bowl of ice cream next to her. A medical journal was there. She had been reading it while waiting for me. I was touched she had stayed up.

"It was hard," I said. I kissed her. "I want to talk to my dad. I'll be right back. Promise." What I wanted to say was that I had had a desperately terrible day and needed to talk to my father. I knew she understood.

I took my phone into my home office. Maybe it was because I knew what he would say. Dad believed the first responsibility of a man was always to take care of others. When Amy and I started dating, I had taken her to visit my parents, driving up to their place in Gilbert, right outside Phoenix, in her little green Volkswagen. Amy had loved the rural Arizona farmland, with its irrigated pastures and horses nuzzling patches of green grass in the sun. My dad did not love her car.

He took one look at her tires and began reading me the riot act. "Look at those tires!" he said once we were alone in the driveway. Amy was enjoying a soda in the cool, shaded living room with my mom and sister, Stephanie, who was over for Sunday dinner with her husband, Curtis, and their two young, boisterously happy sons. "Those tires are bald," Dad said forcefully. "They could blow any time. Do you want Amy getting a flat tire when she is alone on the freeway?" I promised to have them changed soon. "Change them now," Dad said, and went back in the house.

Dad listened to the stress in my voice. I had pulled him from bed. He waited until it all came out. "Son, remember that time when you were little and your sister bonked you on the head with a hammer?"

"How could I forget?" I said, laughing.

"And what did I tell you?"

"I should have ducked."

"That's right. Not because she was right to hit you. But life isn't always fair or easy, and the sooner you learn to handle it, the better off you will be. Now, you wanted this, right? Then figure out what you can do to make it work. You got that smart wife of yours. Isn't Amy an adviser on this van?"

"She is." When her father gave us the gift from their family trust, we had created an advisory board. I had remembered how important her father's questions had been and asked several professionals to sit on a board to give us guidance and ask those hard questions. Amy was now on the board, as were several hospital and social service administrators.

"Then why are you talking to me and not talking to her?" he asked pointedly.

Good point. Because I'm embarrassed to tell her how horribly it went, I thought.

"That's what an adviser is for," he said. "They give advice. But you got to ask for it." He waited a moment. "Don't be too proud to ask for help, son."

"Thanks, Dad."

He chuckled before hanging up. I pictured him and mom in their house in Gilbert, a home with its neat rows of family photographs in the hallway, the hobby shelf with my mom's miniature adobe houses, and the little guest room with my childhood bed. Whenever I thought of my dad, I would remember Kremmling, Colorado, where my sister, Stephanie, was born. It always came back in the bright memories of childhood: the times spent fishing at the lake, the gentle jokes at the dinner table about our Lutheran gringo dad marrying a Catholic Mexican girl. We were proud of how my parents were so in love they weren't going to obey the rules of the time. My dad had always lived by his own heart. When I was growing up, I wanted to be just like him.

"Amy?" She was barely awake. "Sorry that took so long." I

crawled into bed, wearing my pajamas, my breath clean. I curled against her back. I smelled her clean damp hair, and I felt a lot better.

$$\square\square\square\square\square$$

The next few days were a firestorm of activity. We ordered many of the supplies we had found ourselves needing, including clipboards. At home I began regularly running problems by Amy. She immediately had an answer to the laundry problem: disposable paper gowns. It was a genius thought, and I ordered them immediately.

Jan was busy creating new intake forms. She had reviewed dozens on the Internet and found none to her liking. Not one, she told me, was appropriate for a homeless child. There were intake forms for regular children, the kind that parents fill out, and there were forms for adults. But none was for an unaccompanied teenager. So she was making her own. One morning I went into our offices at HomeBase and found ten different samples waiting on my rickety swivel chair. "What do you think of this one?" Jan asked, handing me a form. At the top was a place for the kid's name. The first question was, "Where are you currently living?" Under the answer section the choices read: "Street," "Shelter," "Friends," and so on. The second question was, "How long have you been homeless?" On down the list the questions went, from abuse at home to depression and suicide attempts.

"This is great," I said.

"Can we use them?" she asked.

I thought for a moment. "Sure. But let's run them by administration first."

Jan frowned a little but didn't say anything. It occurred to me that I was used to working with bureaucracies while Jan was not. I didn't want to upset anyone in administration by using intake forms it had not approved. The van was considered a clinic under the Phoenix Children's Hospital; the administration was essentially our boss, I felt, and we needed to follow its rules and regulations.

Before I knew it, we were parked again in Tempe. A week had passed since our first visit. I was hoping to see the girl with the cherub's face, but she didn't appear, and when I asked the other kids, no one seemed to know who she was or where she had gone. The kids came all day, in dusty waves. They came with uncontrolled asthma, injuries from fights, broken teeth and noses, tooth abscesses, old scars from beatings, and long lists of symptoms that sometimes began in early childhood. I was already learning that this would be a typical day. None of the kids came with easy solutions either. As soon as I treated one symptom, a child would nonchalantly mention another. "I've had this bad cough now for months," he or she would say, or, "My tummy hurts all the time." Under it all was a desperate need for help: for shelter, housing, a search for relatives or friends to take the child in. But at least today I felt the day was going better. Jan had the kids organized and the new intake forms made care much easier. Jan was seeing as many patients as I was, or even more. We dashed in and out of the rooms, calling names.

The day whizzed by. My last patient left, carrying a new inhaler. It had to be close to quitting time, I hoped. I stretched my back and looked at my watch. It was past eight, and I was starving. I hadn't eaten all day, let alone taken a break. I stepped outside the van to take a breather. Dusk was falling. The heat was still a heavy mantle over my shoulders. Fresh sweat trickled down my back.

That was when I saw her. She was sitting in one of the lawn chairs outside, as if waiting for someone to notice that she was there. I hoped she hadn't been waiting the whole day. I grabbed a bottle of water and took it to her.

She was slender and waiflike, almost ethereal. She had dark hair cut in elfin wisps around her face. She was far too pale for Arizona, a porcelain girl in the desert heat. Her jeans were stained, and the hems dragged in the dust. Thin adolescent shoulders jutted out from her T-shirt. She was just sitting there, slumped in her chair, looking exhausted. Her arms seemed immobilized from weariness, almost dead in her lap. I noticed she wore something on one wrist, a bracelet.

I sat in the chair next to her.

"I'm Dr. Christensen," I said. "What's your name?"

The moment stretched out. Finally she answered. "Mary." It was a small and unimportant voice, the voice of a girl who has learned how to be forgotten.

She took the bottle of water, reaching in slow motion. The bracelet swayed. The pockets of her jeans were pouched and grimy, and her fingernails were dirty. She obviously needed a bath and a change of clothes. She slumped back in her chair as if I weren't there. The sun was setting, and the sky was aflame in streaks of magenta and orange, while the red stone mountains stood in sharp relief. The smell of citrus from ornamental orange bushes was heavy and florid, a thick perfume. In other places of the city people would be getting ready for dinner. They would be having meals in air-conditioned restaurants and later strolling in cool malls where fountains tinkled. Tempe was such a beautiful city, crowned with tall palm trees and rimmed with red mountains. Yet even here, like everywhere else, there were children like Mary.

I sat next to her for a moment, making conversation, trying to help her feel comfortable. I sensed a fear about her, and I worried she might bolt. She sat with her hands loosely folded in her lap. We watched as a group of kids played hacky sack outside the van against a backdrop of the setting sun. Even in one-hundred-degree heat they would play, stopping every now and then to pant. Jan came out with several water bottles and left them on a chair for the kids.

In that crystalline moment, my eyes dropped to Mary's wrist. It was very thin and white, and I could see the tender knob of the ulna bone. The bracelet, made of large letter beads strung together into a sentence, was large and conspicuous.

I read the beads she had strung together. It took me a moment to absorb what they said:

ASK ME WHY I HURT

For a moment I was so caught off guard I thought my heart had stopped. My breath caught. I wanted to ask her what painful memories had left their mark so deep that she needed to wear this naked plea around her wrist. But she suddenly turned to me with a look as if to say, "Don't ask. Not yet." Her eyes were dark.

I saw Jan poke her head back out of the van. She was looking at us. "You're next, honey," she called, smiling at Mary.

"Let's get you taken care of," I said to her, and the words I had often spoken to children as a doctor now seemed to have special meaning. I stopped at the van steps and let her go first. I watched her as she entered the exam room and slowly climbed on the table. I watched her breathing rate and how she spoke, to see if she showed signs of a condition like asthma. I watched her eye movements, mouth, head, and neck to evaluate what we call the twelve cranial nerves, or the main nerves of the head. I observed her skin color, which can give clues to problems like anemia. From the way she moved it appeared she had good muscle function, but she also moved slowly, as if depressed. I wished at that moment I had a psychiatrist on board. Even in our first week we had seen kids with mental health issues. Some had been outright delusional or suicidal. I felt poorly equipped to deal with these problems.

I fell into the doctor role, smiling and calmly explaining the physical as I went. First I checked her eyes and ears and the lymph nodes of her neck and head. I listened to her heart and lungs. "Can you lie down?" I asked, and she reclined slowly and, I thought, suspiciously. I felt her abdomen for liver, spleen, and masses. She looked away, tuning me out. She kept her head turned. Her body was tense when I touched her. I couldn't tell if it was because she had pain or because she was emotionally uncomfortable. "Does that hurt?" I asked as I gently felt her liver area. She gave a quick shake no. She doesn't want me to touch her body, I thought, and quickly finished.

I stood back. Mary's general physical health seemed good. She was slightly malnourished. She had a lot of scrapes and bruises.

"How old are you, Mary?"

There was a very long silence. "I don't know," she whispered.

I stopped when I heard that. She had spoken so softly. Instantly I felt my own voice soften.

"Don't you remember when you were born?"

She didn't answer. The blank quality to her face gave her a strangely ageless look, like a blurred photograph. She could have been eighteen. She could have been younger.

"What's your last name?"

She turned her head away and looked out the exam room window, to where dusk was falling rapidly. The sunset had tinged the blinds orange and purple. It was as if a curtain had fallen over her features. She tucked her hands inside her legs. I felt a sudden, completely unexpected flood of emotion. Maybe it was the lack of animation in her face and the emptiness and despair it suggested. Maybe it was the slightness of her body and how young and vulnerable she seemed. I had come for this, but the reality was not what I had expected. It hit me in my gut. This child had no home. She would not bounce off my table and return to the loving smile of a mother or father. She would leave my van—for what? What was waiting for Mary outside on the streets?

In that moment I thought of my little sister Stephanie. I remembered one Christmas when Stephanie was about three. Wearing a Christmas red smock, she was sitting in a tiny chair under our fake white tree. I was standing by her, proud to be a big brother. The memory was as bright as a snapshot. Then another came: Stephanie, diagnosed with multiple sclerosis, rising from her hospital bed in a Christmas red nightgown, leaning on a walker. As the doctor in the family I was the one who broke the news to my sister and helped in her treatment. Mary reminded me of Stephanie in some way. Maybe it was the sense of vulnerability about her, the feeling that under this blank exterior a real girl was hiding.

"Do you have a place to sleep, Mary?"

"Sure," she said. Her eyes slowly moved toward mine.

"Couch surfing?"

There was no answer.

"Do you have any identification, Mary?" She shook her head no and gestured toward her grimy jeans pockets, as if to turn them inside out. I had discovered in the past week, much to my shock and frustration, how much identification mattered. Identification was the key to unlocking so many services, from housing to employment to education. Yet very few of the kids had identification. Why would they? I thought. Not many homeless children are going to have driver's licenses. It was a major stumbling block for getting help.

Mary got up as if to leave. I wanted to talk her into staying, but I felt if I pressured her, she would bolt for good. Outside the exam room I heard voices. Jan was dealing with a new group of freshly arrived kids, telling them we needed to close down the van for the night. She was telling them we would be back at this site next week, that tomorrow we would be in Phoenix. There was a chorus of complaints.

I looked again at the intake form Jan had filed out. Mary had answered few of her questions. "Says she has a headache," Jan had written, with a question mark after it. That was our new code for suggesting that maybe the kid was using one complaint to get help for another problem.

I gave her some Tylenol. She smiled at me for the first time, a shy smile that she almost immediately hid behind her lips.

"Can I make some calls for you, Mary? Is there anyone in your family—"

She looked alarmed, shook her head rapidly, and began edging toward the door. For the first time I saw panic on her face.

"Hold on," I told Mary.

I got her a pair of fresh socks and a hygiene kit, which contained a toothbrush and soap, as well as bus tickets and brochures for help. I handed this to her up front.

"Come back please," I told her.

For a moment she stood there, and in the final vestiges of sunset I again thought of my sister. Could Stephanie have survived on the streets? I knew the answer: of course not.

Jan and I watched Mary walk off toward Mill Avenue. She was small and slender under the large dark sky. She looked no bigger than a child and walked quickly, as if afraid of the coming night. She carried the bag with supplies under one arm. I didn't want to think of what awaited her on those streets.

"She's just a baby," Jan murmured.

I nodded.

"What's her name again?"

"She said it was Mary."

"That's right. She didn't really have a headache, did she?"

I shook my head, "I don't think so. I think what is wrong with Mary is much worse," I said. "But I can't say what it is. She wouldn't talk to me."

Jan nodded. "If only headaches were the only problem these kids had."

Night was falling, driving a final sweep of colors across the sky. Soon the stars would come: bright desert stars. The streets had fallen into that peculiar desert silence, permeated with clicks and buzzes and insect sounds, yet seeming utterly still. Mary's figure retreated until it was just a small shape, and then she turned a corner and was gone. From down Mill Avenue came the faint hoot of music from a bar, and in the distance there was a sudden blast of a car horn. I felt a tremendous guilt. If I could, I thought, I would lock her up to keep her safe. I looked at the stars and made a fervent wish that Mary would travel safely into the next day.

"She could be my daughter," I said softly.

Jan shook her head. "Heaven forbid, she's someone's daughter." Jan had a son and a daughter, both teenagers. The sadness in her voice was clear.

"Yes," I said, this time with anger in my voice. "She's someone's daughter."

2

MOEUR PARK

The van was a disaster. The jacks kept malfunctioning despite repeated repairs. It seemed that as soon as we got one problem fixed, another cropped up. My dad came out several times, driving down the freeway from Gilbert to work on the engine. I'd call him from blighted urban areas of Phoenix or outside shelters or Tempe, and somehow he'd find us, tooling up in his little truck with his green army bag on the seat next to him. For as long as I could remember, he'd used that same oil-stained army bag to hold his tools. Soon he would be under the hood, grease smeared up his brawny forearms, a cap perched on his fluffy silver hair. The homeless kids adored my dad. They called him Gramps.

But my dad couldn't help with the biggest problem, which turned out to be the generator. It simply couldn't produce enough power to run all the medical equipment and refrigerators and keep the air conditioning running too. I would be right in the middle of a busy day, up to my armpits in kids, and the generator would conk out. With a hiss the air conditioning would die. Without air conditioning the heat inside the van climbed to more than a hundred within minutes, and all our refrigerated supplies were at risk.

One day, soon after meeting Mary, I was complaining about my general predicament to one of my best friends, Ron Couturier. His father was a member of a charity group called the Jaycees. Ron's dad and friends had formed a group of older men who called themselves the Old Timers. "Why don't we ask my dad's group for help?" Ron suggested.

I really didn't want to impose on people, but Ron insisted, and so the following night I found myself knocking on the door of his house for one of the Old Timers' meetings. I had dressed up in a suit and a tie, my unruly hair brushed back. When I walked in, all conversation stopped. Sitting in a circle in the living room was a bunch of old cowboys dressed in worn jeans and dusty boots. After a few friendly laughs and jokes about my attire, I stammered into my speech. I stood in the living room and talked about how we were trying to help homeless kids with medical care, but the problems we were having with our generator were making it hard. The longer I went on, the more I felt my cheeks color. I was overly conscious of my stutter and tried to choose my words with care so the dreaded "uh-uh-uh" wouldn't start. I wasn't sure where I was supposed to be looking either, so I looked at one wall over one cowboy's hat, seeing the brim under my eye and aware of everyone's attention on my face.

When I finished, the cowboys were polite and I thought probably embarrassed for me. They offered a slice of their pizza. I ate it without tasting it. I felt I hadn't done well at all. Clearly public speeches are not your thing, I thought as I drove home, feeling the sweat still dampening my suit jacket. I had barely made it home when I got a call from Ron. He said the Old Timers had started writing the check as soon as I had left. I made a joke that it was probably out of pity, but Ron stopped me there. "They like what you are doing," he said matter-of-factly.

So the next day, from the generosity of the Old Timers, I was shopping for a new generator. It was too big to put inside the van; we had had to mount it on the back, and to start it, I had to go outside in the blazing heat and yank on a cord, like starting a lawn mower, sometimes for ten or more minutes. It wasn't easy, but I

wasn't about to complain. I was just grateful we had air conditioning, and my sweaty exertions always gave Jan the opportunity to
joke that I needed the exercise. She usually flexed as she spoke,
showing off her buff muscles.

A few days later we were back in Tempe, and in the 109-degree
heat I was out behind the van, yanking on the generator cord. Arizona heat is an all-encompassing thing, more like a physical object
than just air: it surrounds you like an inescapable blanket, sometimes so unbearable it is hard to breathe. The idea of the homeless kids being out in such heat waves, forced to walk blocks or
even miles for food or shelter, frightened me. I immediately began
pouring sweat. It ran into my eyes, stinging, and made a sightless
wet fog out of my eyeglasses. My shirt was soaked. The sweat ran
down my arms and dripped off my wrists.

Suddenly I was aware of someone standing behind me. It was
Mary. It had been a few days since we had gotten the generator
and several weeks since I had first met her. She had come back
once since, but the minute I started pressing her she had run off.
I had felt sick at heart about it and resolved not to make the same
mistake again.

As before, she was alone. Most of the homeless kids seemed to
move in protective packs. But Mary was alone.

"Please wait," I told her. The generator had finally roared to life.
I led her inside. I couldn't see out of my glasses and felt around
for a towel. She sat in the front of the van, in the little intake seat
near the door. She seemed to like sitting in the little chair. Mary's
face was a mask. She looked miles away, lost someplace behind
the curtain of her eyes, as fearful as a small animal. "How are you
today?" I asked. She looked at me suspiciously from the corner of
her dark eyes.

I felt a new awkwardness. When I worked in the hospital, it was
easy to know how to act around children: I was professional with
the parents and warm with the children, but I could always assume
the parents would explain things to their kids and, if necessary,
share information. With the homeless kids I wasn't sure how to
act. I needed to bridge a distance that didn't exist in usual pediat-

rics. These kids had built fortresses around their hearts. They were not about to share with me secrets that they had never told anyone. Mary was so closed off that I didn't think my usual professionalism would work. She seemed so shut down that I wasn't sure if anyone could reach her. I can't get across this divide, I thought. I can't figure out how to get her to talk to me. I wondered if it would be possible to act professional yet also connect as a caring adult.

I decided that for the moment I'd stop being the doctor. I'd drop that persona, and I'd just be Randy Christensen. "Whew," I said, sponging off my face.

Mary stared around the van. Boxes of gloves were mounted on the wall. Vials lined the counters. I often felt like a bull in a china shop, trying to maneuver around. When Jan and I passed in the narrow hallway, we both had to turn sideways. I handed Mary a pack of peanuts from the dashboard. She secreted it in her clothes. Everything she did seemed to be in slow motion, as if her movements were underwater. I saw her looking at the wall. Both Jan and I had stuck up a few personal pictures. One of Jan's photos showed her winning a BMX trophy, her husband and teenage son at her side. Mary was staring at another photo.

"That's my wife, Amy," I said.

She stared at Amy's wide smile, at the way her hair curled over her ears. She asked a question in a voice so low I almost didn't catch it.

"We don't have kids yet," I answered. The truth was Amy and I had been trying. We both wanted children. But that didn't seem like something to say to a homeless girl.

Her feet hung off the little chair, not even touching the floor. The soles of her low-top sneakers were cracked and worn. She had drawn designs in marker across the tops of her shoes, strange designs that made no sense to me. The bracelet was still on her wrist. She looked so distressed yet incapable of communicating. I was aware of myself as a big man, sitting across from her. Is it me? I wondered. Maybe a female doctor would be better. A woman might be less intimidating. I could hear voices outside. More kids, coming for help.

"Where exactly are you staying, Mary?" I asked nonchalantly.
She spoke suddenly. "I have a cozy place. A cozy little home."
A cozy little home? The phrase seemed odd.
"That's nice." I spoke carefully. "Where?"
The look of suspicion came back. "Moeur Park."

I knew Moeur Park, an empty slash of desert just north of where we parked our van. It was known for its homeless camps. It was not really a park, but rather a desert wildlife area protected by law from new housing developments. During the day hikers and joggers sometimes used the trails. But at night the homeless found shelter among the hills and desert shrubs. Although relatively near the city of Tempe, the area was secluded, and there were no police stations nearby, no homes, no one to hear a person cry for help. I knew that for homeless kids, violence was an expected part of life, and for a loner like Mary, Moeur Park could be especially dangerous. I shuddered inside to think of Mary alone, hiding there in Moeur Park. And what did she mean by a cozy little home?

I asked her, even as I heard the tentative climb of feet up our steps and saw the long shadows cast by other bodies, knowing that soon I would have to turn my attention to the waiting children.

"What kind of cozy little home, Mary?"

"Oh." She looked at me with a strangely hopeful expression, the first light I had seen in her eyes. "It's a *nice* home."

"I'd like to see that sometime."

"Really?" She sounded as if she didn't believe me.

⌐⌐⌐⌐⌐⌐

I didn't want to miss this opportunity to connect with Mary. I asked her to wait while I took care of a few patients. Jan agreed to cover the van while I took Mary in my truck. Mary slid in the back. After being in the clinic all day, I felt the air conditioning of the truck with relief. Mary quietly sighed with pleasure. I heard a rustling. She was looking through all the fast-food wrappers in the back, examining them like artifacts. She held up one Arby's roast beef sandwich wrapper, then another, and an empty curly fries container. I suddenly wished I had cleaned the truck.

The scenery sped by. We were crossing the Mill Avenue Bridge on the way to Moeur Park. Below us was the man-made Tempe Town Lake, with serene, shallow blue waters. People were out paddling on the cool water and walking on the esplanade. I could remember when the lake had been a dry extensive wash full of rocks, and the homeless had camped there. The new lake was pretty, but it had pushed the homeless even farther away from social services.

"Here we are," I said, as we turned into a small parking lot on the other side of the bridge. Someone had defaced a NO LITTERING sign with an obscene spray-painted picture. Moeur Park reached around us. A lunar landscape of sandy hills capped with shards of rocks and stunted cactus, it was the sort of place where you never knew—and maybe didn't want to know—what waited over the next rise. Mary got out of the truck. She pulled a hank of her limp dark hair forward and stuck the end in her mouth with a blank expression. She nursed the strand of hair as she contemplated the expanse that was her home.

I was struck again by how young she looked and how devoid her expression was of any emotion, any hope. Wordlessly she trotted off over the rocky hills.

I followed Mary over several hills, until we were out of sight of the truck—out of sight of everything, as a matter of fact. The desert spread around us, the clear blue sky endless and daunting. The homeless had set up their camps in the washes, spreading old blankets and tarps over the bushes for shade. Abandoned sleeping bags and rags lay about like dead animals. The sandy ground was littered with broken glass. Lizards scampered over hot rocks. The temperature was still over a hundred. Mary seemed strangely impervious to the heat, as if something else had already sapped her energy and left her like this, desolate and empty. I could see no other people around. At night this was no place for a young girl.

"Are we getting closer?" I asked. I had sweat rings under my armpits. Dust marred my new loafers. She stood at the top of a rocky cliff and pointed down a long valley cut between two hills.

Thick desert bushes grew along the bottom. I slid down sharp shale, the thorny bushes pulling at my cargo pants. I felt the reassuring bump of my codebooks in my pockets. Mary didn't answer. At the bottom she stopped on what looked like a concrete lid set in the desert floor. There were storm overflow sewers set in washes like this for when the torrential rains came. In Arizona's monsoon season, it poured, and washes played host to flash floods. Even deserted areas were underlined with a network of storm sewers.

Mary stopped in the middle of the concrete lid. She waited expectantly. I looked around.

It wasn't until I was right next to her that I looked down. I saw what she meant. There was a small square hole in the top of the concrete lid of the overflow trap. The hole was barely large enough to admit someone her size. I knelt and peered in. The inside of the storm drain was a concrete slot, a sewage trap, bordered by dank concrete walls. The bottom was piled with dirty rags and food wrappers, some stuffed into the drainage pipes. To keep out the rats, I thought with a dismal, sick feeling. It looked like the den of a small, frightened animal. It was exactly the size and shape of a coffin. This was where our little Mary slept. This was her cozy home.

I stood, reeling. I knew I was staring off in the distance. Tears stood in my eyes. I couldn't speak. Mary waited, like a child expecting praise. A faint look of worry crossed her face, as if she were contemplating the possibility that I might not like her home. I could picture her there every night, crouched, eating food pulled from her pockets, food that had been culled from Dumpsters, the bag of peanuts I had given her that day. I could imagine her trying to sleep curled up against the fearful noises of the dark. I wanted to whip around and ask her what had happened in her life that had led her to this concrete hole. The injustice of it seemed so wrong. Part of me rebelled. There is no reason for a child in our country to be living in a hole, I thought. But then I looked down at Mary, standing next to me. She was a dirty, damaged-looking teenage girl living in a drainage pipe. She barely came to my shoulder. The same shadow crossed her face. She looked worried. She had shown me her home because I had shown personal interest in her, because I had acted as if I cared. Her gesture was one I could not ignore. Mary had reached out to me. I had to reach back, and the way I did it would show her either my respect and caring or my lack of understanding. It is the first time she has opened up, I thought. Maybe this is the beginning. Maybe I can do this. I knew that whatever I said next was of the utmost importance.

"I'm glad you showed me your home," I said, my voice hoarse.

Back in the truck Mary fiddled with the window buttons, just like a young kid. I was weighing what to say. Something had happened to her that was so traumatic she had either stopped remembering or deliberately tried to forget. I felt that she was hiding from something or from someone. She was hiding not only psychically but also physically. Why else would she have retreated to this hole in the desert? I had realized that asking her blunt questions would only earn me silence or that panicked, blank expression. On the other hand, I could not afford to take more time. I couldn't be patient. Not when she slept in a drainage hole, not when every day was a risk for her. Time was running out against the day when something bad would happen to her. When I thought of her spending one more night in that hole, it hurt inside.

I turned back to her. "How long have you been sleeping out here, Mary?"

Mary got the strangest look on her face, like an anxiety attack in reverse, a sweeping away of memory that took her to a place where no one else visited. She blanked out. Unsure, she stared out the window, blinking. "I don't know," she said slowly. She looked up at the sky through the window. Her face told me that she honestly didn't have the answer. Time, just like her last name, was something that Mary was trying to forget. Just like whatever had happened that had chased her to where she was now.

When we got back to the van, gently I tried to talk Mary into staying or at least into telling us her full name so we could figure out more ways to help her. But she quickly ran off again, toward Mill Avenue. My stomach was in knots, and I felt depressed. I thought, How can I help them when they keep running away?

It was another late night. It was almost 10:00 P.M. by the time we got the van parked back in its loading dock that night, safe behind a high locking gate. Jan's usual cheery good-bye seemed muted. I was so tired I kept relocking the gate before I realized what I was doing. My eyes were burning with exhaustion, and I felt unshed tears.

I stopped in at the children's hospital to check my work there. I was still a staff physician and had many responsibilities, including the supervision of medical students. Instead of being able to go straight home I had to check e-mails and messages and notes. I sat at my desk, feeling the cool silence of the hospital around me. That late it was quiet. I opened my computer. The e-mails and notes waylaid me. There were conference invitations and meetings and a diabetic camp that needed a director. I was facing upcoming certification tests in internal medicine and pediatrics. The thought made my stomach suddenly roil with anxiety. The certifications would require hundreds of hours of study. How was I going to find time to do that? What if I failed my tests? My job might be in jeopardy. My peers might say I wasn't up to the work. If I failed the test, I'd be humiliated and judged by my peers. By taking on the van I had added one huge responsibility to my workload without reducing anything else. The panic gremlin scurried up and gnawed at my stomach. It told me that I had not planned this well. Not at all.

Just stop worrying, I thought. Go home. Eat. Sleep. See Amy.

I crawled into my truck. The dashboard time blinked at me: 11:13 P.M. I would have to be up by 6 A.M. I drove home in the desert night, the wind like black silk outside. Tidy, uniform bungalows passed by. So many lights were already out. Other people were safely tucked in bed.

But I knew Amy would be awake. She would be waiting for me in the kitchen, sitting at the counter, flipping through a magazine, a mug of tea at her side or an empty dish of her favorite ice cream, peppermint. Her hair would smell like vanilla and coconut shampoo. She would have changed into a pair of my boxer shorts and a matching clean cotton shirt. It was something I found touching about Amy: if she couldn't find a shirt to match my boxers, she would change. It was only nighttime, and no one but I would ever see; still, the boxers had to match the shirt.

I was looking forward to our sitting together for a few minutes and telling each other about our days. It was a profoundly comforting thought.

☐☐☐☐☐

The next day the boy who had almost died from pneumonia and blood infection stopped by the van while we were parked in downtown Phoenix. The hospital had released him, and he was back to being homeless and sleeping under bushes. It was strange to see him looking so healthy after he had come so close to death. His brown hair was shiny, and his face was calm. Without the shroud of sickness he was even more handsome than I had thought. The blue eyes that had been blinded with shock were now clear.

I took his vitals. Once again they were normal; only this time I knew they were true vitals. "Are you having any health problems from the infection?" I asked.

"Naw." He sat on the exam table, hands calm on fit legs. He still had the athletic build of a football player, with broad shoulders under his T-shirt. "I can't believe I was almost dead. That's what they told me at the hospital. Is that true?"

I nodded.

"Wow," he said in a muted voice. "I came that close."

"You did." I listened to his lungs. After such a severe pneumonia we would need to pay close attention to his lungs. They might not heal well. A bad pneumonia can cause adhesions that lead to collapsed lungs. In some cases patients lose parts of their lungs.

"No white light," he said, laughing nervously. "But you know what I remember?"

"What do you remember?" I asked. I moved the stethoscope to another place over his lung fields. He winced a little at the feeling of the cold metal. I listened. So far so good. His lungs were clear.

"This guy out in the desert who told me about a van called the Big Blue. I thought it might be a dream when I saw you parked here. I don't really remember you at all. Are you the one who helped me?"

"Me and Jan. She's the nurse-practitioner out front." I moved the stethoscope again for another listen. "Take a deep breath for me."

He breathed. "Doctor?"

"Yes?"

"I can't believe I almost died." His clear blue eyes met mine. There was a grave realization there. He knew he had almost died. I wanted to tell the young man about the first time I had touched death and how much it had influenced me. It had been only ten years before but felt like yesterday. I had taken the year off to save up money for medical school. I was working for a drug company in San Francisco. One day my bosses sent me to Tucson to pick up supplies. I had lived in Tucson from age ten until my college years and was looking forward to the visit. Coincidentally, there was going to be a party in Tucson for the new members of my fraternity, Kappa Sigma. I thought seeing old friends would be good, especially since I'd been feeling down about not being able to start medical school right away. I was standing in the middle of the courtyard between the cheap little cottage apartments that the guys in the fraternity used to rent, talking to an old friend. The sky was black and starry. It was one of those hot electric summer nights when you just feel there is going to be trouble. A strange man suddenly appeared in the middle of the party. He had wandered in off a busy downtown street. He began arguing loudly with my companion. I wondered if he was drunk. I moved to intervene when there were shouts. Another man had come into the courtyard, and it was with disbelief that I saw he had a gun. He was pointing it at the sky and shooting as he came straight at us. The sound was strangely anticlimactic yet chilling, little popping sounds in the night. Instinctually everyone ducked and panicked. None of it made any sense to me, but without thinking I moved toward him, gesturing peacefully with my hands. "Drop the gun," my hands were saying. Behind me police cars arrived, and officers came running. I was thinking, This makes no sense. Why is someone with a gun here? How did this happen, and so fast? The police must have been looking for this guy. One of the officers dived for the gun. Shots rang out. Others chased the shooter out the back entrance as the officer collapsed next to me.

I crawled to him. There was a jet of bright red blood coming out from under his armpit. I knew this was arterial blood, from the heart. He made no sound. His face was quickly turning blue-gray. There was no pulse. I tore open his shirt only to find a bullet-proof vest underneath. How had the bullet gotten through that? With my hands I felt under his arm. The bullet had entered right under his armpit, in the one place not covered by the vest. I tried to do CPR, but with each compression a big squirt of blood came out of his armpit. How do you get these things off? I thought in panic. Blood was pouring out, bathing my hands in thick warmth. I shouted, and someone handed me a towel. With my fingers I pushed it into the wound, trying to stop the bleeding. But within moments the end was clear.

They pulled me off his body. I was taken to a police car, where I sat for three hours, waiting my turn to be interviewed. "What was his name?" I asked the officer sitting in the front. He wiped his eyes before answering. They had worked together, I thought. "John Barleycorn." It sounded so American, so innocent. The death of Officer Barleycorn was a turning point in my life. My own problems suddenly seemed small in comparison. I realized how quickly someone could lose it all. I had tried to save someone and failed. But what I remembered most was the sudden realization of how precious life was and the reality of the man in front of me in flesh and blood and how desperate I had been to save his life. From then on it seemed life was more meaningful.

I wished I could tell the boy sitting on my exam table how being touched by death can inspire one to live a better life. I wanted to tell him he could use his brush with death to fight for himself. But the words just weren't there.

"You can put your shirt back on now," I told him instead. "Your lungs sound pretty good. Your general health seems good. I want to get you a follow-up X-ray." Suddenly I pictured a hospital bill. I realized this boy had no insurance. The hospital had seen him because it was an emergency. Without insurance, paying for an X-ray was going to be impossible. I worried that he might not be able to get the X-ray at all. I'd have to find out. One more thing to add to the to-do list, I thought.

The question remained in his face.

"I don't want to see you sleeping under bushes," I said. "We have some good friends who work at a place called HomeBase. They have a nice shelter for kids your age to stay at. I'm going to call them for you, OK? We'll see if they have a bed."

"OK," he said with a smile back.

3

TELL ME

M ary was there when we parked again on the next weekly trip to Tempe. I suspected she had been lurking around corners from the early morning, just waiting for us. She appeared shyly at the bottom of the steps as soon as we parked, and Jan said, "Look who's here. Come on up." Jan gave her an extra fob chain to wear over her shirt. "She's our new assistant," Jan said. Mary looked delighted.

She sat in the front, opening up bit by bit. I could see the relaxation in her shoulders and a tiny smile peeping out of the corners of her mouth. Once or twice that morning Jan made a joke, and Mary's eyes lit up, while I saw other patients, darting in and out of the rooms. Coming out once, I was startled to hear Mary laugh. It was a bright, sharp laugh that made our heads turn. The other homeless kids accepted her presence without comment. I realized that some things were sacred with these kids. Mary's need for family resonated with them. They understood. No one questioned why the tiny girl with a fob chain sat all day in the front of our van.

That day she let me give her a physical exam and do blood work. She fidgeted during the physical, looking abashed. "We're glad you're here," I told her, and didn't pick up on why she seemed even more uncomfortable than usual.

Jan came in to take the blood. She took one look at Mary and figured it right out. "Can I talk to her?" Jan asked. I left the room. Jan told me later she gave Mary a girl talk about periods and using sanitary napkins. "She was using wadded-up paper towels from the public restrooms," Jan said when Mary went outside. She lowered her voice. "She's so out of touch with her body. She doesn't even know why she has periods. I tried to tell her, but she shut down."

We both looked to where Mary was now sitting outside, her exam over. She still wore her bracelet. "Ask Me," it said, and I hadn't yet. I was afraid I didn't know how to ask. How many weeks had passed since she had first started coming to the van? Too many. What if I just scared her more? What if she left and never came back? I realized that I was better at helping the kids with their medical needs. It was everything else they needed that I didn't know how to handle.

She sat outside in the heat, sipping water and watching the other kids play. Jan had given her a white bag with extra sanitary napkins, and she held this in her lap like a prize. This made me ache inside. I thought about her going back to her hole once again. I made phone call after phone call in between patients, trying to find help for her. I was shocked at the lack of resources for kids like Mary. I wanted to argue with the people on the phone. "She's living in a hole," I wanted to yell. "We're sorry," they said, and behind their voices I heard budget cuts and high caseloads and people sick with stress themselves over all the help they wished they could give but could not. I said I understood. I did understand. None of these people was making it rich by denying homeless kids. All of our hands were tied by lack of money and other resources.

I put my phone in my pocket and looked out the door, and Mary was gone. I stepped outside and looked around. Once again she was gone. "Mary," I wanted to yell. "Come back." I went home feeling sick with worry. I can't keep doing this, I thought. I felt like a failure. Someone else would have saved her by now. A better doctor would have helped her. I waved good-bye to Jan that night, knowing that she too carried that weight home on her shoulders. When I curled up next to Amy that night, I thought about Mary, living in her hole. I had a dream in which I went and rescued her, and when I carried her out, she was as small as a kitten. I woke in the night with longing. If only it was that easy, I thought. If only.

⌑⌑⌑⌑⌑

The following Monday I gave Mary a set of brand-new clothes, including socks and shoes. The jeans were dark blue Wranglers, stiff with newness, and the shirt had a pop star on the front. It was a nice, fashionable outfit, the kind a teenage girl could wear without shame. Afterward she sat on the paper-covered exam table, pressing her new jeans with her hands and giggling. I had never seen her act so much like the child she was. She seemed all of twelve. I imagined her having sleepovers and talking about boys and eating junk food. She had missed so much from life. Was it possible to give any of her childhood back to her? Or was it more important to help her find her way as an independent adult?

"Look at you, with those nice clothes. Now you're ready for a new life," I told her. She blinked, as if this idea had never occurred to her.

I thought about what to say. I needed her to talk to me. I had been taught not to get too involved, not to care too much, to keep a professional shield between the patient and me. "You don't want to get too close" was the mantra of the medical field. I remembered that, encouraged by my friend Danny, I took the special medical program in high school. I soon found myself going to actual surgeries and teaching rounds. I was able to shadow heart surgeon Dr. Jack Copeland. I was very lucky; Dr. Copeland and his team were often in the national news. I couldn't believe I was sitting in on their meetings. During one, Dr. Copeland turned to me and asked, "Randy, can you research this technique?" I stayed up all night writing the report.

Most of Dr. Copeland's patients were older, but there was one teenage girl, who was sick with a failing heart. She needed a transplant. She was on the waiting list but grew sicker day by day. Her name never seemed to move up the list. It upset me that a girl my own age would be so close to dying. I sat by her bed, feeling gawky and adolescent and all arms in the new striped shirt my mom had bought just for my new job. My wrists seemed too long, my neck was too thin, and at that age I never seemed to gain weight no matter how much I ate. My voice kept cracking. Still, she seemed to like my company. We talked about the average stuff: music, bands she liked, how she wanted to learn ballroom dancing even though it was kind of nerdy.

Family members had left a gift basket by her bed. It had a sign on it that said FOR AFTER YOUR OPERATION. She often looked at the basket. You could see the treats inside, under the red cellophane wrapper. It was a reminder to keep hoping and fighting. She saved it. "For when I get well," she said.

Then one night she died. I came in the next day, self-consciously petting the sparse mustache I was trying desperately to cultivate, wondering if she would notice it and say anything, and I walked into her room and saw the bed was empty. My throat trembled. The blankets were gone. The basket was gone. She was gone.

Losing that patient taught me that there are times when you do get close to your patients. The mantra of the field was wrong for me. It seemed to me that I could get close but also maintain my objectivity. It would make me a better doctor. There would always be the risk of attachment, and with attachment came the potential for loss. I felt it sharply at that moment, looking at Mary. I cared for her. It was as if she were my child. Whatever happened to her would affect me. I didn't want to make any mistakes. I knew people who cared deeply but had trouble maintaining their professional boundaries and critical thinking. I knew others who didn't seem to care at all about patients. If I was going to do this work, I thought, I had to find the balance.

I cleared my throat. "You know, Mary, I really care about you." I was looking at her directly. "I think about you sleeping in the hole, and I worry."

Her eyes jumped, and what passed between us was like electricity. It hit me that maybe no one had ever told her he cared about her. I saw something in her eyes that was like hope. Under that hope was a terrible black fear. It was the fear of everything that had ever happened to her. It was time. Maybe it was past time.

"Mary, please tell me: Why do you hurt?"

She didn't respond, just stared, her eyes dark and huge. I had a sudden, deep conviction that what had happened to Mary was deeper than memory. Even acknowledging it would bring it all back. She reached down and rotated the bracelet with one hand.

She began talking. The words came out in a monotone at first. Each one was laced with acid because what she was telling me was so painful. Her voice was flat. I could sense her shame. It was almost like a physical presence. She spoke for what seemed like a long time, her hand ceaselessly circling the bracelet. The more she spoke, the larger and darker her eyes grew. She got closer to what she needed to say. Tears formed almost unwillingly, increasing until they finally slid down her cheeks. I felt dizzy with pain myself.

As she talked and cried, the daylight outside seemed to grow brighter, and I could hear each and every sound of the van around us: the clink of metal in a tray, a series of low voices, the hum of the machines, a bird singing in the distance. If Mary had looked up, she would have seen herself, reflected in my glasses, a little child alone on an exam table, a doctor standing nearby. The tears were all over her hands, like raindrops from a passing storm. And still her story kept coming, in little choked pieces and brutal bits, with a hurt that ran so deep I could see her skin crawl. She told me, and I listened.

When I walked into my house that night, I was feeling wrung out, emotional, exhausted, sick, hopeful, angry. There wasn't a feeling I wasn't having. I thought about what Mary had said her father had done and how unthinkable it was, how it was the worst betrayal. Even to think about it roiled my stomach. I wanted—I needed—to talk to Amy.

People didn't understand why Amy was so supportive of my working on the van. After all, I could have chosen a field that made better money. Instead I had a job that paid less than many of my colleagues' salaries, and I was gone for sixty hours a week. Yet Amy always encouraged me.

I had been smitten with Amy since the first time I'd seen her. "This is your new boss," one of the doctors had said, introducing her. I turned to see cute curly hair and a nose that wrinkled with laughter. Amy was the senior resident, and I was her new intern at the children's hospital. I was bowled over. She was warm, with an infectious smile, but she was also vulnerable and reserved. She was as interested as I was in serving the poor. She had requested her weekly clinic to be at the Thomas J. Pappas School–based clinic for homeless children, just as I had. I got to know Amy well during our weekly rotations at Pappas. I saw how gentle she was with children, how easy to laugh and have fun, and how stoic and strong when something went badly. Amy had integrity.

I surprised myself by asking her out after only a few weeks. Usually I would have been too shy. She gave me that huge smile. "Nope," she announced. I was taken aback. She saw my hurt look. "Look, I don't want a relationship. I'm a senior resident. Next year I'll be out of here. I could get hired in Minnesota for all I know. Or Guam," she said, with a teasing look that I came to know well. So we became fast friends instead. She invited me to go house hunting with her. For months we went to look at little houses in the Willo and Encanto districts of Phoenix, older houses with few modern conveniences. I watched as Amy made plans to buy a house that would contain only her. "I don't have a lot of clothes," she once said, excusing the fact that a little cottage had no closets.

I cleared my throat. "What if you get married?"

Amy looked as if that were way off in a foggy distance. I began to suspect her reservations about a serious relationship ran much deeper than just job choices.

Amy was there for me when my sister, Stephanie, began having troubling symptoms of MS, including numb feelings below the waist and difficulty walking. She listened when I told her that Stephanie's doctors had told her it was all in her head. They wanted her to see a psychiatrist. In the meantime they ran an MRI. I was doing a rotation at the hospital when the neurologist called. He sounded humbled. "We think your sister has multiple sclerosis," he said. I immediately went to my boss and asked to leave early, so I could talk to my sister.

It was Amy I turned to later for support. We sat on the back porch of the house she rented with her roommate, Angel, a southern girl from North Carolina, drinking Diet Cokes. "Look," Amy said, and pointed to a shooting star. "What do you wish for, Randy?"

I looked at her profile. "I wish my sister's MS would go away," I told her. She turned and looked at me abruptly. Maybe, I hoped, she was seeing something new in me.

But after months of friendship I was starting to feel Amy would never develop romantic feelings for me. I wondered if the loss of her mother when she was young had made her fearful to grow attached again. Her father lived in California. Amy was alone. Maybe she wanted it that way. I reflected on my life so far. Each time I had fallen in love, it had been hard and with a woman who never felt the same way. These infatuations had lasted for years. When it finally became clear that a relationship would not happen, I fell into a deep depression. Now I worried I was falling into the same trap again.

In April 1997, when I was ready to give up, we both were invited to the wedding of her roommate. It was in Las Vegas and two months before the end of Amy's residency. We were coming out of the parking garage elevator, talking about nothing, it seemed, just the comfortable everyday stuff we always discussed. Amy suddenly stopped. Her eyes were large and bright. We stared at each other, and she stepped forward and kissed me. The kiss seemed to last forever. When it was done, Amy tucked her face against my pounding chest. "What are we going to do now?" she asked. It was a telling sign of our relationship that after we returned to Phoenix, we started the process of buying a house together. We had been looking for weeks before one day Amy turned to me in my truck and said teasingly, "We love each other, and yet we've never even said it."

I turned around, took a deep, delighted breath, and responded, "I completely and totally love you."

I was thinking of that magical moment when I came through the door and unloaded the contents of my pockets onto the side table. I jerked them out in a hurry: phone, keys, codebooks. I opened my mouth to call Amy. But there was something about the atmosphere in the house. The air felt different. There was a palpable tension. I walked into the kitchen. Amy was sitting where I expected her to be, an ignored magazine in front of her.

"Honey?" I asked, coming in.

She turned to me, her face bright, incandescent, and beautiful.

"I'm pregnant," she said.

I felt all my worries about the van fall away. I stepped forward and gave her a huge hug. Amy was ecstatic. I felt that together we were seeing the same vistas, embarking on the same journey. My heart raced with excitement. I'm going to be a father, I thought, I will have a son or daughter. I realized that along with my joy came brand-new concerns. Suddenly I had worries I had never had. Was our budget enough? Did I need to plan for college? I remembered all the times as a doctor I had seen new fathers, and they had told me about the pressures of fatherhood. Now I understood. Along with those worries were some that came from my experiences on the van. My world was full of kids who had diseases and problems. I wanted desperately not to have these worries for my own children. I held my wife and kissed her, rocking back and forth in our joy.

4

MARY'S JOURNEY

When Mary told me her story, she disclosed her real name. I called Child Protective Services the next day. Mary, it turned out, was seventeen. Her father had been sent to prison for sexually abusing her. The original charge was rape, but he had pleaded guilty to the lesser charge of sexual abuse instead. During the years he molested Mary he had kept her secluded from her other family members. He threatened to kill her if she told anyone what was going on. Mary was terrified. After his arrest Child Protective Services had found Mary a home with an aunt who lived in Chandler, right outside Phoenix. But when the aunt went to school to pick Mary up, she had already run away. "Mary was sixteen at the time," the social worker said. "She's been missing ever since." She paused and then asked curiously, "Do you know where she was hiding?" I thought of the hole in the desert. I wondered how long Mary would have kept living there if she had not come to our van.

There was a storm of phone calls. By the time we were back in Tempe the following week the aunt was coming to get Mary once again. The social worker assured me that the aunt was nothing like her brother: "The two haven't talked for years. He never let her meet Mary." As remarkable as this story sounded, I wasn't surprised. In my work as a pediatrician I had often been struck by the fragmentation of the American family. I asked what the aunt was like. "She works in a nursing home. She's a nice single lady, a bit of an old maid, to use an old-fashioned term. No criminal history, not even a traffic ticket. Apparently her hobby is needlepoint. She's never had any kids of her own but said she'd be happy to take Mary."

Mary was waiting outside in one of the folding lawn chairs, biting her lips. "I didn't even know I had an aunt," she mumbled. "Maybe she won't like me."

"She'll like you just fine," Jan said. "What's not to like?"

I felt just as nervous as Mary. Her aunt drove up in an old Datsun. When she got out of her car, she was crying. She hugged me, tears wetting my shirt. She was crying so hard she could barely speak. "I almost gave up," she said.

Mary stood off to the side. Her aunt approached slowly. She touched Mary's hair and then gently brought her close. "I know we've never met," I heard her whisper into Mary's hair, "but we're still going to be family."

We hugged Mary good-bye. I gave her a little stuffed bear I had found. It had a heart sewn on the chest. "Friends Forever," it said. Hokey, I thought, but I wanted her to know she could always come back.

"If you need medical care for her, or for any reason, bring her back," I told her aunt, whose name was Diane. "We'd love to see our Mary."

Once inside the car, Mary waved a little. She held the bear up, bending its arm as if it were waving good-bye. I was shocked at the changes in her life. It was as if Mary had been a piece of luggage sent here or there. I knew it was wonderful she had a place to live. But I had mixed feelings. I wanted Mary to be safe. I wanted her to be successful. I wondered if this was possible after what she had been through. Could a girl who had lived in a hole make the transition to a normal life? Would she be able to go to high school? How would other teenagers treat her? Could she fit in? Could she recover? Or did her past mean she was damaged forever? Still, I knew she had to try. And we all had to help. There was no alternative.

Monsoon season struck a month later. Dark and gray, the dust storms came over downtown Phoenix. We called them Arizona dusters; they were great black and gray roiling clouds that came in solid walls over the city. It was like watching something from a natural disaster movie. The man on the radio had warned drivers to pull over, far off the road, and turn off their lights. If you were driving and got caught in those storms, it was like being immersed in black soup. When the monsoon season came, I worried for the homeless kids. Arizona storms are nothing to ignore. Homeless people have drowned after falling asleep in the washes and getting caught in a flash flood.

When the rush of patients subsided, we stood for a moment in the van doorway. The distinctive smell of the creosote bushes drifted from the desert, and the hum of the cicadas was so loud it sounded like the buzzing of hundreds of rattlesnakes. It brought back old memories of monsoons, time spent as a kid playing board games with Stephanie inside our house and listening to the rain roar down the washes, or sitting in a café while the rain poured in sheets outside. After, I knew, the air would smell fresh. The streets would be washed, and all of Arizona would seem clean. But for the homeless kids it was different. The storms left them soaked, miserable, and sick. Their socks and shoes and sleeping bags became sodden. Infections and illnesses quickly set in.

We watched as the sky turned the thick, menacing dark color of dust clouds. A boy came running ahead of the storm toward us, the sheet of black dust behind him. He was coughing as he ran—asthma, I thought. "Hurry!" Jan called.

She interviewed the boy with the new intake forms she had created. He said his name was Matthew and he was seventeen. He had been sleeping under an overpass since his stepdad had kicked him out of his home. He had been mugged repeatedly. "He's lost count of how many times he has been assaulted," Jan had written. I took a deep breath and went into the exam room.

He was small and thin, with thick blond hair. He wore a dusty long trench coat over black clothes. My heart knitted a little bit at seeing the outfit. It looked like the sad posturing of a boy trying to look tough. But he didn't look tough at all, not with thick glasses mended with Scotch tape and rubber bands. One lens was shattered inside the frame, and he kept turning his head to look at me through the good lens. I could see from their thickness that he had very poor eyesight. I thought he looked like a walking target, a boy so demoralized he was open to attack.

"What happened to your glasses?" I asked in a friendly voice.

"I got jumped. I was trying to fight them off."

I examined his teeth. The ones up front were OK, but there were huge gaping holes in his back molars, the result of years of untreated cavities. He would need intensive dental work.

"What can I help you with?" I asked.

"My feet. They hurt."

I looked down. He was wearing heavy boots.

"OK, how about we take them off for a look?"

He hesitated. "It's OK," I told him.

When he unlaced his boots and pulled them off, the smell was profound, putrid. I struggled to keep my face even. I carefully lifted one foot. Humiliated, he put his head down. His once-white socks were stuck to the soles of his feet. I could see damp blood and pus through the thin fabric. Parts of the socks were embedded in the rotten flesh. He probably hadn't changed the socks in weeks. Months even. How could he change them? He was homeless. He didn't have access to a bath. The lack of shelters meant the kids had no way to get clean.

He began slowly peeling one of the socks off his foot. A layer of skin and pus came with it. I could tell immediately his feet had a bacterial superinfection from an untreated fungus. I examined the soles. Along with raw infected flesh there were deep holes that looked to be a good quarter inch deep. Of more concern were his toes. The tips of two were black and spongy. It had to be incredibly painful just to walk. He kept his head turned down, his eyes at his knees. The smell filled the room. He was embarrassed. How hard this must be on him, I thought. He was at a time in his life that he should be feeling ready to take on the world. Instead he was at rock bottom.

"I can take care of this," I said, trying to reassure him, to take away the humiliation.

"Really?"

"Sure. These kinds of foot infections go crazy in the heat, especially in monsoon weather like this. First I'm going to get rid of these socks," I said, picking them up with my gloved hands and dropping them in the trash. "I'm going to get you some new socks and shoes. We've got extras up front. But before that I am going to treat your feet. I need to spray them with medicine. Then we'll get some clotrimazole cream. I'm also going to put you on Keflex, since the infection is bad. It's an oral antibiotic. You're going to get the triple whammy."

After I had treated his feet, I finished the rest of his exam. What I'd thought was asthma turned out to be a mild case of bronchitis. On his arms I noticed a series of unusual symmetric scars. They were neat, almost orderly, as if his forearms had been caught in some form of machinery. I turned his arm gently and examined the scars further. They weren't identical. They had a hand-hewn look, something I had seen as a pediatrician, though usually in girls.

"Do you cut yourself sometimes?" I asked.

"Yeah."

"What with?"

He took out a folding knife from his back pocket. "With this."

I took the blood-flecked knife. "It's hard to hurt so much, isn't it?" I asked him. "You must hurt an awful lot to do this to yourself."

He nodded, his eyes watering behind the broken glasses.

"When kids hurt this much, there is usually a reason," I said. "You know, this is a clinic just like any other doctor's office. We are real doctors and nurses. That means we maintain confidentiality. But I'm also what they call a mandated reporter. That means if you tell me you are going to hurt someone or hurt yourself, I have to report that."

"What if someone hurt me?" he asked.

"That depends on when it happened."

He nodded.

I touched his arm very briefly. "Why don't you tell me, and we will figure it out together?"

"I'm scared a lot."

"Why?"

"I don't have anyplace to go. I keep getting beat up."

"How about your home? Your mom?"

"My stepdad kicked me out. He was always beating on me anyhow. You can call him. I don't care. He's just going to tell you he doesn't want me around." He willingly gave me the number.

"OK. We're going to get you help. In the meantime I want you to sign a contract with me not to cut yourself. If you feel like cutting yourself, I want you to call us. I'm going to give you our phone numbers."

He wiped his eyes. "How about that nurse?"

I smiled. "Jan would love to see you. Did you know she's one of the top BMX racers in the country? You should ask her about that sometime. She'll love it."

"Really?" He looked surprised. "I used to motocross . . . a long time ago."

"Ask her about it. She's got medals and the whole nine yards."

Before he left, Jan had set him up with an appointment with an optometrist for new glasses and another appointment at a dental clinic for the homeless that primarily handled emergency cases. I had taken a full set of labs, testing for everything from HIV to hepatitis, and given him a ten-day supply of Keflex, the antibiotic. He had three new pairs of socks, new running shoes, and a pair of flip-flops to wear while the foot infection healed. He opened up his backpack to put in the extra shoes and medications. The backpack was almost empty. There was a crumpled shirt in the bottom.

He carefully took out an old and creased photograph. "This was my dad." I saw a bigger version of the boy, a ruddy-faced blond-haired man sitting on a couch. "He died when I was five. He got killed by a drunk driver." He carefully slid the photograph into the now-bulging backpack. For a moment his face was transformed by anger. "Then my mom marries a drunk. Go figure."

"You're not out of here yet," I said. "I'm calling a shelter program I know about called HomeBase. They serve young adults and teenagers. It's a great program."

"You mean I can go there today?"

"Yes, I hope today."

I glanced at my watch. Almost two hours had passed since the boy had shown up. For once I felt I had done it almost right. The boy was relaxed, happy. I watched him joke with Jan up front as we finished. It was instructive for me to watch how she handled the teenagers. Instead of reacting negatively to her firm and take-charge tone they seemed to eat it up. I can learn something here, I thought, watching Jan. She was very authoritative, and the teenagers seemed to bend over backward to please her. The two of them went off, chatting like crazy about motocross racing. When he was gone, I called the number he had given me for his home. A gruff voice answered the phone: "Yeah?" I identified myself and told the man why I was calling. His stepson was a minor and had seen me for medical care. I wanted to know about the possibility of his returning home. "Oh, yeah?" the stepfather said. "Tell that little asshole not to bother coming back."

I recoiled. "Why?"

"Little shit called the cops on me."

I listened to the man rage drunkenly for several minutes, threatening to do worse than he had done, he said. I was unable to get a word in edgewise. Finally I hung up. I decided to try again, later, to reach the boy's mother. As much as I believed in keeping families together, I realized there were times when it wasn't going to happen. Some of these kids were never going home. What future they had depended on what they discovered, or didn't discover, on the streets.

Jan and I were in our ramshackle office the next day, trying to
stretch our budget to include more socks and shoes for the kids.
The phone rang. It was Mary's aunt. "She's gone," she said through
tears.

My heart fell to the bottom of my stomach. "Gone?" Mary had
been with her aunt for only a little more than a month. It seemed
as if just days had passed since she had waved good-bye. The sky
outside the dirty office window was dark and threatening with
coming monsoon rains.

"Her father is out of prison." She said his name as if it were
poison, spit out. "I just found out. He was paroled. I had no idea.
He's back. In Phoenix."

My heart jerked. I was appalled. He had served only a year in
prison? For what he had done to her?

"I'd got her in counseling." She took a deep breath. "I've been
doing everything. You *know* what he did to her. He's not even
supposed to have contact with her. He lost his parental rights in
prison. I didn't even know he was out. I came home and Mary was
gone. There was a message from him on the phone."

"Did she leave a note?"

"Nothing. I'm so scared he got her. I called the police, but I
don't know if they know where to look or what to do. I thought
maybe you knew."

I thanked her and hung up. I stared off in space, then got up
and told Jan I had to leave. I was barely aware of getting into my
truck, and somehow I drove without seeing anything at all.

I made my way to Moeur Park.

The sky had been moody all day, in the dark, threatening way
that promised severe storms. The weatherman had said the rain-
storms would come again that afternoon. They would be real
doozies, he said. Stay inside, he said. There was a sour, decaying
smell on the wind, and I thought of war-torn countries and what

the dead smell like. It was the same sour smell the street kids brought with them, enmeshed in their clothes.

I made my way across the desert by memory. There was a dense, electric feeling in the air. The birds had roosted in the bushes. A few warning calls broke the air. There were broken bottles in the sand and cans with their lids pried off. I crossed the remains of a fire and caught whiffs of urine. A drunken man rolled out of the bushes into my path, mumbling something. I stepped over him as if I had no time. I didn't.

The sky was electric by the time I came to Mary's camp. The bushes seemed to sizzle from wanting rain. The bottom of the wash was hot, claustrophobic, the wind both still and anxious. It was a dangerous time to be out in the open. There would probably be lightning, and once the rains came, a wash like this could turn into a flash flood.

I stood on the concrete lid of her home. The hole below me was square and dark. Please, I thought. Please let her be here, and not with him. I crouched down. Above me the sky went dark, and there was a smell of ozone. Any minute now, I thought. At any minute the rain will come sheeting down.

"Mary?" I asked.

My voice was too soft.

I made it stronger: "Mary."

I knelt closer to the hole, until my face was almost inside.

It was then that I saw her, in a flash of light from the dark sky above, illuminating her form. She was crouched in the farthest corner, huddled like an animal in her cave. The relief that overcame me was immense. I could see now why this hole in the ground was preferable to other places. I felt a surge of gratitude toward Mary for teaching me this.

"Mary, it's me, Dr. Christensen. Please come out." I had my head in the hole now. "Please." I paused. "You know I'm too big to fit in this dang hole."

I saw a sliver of her face.

"I might get stuck, you know. OK, you want to know the truth? I'm too scared to crawl down there."

I saw a little more of her face.

"The rain is coming, Mary. You could drown in there."

There was a shake of the head.

The sky cracked above me, and the deluge came pouring down. The concrete pad was immediately a freshet, the wash around me two inches high, rushing in alarming sheets into Mary's hole. My shirt was drenched to my back, my hair over my face, my glasses blinded with water. When I opened my mouth, the rain poured in. It ran around me and down into the sordid hole. The smell that arose from the hole was indescribable.

"Please, Mary," I yelled.

She moved maybe a fraction of an inch.

"You won't ever have to go back to him, I promise," I shouted through the rain.

Her face turned. Her face was distrustful. She crawled over. Her pale face turned up at the hole, her dark hair against her cheek. The rain above fell onto her skin. It poured off the curving pale form of her ear. She didn't say anything. Her eyes were pleading. I reached a hand down to her. Nothing felt more important in the moment than my desire that Mary take my hand.

"Mary. Please. I promise."

Mary was taken back to her aunt's house in Chandler. Everyone reassured her that no matter what happened, she would never again live with her father. He was arrested for parole violation for trying to contact her. The police said he would probably be out of jail the next day. They were right. Mary's aunt created a safety plan. Every day she took Mary to school; every day she picked her up. She decided to move across town to a new apartment and change her phone number. "I wish I could just move out of state or something," she said on the phone. "But I've got my job here, and I can't afford to move. What do you think?"

"I think you need to do what works for you. The safety plan sounds like a good idea. Can you ask the school for help?"

I was filled with outrage. This man had hurt his daughter in the worst way possible and had served only a year in prison. Now he was stalking her, and again nothing would happen. Never before had I understood how lightly abusive parents got treated. For the rest of her life Mary would have to deal with the knowledge that her father could be around the corner. The thought made me angry and sick. No wonder so many kids are homeless, I thought, if this is all that happens to their abusers.

I went home that night and found Amy sitting on the living room couch folding laundry. I was trying to find a way to bring up Mary's father and what had happened. It seemed like such a terrible thing to discuss, yet I wanted my wife's opinions and support. Amy looked up and smiled at me. I looked at the framed photograph on the mantel over her head. It was a picture of her mother, Jane, during the last months of the breast cancer that killed her when Amy was just fifteen. Her head was covered with a blue kerchief and a straw hat, but the woman's warmth and kindness shone on her freckled face. They were the same qualities I loved in Amy. I remember Amy's telling me how her mother used to sing to the homeless at their Quaker meeting in Whittier, California. Sometimes when I told Amy a little about the kids on the van, she told me about her childhood and how she wished all children could experience the comfort and faith her mother had given her: the stories every night at bedtime, the family dinners at the table, the homemade bunk beds her mother had made, how she had taught Amy how to sew when she was little. When Amy shared these memories with me, it was as if she were passing secret messages over a high wall.

When she was a mother, Amy said, she would do the same things her mother had done. Once again Amy would be part of a sacred loop of family. She had missed it for so long. I thought maybe I would tell her later about Mary. It is too much right now, and I don't want to burden her with my sorrows. I wanted her to be happy in her pregnancy. It should be a time of joy, I thought, not a time to talk about the evils people are capable of doing to children. Amy saw me watching and folded one of my shirts. She was smiling. "I scheduled an extra-early ultrasound," she said.

"Really?" I sat down next to her, picked up a pair of my shorts, and made a clumsy effort to fold them. "When is it?"

"In a few weeks, on Friday." She smiled.

I gave her a kiss. "Can I get you anything?" I asked, standing up to unload my pockets.

"I'm craving ice cream," she said.

"You craved ice cream before you got pregnant too," I said, teasing her. As I went into the kitchen, I thought it was best I hadn't talked about Mary. Instead I could enjoy this peaceful time with my wife.

The morning of Amy's ultrasound Mary's aunt, Diane, brought her back to the van for some tests. "I don't get paid much and don't have insurance," she said apologetically. "And I'm trying to save money to move." I assured her this was fine. Mary would always be welcome.

"How are you holding up?" I asked.

"It's hard," she admitted. "I never had any kids of my own. This whole thing with her father, well, I used to stay awake because she was missing. Now I stay awake because he is out . . ." She trailed off. "But as far as money goes, you know, there's lots of ways to cook potatoes." I smiled at her. I saw her strained eyes and reminded myself to give her some referrals. We had started a binder filled with the numbers of agencies that helped families, from food boxes to aid to new mothers. Many times kids left home because there simply wasn't enough to go around, and if helping their parents helped them, I thought it was worthwhile. A relative like Diane needed support too. Parenting a child as traumatized as Mary, especially dealing with the looming threat of her father, could not be easy.

I took Mary into a room for an exam. I was astounded at how much she'd changed in such a short time. Her once-dirty hair was now sleek and clean. Her eyes were clear and made contact with mine. She wore clean jeans and a fresh top. She stood up straighter. When she hopped onto the table, her movements were sharper.

She saw me looking at her wrist. She was still wearing the bracelet. "My counselor says I'll take it off when I'm ready."

"I'm glad you wore it. You give me a reason to ask."

She studied me for a long time. "You came to find me."

"You are worth it." I felt that I sounded trite. It was hard to communicate to Mary how sincere I was about her care.

When we were done, she turned toward me. "I was lucky to come here," she said.

Tears pricked my eyes. I never would think of her life as lucky. She gestured toward the outside of the van. The gesture spoke not of dozens of kids but of untold thousands. "Most of the kids out there don't have someone like you. Or my aunt."

What I wanted to say was, "Most doctors aren't blessed to have patients like you, Mary." Instead I held my hand out and we solemnly shook hands. She went out to find her aunt waiting, talking crockpot recipes with Jan. Jan was saying she had two teenage kids who were eating her out of house and home too and how that crockpot was a lifesaver.

I had scheduled that afternoon off for our early ultrasound, and I drove the truck to pick up Amy at our house. I thought the ultrasound would be a special way to start a special weekend. We would meet our baby and then pick up some food for dinner. There was nothing Amy liked more than our cooking a leisurely dinner together, and I couldn't disagree. We had planned our celebration meal. Amy wanted to try a new dessert recipe. We had gotten a fancy little blowtorch for a wedding present from her stepsister, and Amy said we could use it for finishing a crème brûlée. We had never used it, and now seemed like a good time.

"Crème brûlée," I kept reminding her, "is my favorite dessert, just under my grandmother's seven-layer bars." I joked as we drove.

"You keep talking about your grandmother's seven-layer bars, and maybe I will turn that blowtorch on you," she said, smiling out the windshield. "How was the van today?" she asked. "The kids? Anything hard?"

"Fine, fine," I said. The image of Mary sitting on my exam table, her eyes clear, flashed in front of me.

"It'll be neat to hear her heartbeat," she said, looking out the window. There was a misty look in her face. I noticed she was referring to the baby as a girl.

In the clinic we watched the doctor, a friend of ours, prepare Amy's belly with the conducting gel. Amy winced a little at how cold the gel felt. I felt the cool transducer myself in sympathetic prickles across my own stomach. Amy smiled at me from the table. I kissed her. She shifted. The full bladder necessary for the ultrasound was making her uncomfortable. Then it was there, on the screen: our baby. I studied the grainy gray image. A surge of pride filled me. There was my baby. Our baby.

But the doctor frowned. "Are you sure you've got the dates right?" she asked.

I looked at Amy. My wife never got dates wrong. There was a cool place growing around my heart.

"Sure. Why?" Amy asked.

"I don't hear a heartbeat yet. Maybe we're too early. Are you sure it has been six weeks?"

"More than that," I said.

"We should use the ultrasound at the hospital," the doctor said. "This clinic machine isn't quite as good."

"Right now?" I asked.

"Yeah. I think it would be a good idea."

I was tired and hungry and thinking about dinner and sleep and the kids on the van. I didn't want to think about what the dates meant. But Amy wanted to go, and so we did, driving in silence to the hospital only a few blocks away. The joking happiness from before had evaporated. There was a line of worry between her eyes. Another room, another gown, and this time Amy winced when the conductor was applied. Her bladder was now causing pain. The sac, the place inside my wife where our baby lay, appeared on the screen again. The room was quiet. The doctor moved the transducer slowly over Amy's stomach. We all listened. I heard nothing but the sound of my heart. The blurry grayness inside Amy lay still, cupped, and silent.

"I still don't hear the heartbeat," the doctor said.

I turned to Amy. Her face was bleak. All of a sudden she knew. And because she knew, I knew. The doctor's face took on a watchful, careful, and measured expression. I knew the look. I had practiced it enough myself. Soon, I knew, she would turn to us. Her eyes would be kind. They were. I wanted to shout at her for ruining our hopes, for hurting my wife. Amy shook her head wildly, her curls flying. "I'm sorry," the doctor said.

I woke up in the middle of that night, and there was an empty space in the bed next to me. Amy wasn't there. The bathroom door was open, a slash of light showing a damp bath mat. I got up and saw that Amy was sitting on the edge of the bed in a triangle of moonlight coming through the wavy brick glass of our bedroom. The moonlight was very strong, and it illuminated the room. She was wearing one of my shirts and my matching boxers. She was crying very softly, almost in a hushed lullaby sound. Her head was bowed into her hands. It hit me then, with a pain I had never understood could feel so sharp, that we had truly lost our baby. Her devastation was so profound it was a presence in the room. I had never seen Amy so sad, so mournful, and there was nothing I wanted more than to help. "Is there something I can do?" I whispered, and then I went to her.

5

DONALD

We parked the van in a lot near Fifth and Roosevelt in downtown Phoenix, in the midst of an empty urban expanse
bordered with crumbling 1950s buildings. The kids were lining up
outside, and I was pulling a cockroach out of a girl's ear.

When we pulled into the lot, we noticed kids all around us.
They had bedded down for the night in groups of twos and threes,
some in sleeping bags and others just wrapped in their own arms.
There were perhaps twenty homeless kids spread across the empty,
rutted lots, all in their little camps. They had risen slowly in the
early-morning gloom. It reminded me of something out of a zom-
bie movie. A medical student named Scott had joined us after ex-
pressing an interest in working on the van. I was eager to find help
and happy to have him join the team. Scott was a thin, earnest
young man with a long face. Seeing the kids pop up like that, he
got a shocked look on his face. This happened with all the volunteers, it seemed. The first day on the van, I had warned Scott,
could be an education.

Right away it became clear it would be a shocking education
for him. The girl came over screaming with pain, cupping her
ear with one hand. Immediately I suspected a cockroach. I had

learned this was common. The kids would lie down to sleep in abandoned houses and filthy camps, and the cockroaches would run right inside their ears. Baby cockroaches in particular. Every few moments the pain lessened, and she sighed with relief. Then a moment later the screaming began again. The pain came when the insect pinched its spiny claws into her tender eardrum. When it relaxed its hold, the pain diminished. "I think she's got a cockroach in her ear." I spoke in a low voice to Scott as she came up the steps.

"A *what?*" he blurted, and looked at me to see if I was kidding. I wasn't.

Murmuring soothing words, I led the girl into an exam room and examined her ear. Sure enough, there was a large bug deep in her ear. Not only was it a huge cockroach, but it had also wiggled way up the ear canal. How had it gotten that far up there? I wondered.

"Here," I told Scott, letting him take a peek with the light. His face went white. "Can you get me some lidocaine?" I asked him. I was experimenting with different methods to get rid of the insects. At first I tried mineral oil. But that left a thick, goopy mess and a dead cockroach inside the ear, the perfect invitation to bacteria and further infection. A doctor at a county hospital had suggested lidocaine. It numbed the pain and killed the cockroach. Jan jokingly called this the Christensen Method of Cockroach Removal. Someday, she said, I would be famous.

His back against the wall, Scott watched. It was crowded in the little exam room. When I dropped in the lidocaine, the girl immediately relaxed. The cockroach was dead. I carefully removed the pieces of the corpse, dropping them onto the tray. I didn't want to leave any behind because a subsequent infection would be even more painful than a live roach and, from a medical standpoint, more serious. The procedure took a long time. The lidocaine had dissolved the roach into tiny fragments. I had to make sure to get them all. The girl wept during the process, her damp hair swinging in her face. I felt sympathy for her. It had to be like hitting bottom.

Scott had a dazed look I didn't like.

"Doctor?" It was Jan, poking her head in the room. "There's a pastor on the phone. He wants to bring someone in."

"Sure, no problem."

A few minutes later the ear was clean. Inside, the canal looked raw. She had numerous other complaints, including a bad cough.

"Have you been coughing up anything?" I asked.

"Yeah, this green stuff," she said.

I looked at Scott. I waited for him to ask the next question. He spoke nervously. "Uh, how long have you been coughing?" he asked. His eyes kept going to the tray with the dead roach pieces. I whisked them out of the way.

"A week or so, I guess."

I listened to her chest. She had bronchitis. "Have you ever taken antibiotics before?" I asked. "Are you allergic to anything?"

She rubbed her ear. "I have trouble swallowing pills."

"This patient has a raw ear canal and bronchitis. Do you agree?" I asked Scott. He nodded. "Can you write her up a scrip for antibiotics?"

"Sure." He dashed one off and handed it to me. I read it.

"Let's talk outside the room," I said to Scott in a low voice.

"You've got this for fluoroquinolone otic suspension," I told him after we stepped outside into the narrow van hallway.

"Yeah?"

"This girl doesn't have any insurance. The choice you've given her will be far too expensive."

"Oh, boy, sorry." He paused. "Uh, I also wrote an amoxicillin suspension for the bronchitis."

"How come you chose the suspension?"

"She said she didn't like swallowing pills."

I lowered my voice. "With antibiotic suspensions the medicine needs to be refrigerated. This girl doesn't have a refrigerator. She needs medicine she can keep in a backpack."

He looked crestfallen.

"Treating homeless kids is hard," I told him. "You know how I know? Because I've made exactly the same mistakes you just made. I told one kid with asthma he should use a nebulizer. You know what he asked me? 'Dr. Christensen, where do I plug it in?' Just last week I saw rat bites and couldn't figure out what they were. No doubt I'll make more mistakes very soon. This is complicated work and nothing they teach us in school." I paused and smiled. "I'm happy you were paying attention to the patient's needs. That's good."

"What should I give her?" He looked worried.

"Well, what do you think? Give it some thought."

He took a breath. His forehead creased and then relaxed. "How about chewable amoxicillin? It's cheap. No refrigeration. And since she can chew it, she doesn't have to swallow any pills."

"Bingo." I patted him on the shoulder. I was happy to see his face relax and light up. "That's what this work requires. Thinking on your feet. You're going to be fine."

He smiled. "Um, Dr. Christensen?" he asked before we went back in the room.

"Yeah?"

"That cockroach thing? Does it happen all the time?"

"Quite a bit."

He swallowed. "OK," he said. I could tell he was thinking what I had thought before and what nearly all the volunteers had told me: the life of a homeless child was way harder than they had ever suspected.

I let Scott finish with the girl and stepped outside the van. The rocky ground was rutted and littered with trash. An empty Dumpster had been pushed over. It lay half buried in the dirt and sand, with mattresses over the top and around the front. The kids lived inside it like a cave. That's probably where the girl got the cockroach in her ear, I thought. Near the Dumpster the kids had set up a fake Christmas tree. Its limbs were knotted with old silver tinsel that glittered in the hot sun. The rocky ground under the tree was empty except for a crushed beer can. A group of kids were sitting in the chairs Jan had unfolded. She was doing intake forms with them one by one and lining them up for care.

Scott joined me outside. He looked at the kids. One had a lank Mohawk that fell over one eye. In dusty black clothing and with tattoos, the young man looked like something out of a *Road Warrior* movie. "Are you ever scared?" Scott suddenly asked me.

"Of the kids?"

"Yeah. What if they decided to rob you or beat you up?"

"We had some concerns in the beginning," I said. "We were especially concerned about female staff, like Jan and Wendy Speck, from HomeBase; you'll meet her. You'll notice there's a panic button that triggers an alarm in the van. But we've never had any problems. There have been a few raised voices, mostly from kids with mental health issues. But the truth is I think these kids would protect *me* if something came up."

I noticed someone pulling into the lot in a wheezing old Honda that bumped over the rocky ground. That must be the pastor, I thought. He opened the back door. A large boy emerged, blond crew cut shining in the sun. The pastor was a small, wizened African American. The boy was huge and heavyset, easily topping six feet. He was wearing the faded blue overalls of a farm kid. His round shoulders were scorched with sunburn. Just looking at the way the boy ambled behind the man, I thought, There is something wrong with him. He looks delayed.

"Are you Dr. Christensen?" asked the pastor. He held out his hand, which was dry and dusty, as if he had been working drywall. He had a small, narrow face, smiling eyes, and a small head crowned with graying short hair. "I'm Pastor Richardson. I found him this morning," he said, nodding toward the boy. "He was sitting outside our church. He said he's been lost. People been throwing rocks at him."

"How did you hear about us?" I asked, curious.

He pulled a brochure out of his back pocket. It was one of the cheap ones we had made. "Gave the number right here."

"What's your name?" I asked the boy. For some reason it was easy to think of him as a boy, though he was easily as tall as I was, and probably bigger.

"Donald, sir." He had a soft, eager-to-please voice. There was a soft southern accent.

"Pleased to meet you, Donald."

"OK?" the pastor said. He held out his hand to Donald. "You be good."

I took him inside for what we called the H&P, history and physical. Jan's intake forms were now being used by homeless health agencies around the world. We had recently gone to a conference hosted by the Children's Health Fund, and Jan gave a presentation on her new forms, which were quickly scooped up by social service and medical agencies across the globe. But we were still working on the best way to talk to the kids. The standard questions I would ask of an adolescent—about high school, parents, friends—just didn't apply.

Donald sat on the exam bed. The knees of his overalls had hand-sewn patches. His hands were calloused, the nails splayed and horny, from hard labor. He had many scars on his arms and hands and even through his left eyebrow. His work boots were busted, with cracked uppers and a flapping shoe heel. I started with what doctors call the chief complaint.

"How come you're here, Donald?"

With most kids, it's a physical problem: an infection, asthma, or a fight that left broken bones. Donald just looked confused.

"The pastor said people were throwing rocks at you. Did you get hurt?"

He nodded shyly and held out an arm. There was a fresh bruise. I began examining it.

"When did this happen, Donald?"

"Last night."

"Who was throwing the rocks?"

"I don't know. Kids."

I kept up the flow of questions while I looked for other bruises. When I was satisfied that none of the rocks had caused serious injury, I asked permission to examine other parts of his body. When Donald opened his mouth I winced. He had a mouthful of teeth shattered by abuse and decay. He would need all of them pulled. Probably he had never seen a dentist. It had to be hard for him to eat. I felt sad. Here was a boy who probably needed dentures, and he wasn't even old enough to vote.

"How's your throat? Any sore throat?"

"No, sir." His southern accent made him sound courteous.

"You ever wear glasses? Have vision problems?"

"Uh, I can see pretty good."

"You see out that window there?"

He giggled. "It's got shades."

"Well, see there, you aren't blind." I smiled. He smiled back. I listened to his heart. I watched him as I talked to him, sensing his trust growing. He became so relaxed by the questions he looked almost sleepy.

"Do you have any headaches?"

"My head hurts all the time."

"All the time?"

"Yes, sir. All over."

I began to gently examine his skull. My hands stopped immediately. The back of his skull was covered in scar tissue. It was like passing my hands over a warm moonscape of ridges and bumps. I parted his hair with my fingers to examine the scars more closely. There were dozens, hard and thick and raised, crossing his scalp. Some were old; others, more recent. Of greater concern were the hard, raised knobs. I felt them carefully. These bony knobs were the result of skull fractures. When broken, the skull doesn't mend, or what doctors call remodel, the way that other bones do. A weight-bearing bone will remodel after a break to an eventually smooth surface, but the skull will heal with a bony outgrowth. I thought about this as I counted the bony knobs. There were at least eight. His head lolled against my hands. It was as if he were seeking affection from my touch.

"How did you get all these scars, Donald?"

There was a slight pause. Then quietly he said, "My dad."

"Why did he do that, Donald?"

"He wanted to make me mind."

"Did he hit you?" I felt his ear. It was lumpy with scar tissue.

"Uh, yeah."

"What did he hit you with, Donald?"

"A board."

I cupped my hands over his head above his ears again and felt the scars and knobs. He turned his cheek slightly into my hand. I felt I was absorbing his pain as I touched him.

"How many times did your father beat you with the board, Donald?"

"Lots."

"Did he ever take you to the doctor?"

"When I was little, maybe."

"What did he do when you got hurt from the beatings?"

"He put a towel on it."

"Donald, where are you from?"

This time came another smile. "They call it the Heart of Dixie."

It wasn't until later I figured it out. "The Heart of Dixie." Alabama.

I was discovering that many of the physical problems ailing these kids—the untreated asthma or the cutting or the drug use—had roots in their past. They were homeless for a reason. Sometimes it was poverty at home, abuse, or neglect. Other times it was their parents' alcoholism or drug addictions. A surprising number had parents with schizophrenia, bipolar disorder, or clinical depression. Understanding their family backgrounds, I thought, was key to understanding their health.

My questions seemed casual to outside observers, but actually followed a pattern. I started easy and broad. Who was at home when he was growing up? Donald said it was just he and his dad. His mom had left when he was young. Did they always live in one place? Yes. The farm. Did he remember going to school? He remembered a nice teacher in first grade. How long did he go to school? He wasn't sure when he left, but it was when he was young.

Did he ever see a dentist? One time. He couldn't remember. Did anyone ever evaluate him for learning problems? He wasn't sure what that meant. But he mentioned that a home nurse came by a few times and told his dad something.

The longer I spoke with Donald, the clearer it became. He had significant developmental disabilities. The only thing I didn't know is whether the delays were caused by prenatal or birth issues or acquired through the injuries he had suffered at the hands of his father, or both. Complicated questions boggled him. But he was sweet in nature. I began to get more specific, gathering a picture of his past. I asked about his favorite meal when he was growing up. He smiled. He liked spaghetti, the Chef Boyardee kind that came in the can. Did he get fresh milk? Yes. How did he spend his free time? He worked the farm. Did they have a television? Of course, he said. Did he read books? He wasn't too good at reading, he said. Had he ever used drugs? Never. Coffee, tobacco? No. Sex? He blushed when I asked. No. Had he ever left home before? No, he said, suddenly sad, his eyes starry with tears.

"How did you get all the way to Arizona, Donald?"

"My daddy put me on the bus."

"The Greyhound?"

"Yes, sir." He looked at his calloused hands.

"That must have been a long bus ride."

"Oh, it was."

"Did your dad tell you why he put you on the bus?"

"He said I was going to stay with my cousins. He couldn't take care of me anymore."

"What cousins?"

"I never met them. I got their address here."

He handed me an address written in crude block script on the back of a feed store receipt. I knew Phoenix well enough to know there was no such place. The boy's father had put him on a bus to nowhere.

"I kept looking," Donald said. "I couldn't find the place. Those kids were throwing rocks."

"How long have you been looking?"

He suddenly looked close to breaking down. "That nice man found me. I'm hungry."

I asked Jan to get him something to eat. I knew she wouldn't mind running for food; it would give her and Scott a chance to take a break. "Make it soft," I said, looking at his teeth.

Jan came back in a few minutes with a large burrito. We led Donald outside to sit in a chair under our new awning. The Jaycees had given us yet another generous gift, this time bringing shade to our patients. The girl who had had the cockroach in her ear was sitting in a lawn chair. Scott joined her and began talking about why she was homeless and what we could do to help. Donald sat in another chair and began eating with small, hasty bites. Jan and I talked in low voices.

"I don't know if he is brain damaged from the beatings," I said, "or perhaps he has some congenital problem; even some infections can affect the brain at the time of birth. In any case he needs some sort of work-up."

"I'd be brain damaged if someone beat me in the head with a board," she said.

I felt the anger that was there and pushed it down. "We need to get him tested in a hospital," I said. "He needs a full work-up with neurological tests. If he has brain damage, we need to know." Sometimes brain damage came with life-threatening seizure disorders.

"He won't be able to get tested without insurance," she said.

"Do you think we can get him on AHCCCS?" I asked. This was Arizona's Medicaid program, the state insurance for the poor. The initials stood for Arizona Health Care Cost Containment System. I was starting to suspect that the way the state contained costs was by making it impossible to get services. We had discovered very few of the homeless kids had insurance, while getting the insurance was a nightmare requiring multiple personal visits to a building downtown, along with proof of identity. It amazed me that the government expected homeless children to take all these steps by themselves.

"It will take a good three months," Jan replied crisply. "And that is after he applies in person and with identification. If he doesn't have identification, then he can't get on it."

"We'll have to get him identification first then."

"You know how hard that can be," Jan said. We had friends at HomeBase who helped get the kids their identification, which itself was a huge challenge. Before anyone got identification, a birth certificate had to be obtained. Not many homeless children had their birth certificates, and efforts to track them down from uncooperative or imprisoned or addicted parents often proved fruitless.

"We can't just let him wander the streets for three months," I said. "He'll starve or get killed."

Donald ate his burrito while we saw other patients and pondered his future. A homeless boy walked by, looking surly. He let out a cussword at another kid, and Jan swooped down on him. She had her hands on her hips. By the time she was done reading him the riot act he was as passive as a kitten. I held back a smile when she offered to fetch a bar of soap and clean his mouth herself. The next time I checked, Jan was bringing Donald a box of apple juice.

"Have you found my cousins yet?" he asked.

"Still looking," I said. I wasn't about to crush the spirit of this delayed boy by telling him what I really thought, which was that the cousins had never existed and his father had abandoned him, shipping him on a bus to nowhere.

ロ-ロ-ロ-ロ-ロ-ロ

All that day Donald sat outside the van. I was at a loss. I knew the shelters were above capacity, and the current wait for a bed was months. With the budget cuts to social services many shelters had closed or sharply reduced their number of cots. In reality Donald should be in a hospital, I thought, getting those head injuries looked at. But if he walked into a hospital without insurance, he would be turned away.

I felt I was leaving him to get hurt. He'd probably end up spending the night outside with the kids in the Dumpster cave. Maybe they could at least protect him. They did that for one another. But it seemed like no choice at all. I went out to tell Donald we were leaving. He tilted his head back to look at me. The vulnerability of the gesture struck me. His blue eyes were rimmed with pale, sunbleached eyelashes. The scars and knobs of his scalp were visible through his short hair. The scars looked like silverfish against the pinkness of his scalp.

Across the street a familiar car pulled in. It was the pastor. He came quickly across the lot, breathing lightly.

"Sorry, in a hurry," he said. "Suppertime. Wife'll get mad if I'm late. I wanted to check on this boy here. I've been thinking on him all day."

I explained to him the problems of finding Donald shelter or getting him admitted to the hospital for tests without identification. The boy had no place to go. The pastor stopped me with a wave of his hand. "I'll take him," he said without hesitation.

I was flabbergasted. "You'll *take* him?"

"Sure. Got a hot supper waiting. And there's the kids' old room. I've got a cousin staying there, but he can make way."

"You don't have to—"

"There's always room for one more. I'll put him to work tomorrow in the church." He gave a throaty laugh. "He'll earn his keep."

He went and touched Donald's shoulder. Then the pastor turned to me. "I'll be bringing him by, and soon. You'll help him, right?"

"Right." My throat felt thick.

Jan came out as the two were getting into the car. The pastor was opening the back door for Donald. He was crawling in, the dirty back seat of his coveralls visible. "You'll never believe what just happened," I told her.

"What happened?"

"People are good, Jan. That's what happened."

That night I gave Amy a big hug. "It's been a busy year, hasn't it?" I said. "The van, the kids . . ." I trailed off. I didn't want to say the word *miscarriage* out loud. It had been two months now since it had happened, and Amy seemed fully recovered. I was the one who still seemed bruised. She added a handful of fresh basil to the saucepan and gave me an amused look. "I'm trying this new sauce," she said. "Want to try it?" I took a spoonful.

"Spicy, in a good way," I said.

"It's got red pepper in it," she said, taking back the spoon. The cutting board was covered with chopped vegetables, and there was sausage sautéing nearby, along with a bowl of freshly grated Parmesan. I remembered Amy's inviting me over to her place for Thanksgiving right after we had met. I had walked in expecting a few people and maybe a burned college student turkey. Instead I walked into a festively decorated, crowded room, Amy wearing an apron, her table set with linen and candles. She had been cooking for days. Something about the homespun Betty Crocker moment struck me as poignant, knowing that Amy had lost her own mother very early. Here is a woman, I had thought, who believes in family.

"There's something I want to ask you."

"Waiting."

"You know about Camp AZDA?"

"Sure. I refer kids there all the time," she said. Camp AZDA was one of the largest summer camps for kids with diabetes. It was held in nearby Prescott, Arizona. The camp was statted by medical professionals who taught the kids how to manage their diabetes and live healthy lives.

"Well, they want me to be their medical director. It means spending a week there every summer."

"Sure."

"Really?" As supportive as Amy was, sometimes her attitude was startling. The most important thing in the world to her was family. Why would she accept yet another drain on my time?

She was wearing her glasses, which she did only when relaxed. One lens had a smudge on it. With her hair pulled back, no makeup on, and tomato sauce splattered on her apron, I had never loved her more.

"It will be a lot of work, but you'll enjoy every minute." She stirred the sauce. She stopped. "You have good leadership skills. You should put them to work."

"Only if you come with me," I said.

That night I held Amy and felt her heart beating through the T-shirt she had stolen from my drawer for that night. Her bare leg touched mine. "I want to try again," she whispered.

"Isn't it too soon?" I whispered back. Our doctor had told Amy that as long as she had a normal period, getting pregnant again would be OK. But I didn't want her to hurt again. The days following the miscarriage it had hurt even to look at her. Amy had told me several times how normal it was for women to lose pregnancies.

"You know, my grandmother lost four pregnancies before she had my mother," she said. "Almost half of all pregnancies end in miscarriage. It's part of life, Randy."

If only I could feel that way. "What about the baby we lost?" I asked her, our voices soft in the night. Outside I heard a dove call.

"It was never our baby," she said. "It was never meant to be."

I remembered when I had wondered if Amy's losing her mother had made her reluctant to risk falling in love. But in that moment I saw how that loss had made her the woman she was now, strong and willing to take risks.

❑❑❑❑❑❑

Over the next several weeks Donald came by the van regularly. He was still staying with Pastor Richardson, who genuinely seemed to like him. It was clear to everyone that Donald had some kind of impairment or brain damage, but we still had no idea why. We were making headway on his case, though. Pastor Richardson was taking him to HomeBase, and a staff member was working with him on getting identification. The immediate and pressing problem turned out to be his teeth. Donald was having lots of trouble eating, and his pain grew worse by the day. Like all homeless kids, he had no dental insurance and no way to pay for any dental care, let alone the money involved with getting his shattered teeth pulled and dentures made. I called a doctor I knew who provided emergency dental care to the poor.

"We've got a long wait list," he said. "But this boy sounds like he needs help now. Have someone bring him by tomorrow."

"Tomorrow is Saturday."

"Tomorrow." And that was that.

Later Pastor Richardson brought Donald by the van to say hello. Donald came running up, grinning with a row of even new white teeth. "I can eat anything with these!" Donald said.

"And how," Pastor Richardson added dryly.

I was telling him how as a teenager I could put away an entire pan of enchiladas when Jan came into the van. She was suggesting a place that gave out food boxes to the pastor that he could use to feed Donald. But Pastor Richardson shook his head. "Someone else can use that more. It doesn't take that much to feed a boy."

"It's expensive, though," I said.

"True enough. But my wife can make some good beans and rice."

Donald grinned. "Those are good. But not with Tabasco," he said. "Yuck. I hate Tabasco."

I thought about Pastor Richardson often. I saw kids who were homeless because their families were fragmented, destitute, traveling from one crime-ridden apartment to another, ravaged by domestic violence and drug abuse. They lived in isolation. By the time the kids took off by themselves, they'd lost contact with anyone who cared. Pastor Richardson, on the other hand, had a home to offer and a strong community. In his house there were cupboards with food and a stove to cook it on. There were relatives around and neighbors and a whole churchful of people to help out. If the stove broke, someone would have the tools to fix it. If his wife got sick, someone would be able to bring by a few dishes. A whole broken system could fail a child, but one solid family, or even one solid person, could save him.

Amy gave her hair one final brush and adjusted her skirt. It was
Halloween, and HomeBase was having a pumpkin-carving party at
its shelter. It wasn't far from the drop-in center where we had our
offices and parked the van. The agency had converted a nearby
house into a long-term home for homeless kids. Downstairs there
was a kitchen and a dining room with cafeteria tables and a small
community area for the kids to hang out in. A scuffed pool table
stood off to one side, along with a bookshelf laden with well-read
novels and skateboard magazines. Upstairs there were small rooms
where the kids stayed. Each had a single bed and a dresser. A staff
member was always on hand to act as a parent figure. To stay at
HomeBase, you had to follow the rules. No drugs, alcohol, or sexual relationships were allowed.

A skinny, nervous blond boy in glasses came trotting up to me
as soon as we walked in the door. "Dr. Randy! Remember me?" he
asked. I almost didn't recognize him. It was Matthew, the boy who
had been cutting himself. He looked completely different in his
new glasses. The trench coat and the boots were gone. No more
fear in his eyes.

"I'm in the work program here," he said. "I'm getting a job in
construction. How is Jan doing? Is she still racing?" He began asking tons of excited questions. We caught up for a few minutes as
the smell of food filled the air.

"Guess what's for dessert?" he asked.

Amy laughed. "Pumpkin?"

The staff had set out several folding tables in the downstairs
area and spread them with newspapers. The donated pumpkins
all were off size and lumpy. But the teenagers didn't care. They
were rooting out the seeds and laughing as they pulled at the
gooey insides. Soon they were behaving like five-year-olds, laughing and throwing pumpkin seeds at one another. It reminded me

of holiday times with my own family, when something as simple as a pumpkin and an old carving knife could make a memory.

Sitting at the end of one table was Donald. His blue eyes were alive. Amy and I walked over.

"Have you decided what to carve yet?" I asked.

"Dr. Randy! Pastor Richardson said you might be here."

I introduced Amy. Donald took her hand with a blush. "She's pretty," he said to me in a loud stage whisper. We sat down.

"What are you doing here?" I asked.

"Making a pumpkin," he answered innocently.

"I meant, are you staying here now? Instead of with Pastor Richardson?"

His eyes widened. "Oh, no. I'm taking classes here. They're teaching me how to read. The pastor will be back." He paused with uncertainty. "He promised."

"I'm sure he will."

Reassured, Donald relaxed again. I helped him draw the eyes and nose and mouth with a marker pen. He wanted to do the carving himself. He held the knife with surprising dexterity, and I thought he would make a fine artist or sculptor or carpenter. When he was done, he proudly showed his work to the staff.

"My first pumpkin," he told me.

A few days later I had just finished giving a tour of the van to a local magazine writer. We had gotten some media interest. Jan said this was good because if people read about the van, they might want to donate a few dollars. I agreed, though I got tongue-tied and overly emotional during the interview, trying to tell the reporter how important medical care for homeless kids was and how much they deserved help. Talking about the kids and their needs, I felt tears come to my eyes. The minute the reporter left Jan was at my side. Her face was friendly but firm.

"Randy, let's talk."

"OK, what's up?" I sat down heavily in the driver's seat. Jan remained standing, holding lightly onto the back of the passenger seat.

"I've asked you before not to refer to me as my 'nurse-practitioner.'"

"You have?" I looked around for something to eat. I had again let the day pass without eating. I was famished. "A hamburger sounds so good," I said. "With bacon. And cheese." I patted my growling tummy.

"Randy, this is important. I want you to listen."

I didn't see what the problem was. My face probably showed it.

"My name is Jan Putnam. My name is not My Nurse-Practitioner."

"But that's your title."

"All right then, the next time we have a reporter here, I'll introduce you as My Doctor."

"But I'm not your doctor—oh." I saw her point. "I thought I was being respectful," I said. "Not everyone understands what *nurse-practitioner* means and that you have a lot of responsibility. Most people think a nurse is just a nurse."

Jan looked conciliatory. "I'd much rather have you introduce me by my name. You could say, 'This is Jan Putnam. She is our nurse-practitioner.'"

I still wasn't sure of the difference, but I appreciated her thoughtful explanation. She touched my arm. "Friends?"

"Friends. Now, you know what sounds really good, Jan Putnam, nurse-practitioner? Mexican. A huge plate of enchiladas covered with cheese. And some beans on the side. Plus some guacamole."

"Randy, you're always forgetting to eat and then getting hopped up about food. You're going to make me fat just listening to you."

I missed Jan on the days when I took the van out alone. Since there were only two of us, Jan and I had decided it would be more productive to take the van out separately as well as together. Since I still spent many days at the hospital, this freed us both up to reach more kids. We were getting more interns, and we also had the two staff members from HomeBase, Wendy and Michelle Ray, but it wasn't the same, I told myself, on the days without Jan. I had come to depend on Jan more than she probably knew. In addition to being a nurse, she was my role model. I often looked to her to see how she handled surly or reluctant teenagers.

Because we could now have two teams, we were trying new sites. On this day I decided to park the van in a new place. It was in an area of Phoenix known for gang activity and prostitution. I had Wendy with me. Wendy was blond and strikingly pretty. She was also whip smart and good with the kids. At HomeBase she and Michelle been great at getting kids their identifications. But she wasn't a nurse, and for the first time I found myself doing Jan's nursing work as well as my own. It was turning out to be a lot harder than I had thought. Jan was an accomplished nurse who seemed to have the complex world of immunization schedules and blood draws memorized. Different immunizations had to be injected in different places, in different ways, and there were extremely complicated schedules that had to be followed on the order and timing of the shots. I soon felt I was floundering. I had to keep calling Jan. "Is the MMR shot intramuscular?" I asked.

She coughed in alarm. "Randy! Subcutaneous. Under the fat. Do you want me to come in?"

I told her I was fine, even though I wasn't feeling fine. I was glad to have the phone to connect with Jan and others. Even with other staff or volunteers around, there was a feeling of isolation on the van that was unlike anything I had experienced. In a hospital every emergency decision I made was as part of a team, supervised by others, with plenty of help and advice and support. On the van I often had to play nurse, case manager, counselor, and emergency physician, all rolled into one. There was no one to ask for advice or share the responsibilities, and only the phone and computer kept me connected with other doctors and nurses.

The new location turned out to be a good choice, as far as reaching homeless kids went. I soon had a line of kids waiting to be seen. Wendy helped the kids fill out their intake forms. "Where do you live?" I asked one African American girl, as she shyly tugged the back of her shirt over too-tight jeans. Like many of the other kids waiting, she had the obesity that comes from poverty. She had come in for an untreated urinary tract infection. She was fifteen. "I'm staying with a friend of my cousin's," she said. "Can I still come here? 'Cause I'm not like homeless."

"You can come here," I said.

"I'm not like some street bum or something. I got friends."

"Where are your parents?"

"My mom went to Texas to see if she could get a job. She's a good mom. She just can't get work around here. She left me at my cousin's so I could finish high school. But he lost his job and got evicted. So now I'm staying with his friend."

"Where's that?" I asked, taking chart notes.

"This hotel room."

"How many people are staying there?"

"Um, there's my cousin's friend. He's got work. He's a food stocker at Bashes'. Then his girlfriend, her kids—she's got one with that autism—and a few others like me that ain't got no other place to be. So there's like six of us. He's worried we're gonna get caught and get evicted. It's just one room. It ain't got a stove or nothing."

"What do you use for cooking?"

An embarrassed look crossed her shiny face. "We just eat down the street. Plaid Pantry. There ain't no grocery around here."

"What do you eat there?"

"Doritos, you know, Subway if we have money." She smiled. "We buy those top ramens and eat them out of the bag."

"Do you ever get fresh fruit or vegetables?"

"Sometimes, at school. They got canned pears. When I was a little kid, we used to live in this place with a stove. My mama made the best dinners." She yawned and then self-consciously covered her teeth. She looked as if she needed dental care. "I'm tired all the time. It's two buses to get to school."

"What grade are you in?"

"Freshman."

This child, I thought, was one of the hidden homeless. She was not sleeping in doorways, and if you saw her at a bus stop, you would think she was just another girl, a little heavy and probably poor. You wouldn't know she had no real home. She had no one to supervise her homework, no one to make sure she studied or applied for college, no one to take her to a doctor when she was sick. She also had no income and no parent at home and was relying on the strained generosity of strangers. At the most vulnerable age for any child—her adolescence—she was without guidance. If she were lucky, her mom would call with good news and a bus ticket to Texas within the week. If she were unlucky, she would find herself without any place to stay or would attract the interest of a pimp. I thought of these kids as one couch away from disaster.

"Do you have any extended family around?" I asked.

She bit her lip. "My dad passed away. He had sickle cell. My grandma, she lives in Detroit, but she's real sick. She's got diabetes and lost her foot. I got these cousins, but they all out of work."

By midafternoon I had seen a long line of kids just like her. It was depressing, as if I had stepped into a lake of poverty with ripples spreading around me. As with all new locations, once the word got out a van was parked nearby and offering medical care, there was almost a stampede: toddlers held in the arms of big sisters, cousins holding the hands of cousins, sheepish parents holding crying babies in their arms, hoping for help for medical problems they could not afford to have treated. Wendy did intakes until rings of sweat ruined her yellow Crews'n shirt.

Finally around 7:00 P.M. the onslaught slowed. I didn't want to check my cell phone to see if Amy had called. If she had, I would feel bad for running late again; I still had my work at the hospital to check. Wendy and I wearily cleaned up the van, wiping the counters with disinfectant, tossing dirty gowns into the waste bags.

Just then a girl swinging her arms came up the steps. She had a head of curly blond ringlets and a huge, sunny, childlike smile. She wore dirty jeans with frayed bell-bottoms and a pink shirt with a picture of the Care Bears on the front. Her body was plump, with a layer of what my mom used to call puppy fat. It made her look endearingly young. Her tanned skin had a gleam. She looked surprisingly healthy. I opened my mouth to tell her I really needed to close for the day.

"Hey there, doctor man. I think I've got the clap," she announced.

I was startled. "Gonorrhea?"

"Yeah, guess so."

"How did that happen?" I held my stethoscope.

"How do you think it happened?" She giggled.

I was momentarily flustered. "I mean—"

"I got it from a john. At least I don't *think* it came from a toilet seat." She gave a streetwise laugh and winked at Wendy, who had enough experience at HomeBase that she didn't even blink. Instead she just looked at the girl sympathetically. "But hey, you're the doctor. Maybe you ought to tell *me*."

I ushered her to a room. "Call me Sugar," she said, and hopped onto the table.

"How old are you, Sugar?" I asked.

"Oh, I'm eighteen. We're always eighteen," she said with a brazen smile. "Unless you want me to be twelve. A lot of the johns do."

"No." I made my face calm, though inwardly I was sickened by what she suggested. "I'm a doctor. I'm here to help you. Do you have identification?" She shook her curls no. I began asking about her history. I knew that as a sexually active adolescent, she needed a comprehensive exam, including a full reproductive exam. She needed her blood drawn, so she could be screened for anemia and HIV. She needed a mental health screening and vaccinations. I explained all those things.

But Sugar just wanted her clap treated. "Just give me the pills, doctor man."

"I'll need to examine you before I give out medication. Why do you think you have an STD?"

"You know, it hurts. When I do it." I made a note in her chart. Dyspareunia, I wrote: pain during sex.

"Would you like a female nurse to do your exam? She's not here today, but we can schedule you for when she comes back."

"Naw. You can do it." To my amazement she hopped off the table and started to take off her pants before I was even out of the room.

"Stop," I told her firmly. "Wait till I leave, and then put on the gown." Outside the room I took a deep breath. I felt deeply unnerved. This smiling curly-haired girl made me feel off center. She had such a childlike innocence about her, yet she was forced to prostitute for a living. I went to get Wendy. I asked her to be present as a witness and in case Sugar needed support. "I'm sorry this is such a late day," I told her.

Wendy just smiled sadly. "I think about what that poor child does to survive," she said. "I don't mind."

In a few moments we knocked. Sugar was waiting impatiently, her rounded feet and calves dangling over the side. She had little feet and tawny skin. The health of her skin surprised me again. Usually, with the homeless, it was stressed and aged. The minute we came in she lay down and stared at the ceiling. She put her feet in the stirrups, and it was as if she had just disappeared, psychically and personally. She was physically there but not emotionally present at all. I remembered what I had read about sexual abuse victims and how they learned to disassociate from their bodies. Reading about it was different from actually dealing with a real child on my exam table, a child who lay there like a defenseless puppet. When I asked her a question, the answer came as if delivered from a distant planet.

I worked carefully and quickly. I wanted to convey only respect and caring for her. Inside I felt a wrenching sadness for the life she led. She had symptoms of common STDs. I excused myself so she could change. When I came back in, she was dressed again. It was as if her personality had returned with her clothes. The huge friendly smile was back. "Do I have the clap or not, doctor man?" she asked.

"We'll have the results in about a week," I told her. She looked disappointed, as if she had wanted me to pull them out of a hat right then and there. "I'd like to get you caught up on your immunizations," I said, looking at her information. "I also want to give you a vaccination against hepatitis B." I began to explain that this immunization would help prevent a serious disease. But she cut me short.

"Whatever," she said. She looked impatient. She'd had her exam. "I've got to go," she said, putting her shoes on over old and dirty socks.

I tried to discuss safe sex. "The johns pay more for bareback," she said. "A lot more." My face must have shown my feelings. "It's good money," she said defensively.

"It's death," I said.

She shrugged as if to say, "That's life for you, buddy."

"It's your health I'm concerned about."

I tried to give her referrals to shelters. She pushed them away. "I got a place to sleep, most of the time," she said.

"If you are prostituting for a place to stay, then you are homeless."

"I'm fine," she said tersely, as if I were a street-corner preacher ranting about some religion that she was far too wise to believe.

"Why not try a shelter?" I asked. "How can it hurt? I heard there is an adult shelter not far from here."

"I went to one of those places once." She shrugged. "It wasn't good."

"Tell me about it," I said, trying to engage her. She shrugged again. "Stay and we will get you services," I said more forcefully.

But tough love got me precisely nowhere. "Just give me the meds," she said.

Now I saw flight in her eyes. She was going to dash whether I wanted it or not. I prescribed a one-gram dose of azithromycin and a two-hundred-fifty-milligram dose of Rocephin for her symptoms of chlamydia and gonorrhea. They were the common STDs afflicting both child and adult prostitutes. A few minutes later she was gone. I went to the van door and watched her cross the street. Fall in Phoenix means the weather can grow cool at night. She had no jacket, no purse, nothing but the bag with her medicine. At the corner she seemed to sense me watching. She turned and waved good-bye, smiling. Wendy had stepped behind me. Her long blond hair moved in a welcome breeze. "Poor girl," she said.

Later that night, at home, as Amy made last-minute changes to her Thanksgiving menu, I pictured Sugar waiting on a cold curb. I saw the men pulling up. It was a dirty secret of our society. The life of a young prostitute: Sugar, on my table with her soul checked out.

I wanted to talk to Amy about Sugar the way I had wanted to talk about Mary, but once again I hesitated. We had been through so much lately. I felt I was always burdening Amy with sad information and on top of all her own stresses at work. Just the other day she had told me about a child she saw in her practice. His school had kicked him out because he had lice. His parents were too poor to buy the expensive treatment needed, so the boy had missed almost a month of school before Amy managed to get his lice problem fixed. She had been enraged that a child would miss so much school over a fixable problem like lice.

I hesitated, opening my mouth to say something and then closing it. I worried Amy would think I had made a wrong choice. I worried she would get tired of hearing all these sad stories or overwhelmed by the tragedy I dealt with on a daily or even hourly basis. Before I met Amy, I had dated women who seemed intimidated by the life of a doctor. Some had even seemed to frown on my work with the homeless students at Pappas. If those women had known what I dealt with now, they would have run for the hills.

I knew in my heart Amy didn't feel the same way, but part of me worried that if she knew the scope of the kids' problems, she might change her mind. Nothing in my life was more important to me than Amy. If I lost her because of the van, I would never forgive myself.

"What do you think about a ham to go with the turkey this year? We're having over twenty people," she said.

"A ham would be good," I said, bringing her close.

It was the week after Thanksgiving, and Amy was doing her hospital rounds at the Phoenix Children's Hospital. I dropped by to see her and give her some nice news to brighten her day. "Someone at the HomeBase shelter found a puppy in the Dumpster down the street. They want to know if we want it."

Amy and I had been looking for a puppy for some time. I wanted a German shepherd. I'd had a white one for a time when I was a kid. Amy said she didn't care what breed it was, as long as the dog would be good with babies. Amy was too excited to wait. She finished her rounds, and we drove over to the shelter. It wasn't far. The kids who lived there were crowded around on the front porch. As we walked up, I saw the little thing, lying on a torn-up old towel. Matthew, the skinny blond boy I had treated for the bacterial superinfection on his feet, was on his knees, petting the puppy. The puppy was ginger-colored and shivering, with either fear or exhaustion. "Hey, Dr. Randy," Matthew said as we came up the steps. "Isn't this a pretty puppy?"

"The kids were trying to talk us into keeping it," a staff person said, coming out onto the porch. Some of the kids turned hopefully toward her. "I was telling them the shelter doesn't have the room or the time or probably even the insurance for a dog." There was a chorus of protests. "It wouldn't be best for the puppy," she added firmly. "She needs a real home," she said to the kids. They nodded, understanding. Just like all of you, I thought.

"I can keep her," a tall older boy said. He had a leather jacket adorned with punk rock symbols.

The skinny blond boy frowned at him. "You can't raise a dog on the streets," he said.

"Lots of people do," the tall boy said defensively.

"It wouldn't be fair to the dog," the skinny blond boy said. "She deserves better." He picked the puppy up and held her protectively. "I want her to go to Dr. Randy. And his wife here. They can take better care of her." He handed the shivering puppy to Amy.

"Thank you," Amy said, holding the bundle of reddish fur. The puppy licked her face. The kids looked sad for a moment.

"You'll take good care of her, won't you?" Matthew asked.

"We will," Amy said. "Does she have a name yet?"

"We were calling her Ginger," the brown-haired girl said.

"Well, we already have a cat called Gilligan, and a beta fish named the Professor," I said. "Maybe we should get a goldfish and call it Mary Ann. Then we can have the whole television show." Amy rolled her eyes at my dumb humor. The puppy licked her face again.

"Puppy breath," she said with a grimace, and the kids laughed.

Amy and I took Ginger home. She was so tired she fell asleep in Amy's lap on the drive, almost as if she had known she was finally in a safe place. It was similar to the homeless kids like Mary and Donald, I thought. Once they were in a safe place they blossomed. Once we got home I let Ginger on the bed. "She's so tired. Just this once," I told Amy.

"Oh, boy," she replied. "I can already tell you are going to spoil your own kids."

"Randy, is this a good time?" Jan asked in our offices at HomeBase a few days later. We were still teaming on the van when we could, while other times we took separate times out. Jan often took the van out with volunteers and interns while I was caught up in administrative duties like grant writing or my hospital work. I tried to do much of my paperwork in my hospital office, since our quarters at HomeBase were less hospitable.

"Sure, what's up?" I asked, hanging my stethoscope over my chair. I studied a new water stain on the ceiling that was ominously above my desk. I hoped the ceiling wasn't going to fall on my computer.

"Did you hear? A young man in Phoenix died the other day from tuberculous meningitis." Her face was sober.

"I heard," I said, cautiously taking my chair and giving it a test swivel. One of the arms had a way of dropping off.

I felt bad for the young man. Drug-resistant tuberculosis was becoming epidemic among the homeless. This antiquated-sounding disease was making a huge comeback, and it was a killer. It was sad and frustrating. The young man's death was so unnecessary. But I wasn't sure why Jan was bringing it up.

The sober expression remained on her face. "I've been taking the van out after some of your solo trips. I've seen a few of your patients for follow-up too. You're not giving any of the kids their tuberculosis skin tests."

My stomach dropped. I immediately felt defensive. For the life of me I couldn't think of why I hadn't given the kids this test. My mind raced through all the kids I had recently seen. Jan was right. I hadn't tested any of them.

"If I didn't give them the test, then they probably weren't at risk for tuberculosis," I heard myself say.

"Randy!" Her voice was suddenly sharp. "You mean to tell me that homeless children, living on the streets, going into shelters, and being thrown in jails are not at risk for tuberculosis? What planet do you live on? If they aren't at risk, then exactly who is?"

I felt my cheeks color. I felt like a schoolkid caught doing something bad. Part of me thought how dare Jan talk to me like this. But at the same time I realized I was covering for my own mistake. It was a big mistake too. "Tell the truth, Randy," I told myself. "The truth is you didn't even think of giving kids the tuberculosis tests. The reason is you've had no practice giving it. You blanked it out of your mind because you didn't feel comfortable giving the test."

In the hospital it was something the nurses did. Giving a tuberculosis test was a lot harder than it looked. I knew inserting the needle required exact angles, and reading the test was complicated. The idea that I was capable of forgetting something because I didn't know how to do it, instead of asking for help, disturbed me. What else had I been ignoring?

"Do you need some practice giving the skin test?"

"That might be helpful," I replied in a low voice.

She gave me a knowing look and went off to fetch a TB syringe and some saline. "Right now?" I asked.

"Sure, right now. No time like the present." She grinned at me. "You're the guinea pig. Hold out your arm, and watch how I do it. Then it will be your turn." Her voice took on a warm, educational tone. "It has to be on the forearm," she said as she filled the syringe with saline, "and the needle has to be inserted at a ten- to fifteen-degree angle. It should be shallow enough for you to see the needle under the skin. Like this." She wiped my arm with a swab and delicately inserted the needle under my skin. I watched. "If you go too deep, it won't work. If you do it right, you get a bubble called a bleb. If there is no bubble, you need to try again. The angle has to be exact." Sure enough, a little bubble had popped out on my skin. "Now it's your turn. You can do yourself."

An hour later my forearm looked like a sieve. I was proud to note where I had made the skin bubble, showing I had done the test successfully. And I never again forgot to give a tuberculosis test.

⬜⬜⬜⬜⬜

"Juan is back," Michelle said, her hands full up front. "Can you get him?"

Juan was a slender Mexican boy with smooth golden skin, shiny black hair, and intense almond-shaped eyes. He had grown up traveling the migrant farmworker route with his family, living in a series of trailers and shacks on farms across the country, often in foul conditions. As a child he didn't go to school. He labored in the fields despite laws that are supposed to protect children from such abuses. Eventually times got tough, and he wound up on the streets. "My mom, she got the cancer," he had told me. "My dad, he worked, but he couldn't make enough to feed us all. I was the oldest, so I left. I was sixteen."

Juan was now eighteen. He was a hard worker, but finding a job as an illiterate Mexican was not easy. I asked him how the search for work was going.

"I got a job house painting," he said in Spanish.

"Muy bueno," I said, wishing my Spanish were stronger. I could speak the language well enough from my Mexican mother, but I lacked nuance. And unfortunately, medical terminology often escaped me. My parents had decided not to teach us Spanish when Stephanie and I were little. It was in the days before we knew that learning two languages had many developmental advantages for a young child. At the time parents were actively discouraged from teaching more than one language. My own parents worried I would just be confused and do poorly in school. But because I didn't learn Spanish until I was older, I was not as fluent as I could have been.

"But that job ended," Juan continued in Spanish. "The economy, it is hard to find any work."

"Where are you sleeping?" I asked.

"In this old house. No one lives there. It is cold at night."

"Juan, how come you don't stay at one of the adult shelters? You're eighteen. You could stay at one of the shelters downtown."

"Dr. Christensen, those are bad places."

"What do you mean?"

His dark eyes were grave. "Bad things happen there at night."

"What kinds of things?" I asked, curious. He was the second young person to tell me that some of the adult shelters were bad.

"Bad things, period." I could tell he didn't want to tell me more.

"How are your meds?" I asked. Juan handed me an empty bottle. He had been born with a seizure disorder but never had insurance to pay for his phenytoin. I worried. He could easily die from a seizure. "Have you been having seizures?" I asked.

He nodded, looking as if he were somehow at fault. "Even with that medicine," he said.

I checked his charts. Juan hadn't been evaluated in years. His dosage probably needed to be adjusted. That was not something I could do. He needed to be seen by a neurologist. Once again I felt slammed against the wall of access to health care. Juan didn't have identification, and without identification he could never get state insurance and a referral for a neurologist.

"Juan, I'm going to make a call for you, OK?"

I stepped outside the exam room to the front of the van. Michelle was doing an intake with a heavyset girl with short dark hair. The girl had the frightened look of the newly homeless, her eyes huge in her face.

"Dr. Hendin?" I said on my cell. "I have a favor to ask."

Dr. Barry Hendin was a respected neurologist in the community. He was also my sister's doctor. Setting Stephanie up with him after her diagnosis was probably the best thing I had done to deal with the disease that had taken my sister from being an active mom to being a woman who couldn't get up a four-inch curb without help. Dr. Hendin was a warm, Marcus Welby–style doctor who exuded caring and confidence. He was a healer.

"The problem is he doesn't have any insurance," I told Dr. Hendin after apologizing for taking up his time. "Our program can help out with costs, I think. He desperately needs an evaluation."

He interrupted good-naturedly. "Don't worry. I'll have my receptionist schedule him next week."

I felt a surge of gratitude. A lot of people wanted to help homeless kids; they often just weren't asked. "Thanks. I'll let you go. I know you're busy."

"It's fine. How's your sister? I haven't seen her for a bit."

"She just got back from Mexico. She was feeling good enough to take our mother. I haven't seen Stephanie so happy in a long time."

"Did she take those boys of hers?"

"Yes, and my mom had the time of her life with them. She had wanted to go to Mexico for ages."

"And your sister's husband? Curtis, right?"

"He went too." Curtis had been a rock for Stephanie. He was always there for her and endlessly patient with her MS.

I thanked Dr. Hendin and told him I'd make an appointment for Juan.

A few weeks later Juan dropped by the van. It was early December but as warm as always in Phoenix. Dr. Hendin had evaluated him and adjusted his meds appropriately. His seizures were back under control. Even better, he had found work. "It is roofing. It will be hot under the sun. But I'm used to that." The dark muscles of his shoulders were a stark contrast to his white tank top. I noticed the tank was white and clean. His clothes looked freshly laundered.

"Did you find a place to live, Juan?"

"One of the guys on the crew, he asked me to stay at his place. He's a good buddy. Now that I make a little, I can help with rent." He gave a shier smile. "I met this nice girl too. Her family is from the same part of Michoacán as my family. Her name is Gabriella. She's going to school and is teaching me English." I could picture Juan as a husband and father, a good provider, and a contributing member of society.

I congratulated him in Spanish. "It sounds like your life is looking up."

"No kidding. I still don't have insurance," he said apologetically, handing me another empty bottle.

"One step at a time," I said, examining the dosage that Dr. Hendin had written.

◻◻◻◻◻

When I saw the pastor leading Donald up to the van, I thought, Now he's going to ask us to find him a shelter bed. So far the efforts to get Donald identification had been fruitless, so he still couldn't qualify for any evaluations or services. Without identification he couldn't even get food stamps. His delays were more apparent over time; he was taking remedial classes at HomeBase but struggled with reading. As charming as Donald could be, I was sure there were times he was frustrated. I wouldn't have blamed Pastor Richardson if he had come to a time when he decided he no longer could care for this large, brain-damaged boy.

But to my delight that wasn't the case. Pastor Richardson spoke. "We dropped by to tell you that the HomeBase shelter is having a little Christmas dinner. Going to be tomorrow, if you can make it."

"Can you come?" Donald was excited.

"Sure. Amy and I will be there," I said.

The next day, at HomeBase, the folding tables were laden with serving dishes, a hodgepodge from turkey to casserole. Each table had a homemade gingerbread house as a centerpiece. "Don't eat those," Wendy whispered to me, laughing. "We ran out of frosting and had to use caulking to glue the sides together."

The kids finished carrying out the food, teasing one another with good nature, hailing one another in fake waiter accents, un furling paper napkins as if they were fancy cloth ones instead. Amy and I volunteered to dish out food. When everyone was served, we filled our own plates. The meal began with a brief prayer, and I bowed my head for my own thanks. It was crowded inside, so we went out onto the porch. Pastor Richardson came out with his wife and introduced us. She was a short lady wearing what appeared to be a wig. She had dressed as if for church, with heavy hose and sensible shoes, and when she sat near me, I smelled a perfume that made me think of grandmothers' houses and laundry hanging over the line. It was comforting. The night was pleasant, the air just slightly cool. Stars showed in the sky, and the lights of the city caught the tops of nearby palm trees. The warm winter weather in Phoenix was lovely. There was a distant hum of cars.

"Are you still bringing Donald here?" I asked Pastor Richardson.

He nodded, his mouth full.

"Good place." He cut his food. "He's been getting all sorts of help. Counseling, job training, classes. He wants to get his high school diploma."

"That's wonderful," I said.

He chuckled. "He's got some catching up to do."

"A whole *lot* of catching up," his wife added.

"Might take some time, and they said it would be what they call a modified diploma nowadays, you know, for slower folk."

"Nothing wrong with that," his wife murmured.

They told me how they had two kids of their own, a son, who had gone to Hampton University, and a daughter, who had gone to the University of Washington, clear up in rainy Seattle. The son had a master's in social work, and the daughter taught theater, but her real passion was art, and wasn't the world a funny place? Pastor Richardson's wife revealed that they'd raised other kids, most of them the children of relatives, but some not related at all. Amy asked how many, and she had to turn to her husband.

"Eight, I believe," he said, chewing and swallowing.

"That's not counting the ones who stayed just a bit," she said.

Kids kept coming out on the porch to talk. Matthew, the skinny blond boy, asked after Jan the way he always did. Donald joined us, stretching his legs down the steps. He was wearing new blue work pants and a heavy shirt. His hair was a little longer, covering the scars. I noticed that out of his dirty overalls and with his hair growing out, he was a handsome young man. He bent his head over his plate and said grace. "This is good," he said, and quickly cleaned his plate.

A girl came and sat down on the steps below him. She stared at Donald. She had dark brown hair parted in the middle and round brown eyes. She tucked her hands under her legs.

"Donald?" she asked. "Want to go play pool?"

"Sure." He got up. "But let's have some pie first."

I heard him tread heavily inside. The girl happily followed.

"How long do you think he'll be at your place?" I asked Pastor Richardson.

His wife looked alarmed. "What do you mean?" she asked.

"We don't want to get rid of him," Pastor Richardson said quickly, as if I were going to steal Donald away. I felt a moment's pang. This couple was treating Donald like a prized, desired child. If only the other adults in his life had treated him the same way.

"Having him around is nice," his wife said. "And you know he loves to play basketball with his cousins?"

His cousins? I thought happily. Now they are giving him a family.

"I figure God brought him into our lives for a purpose," Pastor Richardson said. "He left that boy sitting outside our church for a reason."

"Amen," I heard his wife say.

I was wondering about Donald's future. He was a young man now. I didn't know what the Richardsons were planning for him. How long would they be a resource for him? "Are you planning on keeping him for a time then?" I asked hopefully.

"I don't see why not," the pastor said. He stood up, shaking his pants out. "Now, I think Donald had the right idea. Who wants pie?"

After the party was over, Amy and I helped wash up. Amy was wiping down the tables and I was putting away dishes when the pastor and his wife left with Donald. The boy towered over both of them.

"That Pastor Richardson," Wendy said, watching them leave, "ever since he heard about us, he's been helping out around here all the time. He even had his church in to paint the kids' rooms."

Amy folded the washcloth. "He didn't tell us that. That's wonderful."

I felt a wave of appreciation for the shelter and all the amazing volunteers who dedicated their time to understanding these kids. I suddenly thought about what Juan and Sugar had said about the adult shelter downtown. I had assumed that all shelters were as supportive and safe as HomeBase. Maybe that wasn't the case.

"What do you know about some of the adult shelters around here?" I asked Wendy. "Like the one downtown."

Wendy grimaced. "I know that one in four adult men in Phoenix area shelters are registered sex offenders. That should tell you enough." She wrapped a leftover wedge of pecan pie in foil and added it to her stack of leftovers. "I've heard horror stories from some of the older teenagers. Some have been raped. Boys as well as girls." That was what Sugar was talking about, I thought. I realized why she and many of the older teenagers avoided the adult shelters. But there were so few beds that opened up in a place like HomeBase.

Matthew caught up to us on our way to the truck. His blond hair glowed in the moonlight, and the light wind billowed his white T-shirt. "Dr. Randy," he called, trotting up. He handed me several foil-wrapped packages. "We got some extra pie for you." I expected Amy to tease me about this, because she knew how much I liked pie. Instead she just captured my hand and held it all the way home.

6

THE HEART OF DIXIE

It was early spring before the staff at HomeBase was able to get Donald identification. His father in Alabama had been no help. He refused to answer phone calls or letters. Jan told me all about it as we stocked the van one evening, loading medications and checking them off our lists. "Finally they tracked down a birth certificate from a county hospital in Alabama," she said. "If Pastor Richardson hadn't taken him in, who knows *what* would have happened to that boy."

With the identification we were finally able, with effort, to get Donald on the state insurance. As soon as he was approved, I set up appointments for neurological tests for him at the hospital. It was time to get to the bottom of his delays. If Donald suffered from any sort of deteriorating condition or needed treatment, I wanted to know.

I helped him check in one evening at the hospital. He waited on the edge of his hospital bed, looking large and helpless in his blue gown. Mrs. Richardson had given him an old flowered suitcase for his few belongings. I was touched. I had seen kids admitted into a hospital with little more than a paper grocery sack to hold their clothes.

"You're going to be OK," I tried to reassure him.

He looked as if he were going to cry. I could see the scars on his scalp through the bright lights where his hair parted. "I want the pastor," he murmured.

"He had to go to work. He's coming back once your tests are done."

"Ain't going to take no bus," he whispered.

"What bus?" I asked. Donald didn't reply. It took me a moment. Donald was afraid I was going to put him on a bus the way his father had. I realized that Pastor Richardson's leaving him at the hospital had triggered fear in Donald. He had been abandoned before, and he thought he was being abandoned again.

"Pastor Richardson is coming soon."

"No bus." He looked as if he were ready to run. His muscles tensed. I could see the panic rising in his eyes. "No bus!"

"Donald, would you like me to stay?"

His eyes slid toward mine. "OK."

"Let me make a call."

"No bus."

"No bus. I'll be right back." I stepped out the door to call Amy and tell her I would be late.

I waited with Donald for an hour until Pastor Richardson arrived from work. He would help Donald until the tests were done. He was dusty and shrunken-looking and tired from his drywall business. It wasn't until I was driving home that evening that I remembered I had promised Amy before that I would come home early. She had something to tell me. I wondered what it was.

When I walked in, I could smell freshly baked cookies. Amy was in the bathroom, brushing her teeth. There on the counter was an early pregnancy test.

I felt delight bloom in my heart. "When?"

"We'll see. I'm guessing November."

The specialist called us in the next day. Donald had been given an MRI as well as other tests. I met Pastor Richardson and his wife outside Donald's room. The specialist began talking the way neurologists do, about tests and skills and frontal lobes and executive functions. I could see the pastor was not following anything. I barely understood it all myself.

"Can you cut it down for us?" I asked.

"He has permanent brain damage."

"He's always going to be this way?" Pastor Richardson asked.

"Yes and no. The point is we don't know what he is capable of accomplishing. It's hard to tell because I don't think he was given many opportunities *to* learn."

Pastor Richardson looked at the floor. I wondered what he was thinking. "It was those beatings he got in the head, right? He'd be a normal boy otherwise." His voice shook with a thread of anger. I had never heard Pastor Richardson sound angry before. His wife took a sharp breath and held her patent leather purse closely.

"We may never know," the specialist said. "He could have been born this way. If his father was mentally handicapped, maybe that explains why he thought it was OK to beat his son. When I was interviewing Donald, I noted several details that suggested this to be the case. For instance, he told me his father only made food out of cans. A mentally handicapped person often doesn't know how to cook, so they cover it by eating out of cans or fast food places. But for whatever the reason, Donald has limitations. Still, he has a lot of strong qualities. His verbal ability is good. He can speak well. He has good impulse control. I think he can learn. He will probably just always be a little slower than other people."

"Is there any treatment?" I asked.

He consulted Donald's charts. "Most times these scores are pretty static." He looked at Mrs. Richardson, who was trying hard to follow him. Her wig was slightly askew. "What I mean is if he exercises his brain, we could improve connections to help him learn faster. But he's never going to be the proverbial rocket scientist."

"I'd still like to know if it was those beatings," Pastor Richardson said. I could tell he was grieving what I was grieving. If Donald hadn't been beaten, he might have been whole, and the Donald we knew would have been a young man capable of going off to college. I thought we were probably feeling the same fury toward a father who would beat his son this way and then discard him.

His wife cleared her throat. "The Lord blesses the meek; he doesn't ask them why they got that way."

Pastor Richardson gave her a sharp look. "I guess you're telling me I don't need to know."

"I guess I'm saying you got the clay you got to work with. What kind of pot are you going to throw?"

The specialist looked among the three of us. He cleared his voice to make sure we all were listening. "The most important thing that Donald needs is people to watch out for him, to guide him and keep him safe. I can't predict the future for him."

"OK," Pastor Richardson said slowly.

"Let's see him," his wife said, and marched to the door.

Donald was sitting bolt upright on the edge of his bed. He was holding the old floral suitcase in his lap. He looked overjoyed. "Pastor Richardson!" he exclaimed. "Mrs. Richardson."

"You ready to go, son?"

Some social workers from a school had called about several teen-agers living in a house that had no water and no electricity and was extremely dirty. Bouncing over rutted roads that had not seen re-pairs for years, Jan and I found the neighborhood easily enough. We talked on the way. We had been running the van for a year now and still were discovering new places where the homeless kids hid out.

At the far end of the street lay an empty stretch of boarded-up houses and crude adobe huts. Abandoned cars lay in some of the yards. They had been stripped. As soon as we parked, a group of three kids came over, all complaining of severe ear pain. I treated the two boys first. Both had ear infections. They had previously been on the van in another location, so I was able to check their records on my laptop. I saw they had been given oral antibiotics previously. The drugs hadn't worked; that meant it could be a drug-resistant strain. I gave them intramuscular shots. "With these drug-resistant strains we have to use the big guns to knock them out," I told one boy as I prepared the needle. He looked resigned and held his pale arm out. His hair hung in his face.

The girl was even sicker than the boys. She was short and plump and had a wide Slavic face and crystal blue eyes that were watering with pain.

"Where are you guys living?" I asked her. She made a gesture with her thumb to a house outside the exam room window. She held the sore ear with one hand.

"Are you all sleeping on the floor?"

She tried to smile. "Yeah, the maid service forgot to deliver beds."

"Let me take a look." Right away I saw the large mass behind her ear. "How long have you had this bump behind your ear?" I asked, examining it.

"Weeks, I guess," she whispered. She was hot with fever, her eyes glassy and wet.

I looked inside her ear. It was curdling with infection. I returned to the mass. It was large and swollen.

"You've got mastoiditis," I said. "The infection went down into your mastoid bone."

"Is that bad?" She swallowed.

"It can be very bad. We used to see mastoiditis a long time ago. Or at least doctors older than I am used to see it. Nowadays it's more unusual because we have antibiotics. We usually see it in Third World countries and places without medicine." I examined the hot lump while I explained to her how her ear infection had passed down into the hollow mastoid bone behind her ear. Now it was filled with pus. Sooner or later it would explode.

"If it goes backwards into the covering of the brain, you could get meningitis," I told her. "It can be fatal."

"I don't want to go to the hospital."

"You have to go." My voice was firm.

"I'll miss my friends," she said.

I patted her arm. When the ambulance arrived, her two friends helped her into the back. Then they came over to the van, shouldering backpacks.

"Where's the hospital?" they asked.

"Clear across town," I said, giving them directions. Jan handed them bus tickets, and they headed to the nearest bus stop.

When I had a break later, I walked over to the house the girl had said they were squatting in. There was a rusting shell of a car in the front and a sour smell around the place. Aware there might be fecal contamination, I took care as I stepped closer. All the windows were busted out. Glass littered the sandy ground, and thorny bushes grew wild around the sides. I peeked in a window. The floor inside was covered with old sleeping bags and blankets and strewn with garbage. There was an old paperback, a romance novel, open over one unzipped sleeping bag. There was no furniture. It had to be more than 110 degrees inside the room. I was sure that at night the desert wind came in those empty windows and it got bitterly cold. The kids staying there probably sweltered in the day and froze at night. Along with snakes and insects, virulent infections thrived in such places. They spread like wildfire from lack of hand washing and the kids' already compromised immune systems. Everything from the walls to the sleeping bags was probably hot with contagions.

The rest of the day we spent treating the other kids squatting in the area. All the shelters were full, but we did our best to get them on waiting lists. It felt like a productive day. We closed up the van and headed into town. It was blocks away that we passed the bus stop. I wondered if the boys had made it to the hospital for their friend. Phoenix buses were notoriously infrequent. People sometimes waited for hours.

"It has to be hard on them," Jan said. She was apparently thinking the same thing. "They've got such long distances to walk, even just for food."

"Or to visit a friend," I added.

She nodded. The heat shimmered in front of us, and I thought of the journeys these kids made.

Another early ultrasound: I felt jinxed, anxious, bereaved in advance, and, still, madly hopeful.

"Randy, we're running late." Amy fretted. "Just drop me off."

"I'll catch up to you," I called out the door as she ran into the hospital.

When I got inside, I expected her to still be filling out forms. But the reception area was empty. The receptionist looked up. "Dr. Christensen, your wife is in room two." I walked in, and the ultrasound technician got up and immediately left the room. Thoughts began swirling through my mind like a snowstorm. I went to Amy. Her face appeared mystical, perplexed, far away. Bright. This wasn't a smile. It was beatification.

"Both hearts are beating fine," she said.

I was dumbfounded. "Both? Two? You're kidding!" I stuttered. I was too excited to even speak. Two heartbeats, I thought. *Twins.* Two angels on wings.

I held her hand, feeling the warmth between us. The technician came back in and turned on the screen. We watched in fascination. "Remember, Randy, how you used to say you married me because twins run in my family?"

"Maybe Ginger knew all along," I said jokingly. Since we had figured out Amy was pregnant, Ginger had spent every night lying by her bedside, refusing to leave her presence. Amy was convinced that Ginger had known she was pregnant before she did.

I hugged my wife and felt her hair against my lips. After we talked awhile, I went outside to call my mom and dad. The air was clear and bright, and the palm trees stood in vivid relief. The sun always shines brighter when you've had good news. I imagined my mother's manicured hand reaching for the phone. She had left her family in Las Cruces, Mexico, to marry my father. I knew she loved him, but I was sure there were times she missed living near her own parents. I heard in my mind the things she used to say to me as a child, how she would use all my names when she was mad. "Randal Charles Christensen!" she would yell when I got into mischief. But when she was proud, she would only say, "That boy." I saw her holding my hand on the way to first grade, feeling special that my mom was walking with me past the dry washes, watching the early-morning rabbits scatter from the brush. I saw her face in the audience while I received my high school diploma. I was seeing in a rush all that had come before, from boy to grown man. "That's wonderful, how exciting." My mom was crying on the phone. "Twins!" she called to my dad. I knew he would call me later, full of warnings and precautions. For some reason this thought was comforting.

When I came back in, I announced to Amy that we should talk about names.

"Already?" she said, laughing. "We don't know if they will be boys or girls."

"Or one of both," I said. "Well, one girl's name is easy," I added. "Jane, for your mother."

The look on her face caught me off guard. There was surprise, aching, loss, and joy. "Yes, please," she said. "Only let's say Janie Marie. Your mother's name is Maria and my sister's name is Marie. It just sounds perfect." I wanted to kiss her. My mom would love the name.

"What about boys?" she asked after a pause.

"I'm not sure. In my family the men all have the initials RCC."

"Randal junior?" She looked as if she were half joking.

"No, we can't have a junior with twins, and what if there are two boys? Let's think about it," I said, jumping on the bed. "You know what this means, don't you? We have to go buy a minivan."

Now my wife looked incredulous. "Oh, no. I am not a minivan person. I just can't, Randy. I can't."

The technician had come back in the room, peeking to see if

we were done with our private time. "Usually when they say they 'can't' it's because they heard they're having twins—not because of a minivan," she said, smiling.

Amy's curls were shaking. "No way. No minivan."

"Shh," I said, laughing and petting her hair. "Shh. Everything will be OK."

"You dork," she said, and gave me a punch.

As I spent more time on the van, visiting different areas of Phoenix and the surrounding areas, I was starting to hope I would see kids I knew at certain locations. Some of the kids were easier to help than others, and for the hard ones, like Sugar, I held out eternal hope that each visit might be the one where I figured out what they needed.

For the rough area of downtown, I always hoped to see Sugar, and usually I did. Today I wasn't disappointed. Almost as soon as we lowered the jacks, Sugar moseyed over from where she had been standing on a curb. It was hot out, and she was wearing short cutoffs and a tank top. There was still a sense of vitality about her. Some of the kids I treated seemed so destroyed by what they had gone through, but Sugar seemed indestructible. I knew this was a dangerous idea, because at any moment Sugar could be destroyed by her life, either actually or emotionally.

When she bounced onto my exam table, she had an energy that was unusual in street kids. She was starting to drop the brash sexual act around me.

"What's going on, Sugar?"

"Nothing. I heard you got a dog," she said. I was surprised.

"Where did you hear that?" I asked.

"Around. I hang with some of the street kids. But not too much." Her eyes were as clear and bright as a white window. So young, I thought.

"Her name is Ginger," I said. I told her all about the dog while

I made notes in her chart. I showed her a picture of Ginger in my wallet. Sugar gazed at it. Her hazel eyes were unreadable. What was she feeling? The dog had a home. She did not.

"It's been a little while since I saw you," I said carefully. "Where are you staying?"

Her eyes became guarded. "Here and there," she said evasively.

Sugar had chlamydia again. "The state health department asks that we promote partner notification," I told her. "That means—"

"I know what it means. You want me to tell my partners."

"That's right."

"And do you really think I know my partners?"

"Maybe not." I looked at her with sympathy.

"Maybe I don't even know their names."

"Maybe not."

She looked at me expectantly.

"How long have you been prostituting, Sugar?"

"Since I was twelve." Twelve. My God.

"Do you want to tell me about it?" I asked.

"It doesn't matter."

"I'd like to hear. Or maybe you'd like to talk to a counselor?" I was hoping she would go for this option. Whenever possible I wanted the kids to talk to a professional therapist.

She gave that little shrug. "There was something wrong with my mom. She was always hiding in her room. She thought people were out to get her and stuff. I used to take care of my little sister. I'd change her diapers, put her to bed." Her eyes grew hazy with memories. "Her name was Sara. I called her Sara Bear. I made her bottles, and I'd put her to bed." There was a silence. She rubbed one sneaker over the other. "We used to fall asleep on the couch together. *Sesame Street* was her favorite show. When Mom would get food stamps, I'd buy food."

People said that adolescents were hard to talk to, but I was starting to think the problem was that adults often just didn't listen. I was patient. She took a breath.

"Then one day I was at the store. I was buying Sara and me

Popsicles because it was so hot out. This man came up to me. He looked like he was really nice. He had the nicest eyes. He said, 'You seem to like sweet things, I guess I'll call you Sugar.' He took me to his place." She stopped and waited, looking at the floor. I was learning just how many girls are molested, some raped, even by their parents. A few I encountered had even been sold into prostitution by their own parents. At first I had thought, There is no way they're all telling the truth. Now I was realizing how naive I had been.

"At first he kept me for himself. Not too long. Then, well, you know." The sneaker was still rubbing. Under that veneer of bravado, I thought, this girl carries an immense amount of pain. "They liked me," she said, sneaking a glance to catch my reaction. "He called me his Sugar."

Never again would I want to call her by that name, I thought. Never.

The rub of the sneaker stopped. Her clear eyes were wide and full of questions. "I feel so bad I left my little sister. I wonder what happened to her. I think of her all alone in the house. Can God forgive you for that? I don't know."

I took my time before replying. I wanted to make her understand that she was the victim and that she couldn't blame herself for what had happened. But I also sensed how strong her love for her sister was still. If she wouldn't fight for herself, maybe she would fight for her sister.

"Maybe there is a way to see her again," I said gently.

"I'd just like to know she's OK," she said. "I wouldn't expect her to talk to me or anything. I'd just like to know if she is OK."

"If you go into a shelter . . ." I said. I quickly added, "We could find a safe shelter for you. Like HomeBase."

There was a quick shake no of the head.

"Or a counselor. You could tell this to a counselor," I said.

"Naw." She looked as if she were ready to bolt. "Look, it's too late. Hell, the last time I was in school I was in seventh grade. I can't even do math or nothing." She was being tough.

But I saw under that hard shell of sexuality a twelve-year-old girl who had never been loved, a twelve-year-old girl who loved her baby sister. Just like Mary, Sugar was hiding.

When I got home that night, I crouched down to pet Ginger and rolled her on her back for a belly scratch. She was a little fluff ball. I asked Amy if she wanted to go out for pizza. I had to spend the night studying for my certification tests, and I wanted at least a little time with Amy. I was worried about her. The doctors had told her she needed to gain a good fifty pounds for the pregnancy, twenty-five for each of the babies. She was a healthy weight but needed the extra weight to carry the twins. This task already seemed impossible. Amy had been nauseated from day one, and not mild nausea either. She vomited much of what she ate. We kept expecting the morning sickness to pass, but as the weeks went by, it was getting worse.

"You know what sounds good?" she said. "Chinese hot-and-sour soup." On the way to the Chinese restaurant, she rolled down her window and let the cooler air flow over her face to calm her nausea. We drove past a girl standing conspicuously on a street corner. Wearing shiny blue shorts and a blue zip-up jacket, she was under a dome of light. I thought immediately of Sugar.

"How sad," Amy said, glancing at the girl as we pulled up to the light.

"Why do you think a girl like that wouldn't want to get help?" I asked Amy.

"What do you mean?"

"If you offered a girl like that other options, why wouldn't she accept them?"

The girl turned her face toward Amy and then quickly turned away when she saw us looking. I saw a car across the street slow down. The girl's face migrated to it as if by instinct. A frown line appeared between Amy's eyes.

"I imagine she would be afraid," she said slowly.

"Afraid of what?"

"She'd be thinking she didn't deserve any better."

"Why?"

The light turned green. The car across the street had stopped, and the girl was sashaying toward the open window. The man inside had to be three times her age. The girl was leaning through his window as we drove away.

"Why do you think?" Amy said softly.

⌐⌐⌐⌐⌐⌐

Jan was bouncing with pep, having just racked up yet another BMX win. She was now a national champion. I didn't realize how big this was until some of the kids on the van went gaga over the news. Her taut forearms had a fresh set of freckles. She showed off her new trophy. I watched with bleary, tired eyes. Between the van schedules, my hospital work, cramming nonstop at night for my certification tests, Amy's pregnancy, and the troubling ongoing severe nausea, it seemed I never got sleep. I felt constantly stressed, and the pressures were only rising. I was on call for two hospitals along with the van and working nineteen and twenty days straight at a time, with only one or two days off a month. It was becoming typical for me to work eighty- to ninety-hour weeks, and I wondered how long Amy would put up with it. My mind shied away from the worry.

"You won against women twenty years younger than you," I told Jan, yawning. "Aren't you ashamed?"

"Not at all," she said. "Hey, I made a new schedule."

I yawned again. A new schedule, I thought. OK. She handed me an extremely detailed chart. For a moment the lines moved into a wavy pattern and then reorganized back to where they had been. I really needed to start getting more sleep. "What's this?" I asked.

"I told you, it's a new monthly schedule. See? Here is all the places we take the van, here is how many hours we spend in each location, how many times a week, and when we finish for the night.

Over here I have the staff and interns and medical students and their availability. I worked it all out so we aren't so short staffed, and the kids know where to expect us and when."

For a moment nothing she said made sense. I had to think about it. A new schedule. Right.

"When did you do this?"

"Last night, after I got back from the race."

"You must have been up all night."

"Only until one or two or so," she said. "But I had to get up at five to do the laundry and get my lazy teenagers out of bed." She drank a slug of water and smiled.

"You are crazy. Really, Jan. Stone-cold crazy. I'll present this to the administration at our next meeting."

"When will that be?" She looked cross.

I glanced at the calendar on the wall. "Next month."

"You remember how long it took them to approve the intake forms I made," she said. "And then as soon as they did, it was like everyone agreed they had been needed all along."

"We can't just make big changes without going through the administration and our supporters," I said, "no matter how good the idea."

Jan had a reputation for going toe to toe with people. Just the other day she'd had a huge battle with one of our supporters. For religious reasons, he was opposed to giving out birth control. While I diplomatically tried to handle the issue—or so I thought—Jan marched into his office and asked him how many child prostitutes he wanted to see die because they caught HIV. I had heard the fireworks were pretty spectacular. While I agreed with her, I also worried about losing a key supporter.

She pursed her lips and went back to work. We were quiet as we took the van out. It was Jan who made an overture later that day. She touched my forearm. "I have a feeling you're mad at me."

We have to work as a team, or this will never work, I thought. In order for the van to be successful, I have to create a strong team. I can't do it by myself. And one of the first things I need to accept is that I can't always be the boss. I needed to learn to meet Jan halfway. I knew she cared about the kids as passionately as I did. We just had different styles, and it occurred to me I should probably back off and let her do things her own way too.

"I'm used to working with administrations," I said. I explained to her I was willing to work slowly because I knew there could be big results down the line: funding, support, ongoing programs. I didn't want to anger anyone or turn people against our work.

"Yeah, but I like to get things done," she said.

"That," I said with a laugh, "is abundantly clear."

□·□·□·□·□·□

I had been excited all morning. Mary's aunt had called and said they were coming from Chandler into Tempe for the annual Tempe Arts Festival, the local art-crazed street festival that drew people from all over the state. Afterward her aunt was taking her out to lunch for her birthday. Mary was turning eighteen. They had promised to stop by the van and say hello.

I kept peeking out the door of the van to see if they were coming. The street festival was only a few blocks from where I was parked. I was busy. Several kids had told me the festival was a good place to panhandle and get free food. Jan poked her head into a room where I was finishing with a kid. "Guess who is here?" she said.

A suddenly grownup-looking Mary was carrying a balloon and had her cheek painted with a little flower. Her hair was longer, the dark silky strands growing past her shoulders. She had clipped the hair in front into straight bangs. The style showed off her features, her high cheekbones and dark eyes. I suddenly realized what a pretty young woman she was.

Her aunt's face was flushed with heat. A large purse was slung over her shoulder. "This is an amazing festival," she said to me. "We visited all the booths. I got a paint set for Mary for her birthday present."

"Can you come to lunch with us? Please?" Mary asked. "We're having Mexican."

I hesitated. In general I didn't see the kids outside the van. I wanted to maintain good professional boundaries. But we had decided as a team that while it wasn't direct medical care, there were times we might want to celebrate a milestone with a child. Giving cards for birthdays, for instance, seemed appropriate. While cards were OK, we had drawn the line at giving out money or expensive gifts. When a child asked for money for a Greyhound bus home, or there was some other legitimate need, we dealt with it on a case-by-case basis.

"It's not expensive or fancy," her aunt hastened to say. "Just that little Mexican place down the street."

"It's my birthday lunch," Mary said.

"Go," Jan said, making shooing motions. "I can handle it here."

On the way out I opened a storage cupboard up front and took out a small envelope. Jan had gotten Mary a birthday card. She had picked out the card because it looked artistic, with beautiful watercolors on the front. The inside read that we were wishing Mary the most wonderful year. I put the envelope in my pants pocket.

"It turns out Mary is a computer whiz," her aunt told me as we scooped up warm artichoke dip with tortilla chips in the restaurant. She was proud. Mary stared at me briefly over her plate, her cheeks high with color. Her dark eyes studied me intently. I wondered what she was thinking.

"I made new friends at school," she said.

"They're all computer kids," her aunt said with a laugh. "She fits right in. She's smart."

Mary dug into her food. I noticed she held her fork awkwardly, like a spade. Her aunt reminded her gently about "manners" under her breath. Mary immediately switched the fork to the other hand. She soon scraped her plate clean. "Can I be excused for a second?" I watched as she stopped and asked a waitress where the restroom was. Her shoulders were back, and she held her head high. She had gone from looking like a fearful animal to looking like a confident young woman.

Her aunt spoke quietly. "She spaces out sometimes. The counselor says that will get better over time. She's got PTSD, you know."

"You must be proud of how far she has come."

"Dr. Christensen, she's never celebrated her birthday before. Not once in her life did that girl have a birthday."

When Mary came back, I handed her the card. "Happy birthday, Mary," I said. Her eyes widened. She opened the card. This is amazing, I kept thinking. When I met her, she couldn't remember her age.

7

TOO SOON

I t's kind of hard to celebrate the pregnancy when you are puking so much." I tried to tease Amy as she knelt over the toilet bowl. She wiped her mouth and gave me a look. We were enjoying pregnancy, despite the still-sharp memory of the miscarriage and despite Amy's constant sickness. But she was not gaining any weight, and I was getting more concerned all the time.

"What happened to my famous cast-iron stomach?" she said, moaning.

"Remember how you used to drink milk that was weeks old and not even notice?"

"Oh. Don't talk like that." She retched again. Her stomach was empty. "I've got to get to work," she said, standing weakly.

I wanted to argue but didn't. Amy was still putting in her own twelve- to fourteen-hour days as a pediatrician. Part of the reason she understood my dedication to the van was that she had the same dedication to her patients. She was a driven person. Amy was a hard worker. And stubborn too. I knew it wouldn't do any good to argue with her.

"Some ginger ale?" I asked. We were trying everything for the nausea: wristbands with acupressure points, dry toast, frequent meals, and all sorts of liquids. Nothing quelled the vomiting. She shook her head. "You know, sweetie, we're going to have to get you on nausea meds soon, if this doesn't stop," I said. "You're losing weight, and that isn't good for the babies." It was still hard for me to believe that under my wife's still-flat tummy lay two tiny babies, growing minutely each day.

"I know I can't go on like this," she said.

Mercifully, at sixteen weeks the vomiting finally stopped, thanks to a daily healthy dose of an antinausea medication. Amy felt strong enough in June to drive up to spend a day with me at the diabetes camp at the Friendly Pines campground in Prescott, Arizona. The work was exhausting. Thinking it had to be good preparation for parenting, I spent twenty-four hours a day with my young charges, testing blood sugar early in the morning and waking kids up for midnight blood sugar tests. It was around-the-clock work. The kids had quickly given me the camp name of Bill Gates. I told Amy it had to be because of my computer savvy and leadership abilities. Then Amy said the kids had told her the real reason. It was that I wore "nerdy-looking glasses." This just killed Amy. She vowed that as soon as camp was over, she would take me shopping for new glasses.

She and I sat on a fence and watched kids ride ponies. One of the teenage counselors rode her horse next to a boy who was suddenly looking faint. She talked to him, he nodded, and they got off their horses to test blood sugar. Amy patted her tummy and turned to me. "Can we bring our babies here too?"

"I don't see why not," I answered. "Smooth sailing from now on out," I told her.

Another ultrasound had shown us we not only had twins but had a boy and a girl. I thought of the names Amy and I had decided when we had found out we would have both: Jane Marie and Reed Coleman. I sat next to my wife on my break in the summer sun and felt happy.

"Let's go to California for the Fourth of July," she said. Her face was shadowed under the brim of her straw hat. "We can stay in my dad's cabin at Lake Arrowhead." It was a great idea.

"Bill Gates says yes," I said.

"That reminds me." She laughed. "We're buying you new glasses first."

Amy and I spent the Fourth of July weekend at her father's cabin in California. We had taken my best friend, Ron. It was his father who was one of the Old Timers who had helped us so much. After two wonderful, relaxing days on the lake we drove back. I was thinking how nice it was to escape all the stresses of our lives, even for just a short time. It was on the long drive home that Amy began looking pale. Ron was driving, and Amy was sitting in the backseat behind him. I turned around and noticed the sick sweat above her upper lip.

"Are you OK?" I asked her anxiously.

"It's just car sickness." She adjusted her belt and took a deep, shuddery breath. Amy often got carsick, but I suspected we were dealing with something else.

"Let's trade seats," I said, and Ron pulled over. Sitting in the front didn't help her at all. Oh no, I thought, the nausea is back. "Have you been taking your meds?" I asked Amy. She nodded, wiping her mouth with a tissue. By the time we drove into Phoenix she was leaning against the window, breathing hoarsely. Her face was actually a pale shade of green.

"What is it?" Ron asked.

"Stomach cramps. Must be something I ate." I remembered the weeks of vomiting and felt a chill.

After we had dropped Ron off and pulled into our driveway, there was panic in her voice. "Randy, I'm having contractions."

My heart went cold. It was early July, and the twins weren't due until November. Not again, I thought, remembering the miscarriage. We spent a long, anguished night in the emergency room. "You're having premature contractions," the doctors told her. They were finally able to get them under some control with medication. Amy kept hold of the babies, as if through the power of her own will. I pictured them as small as slips of paper, little paper cranes, tucked inside her, feeding gently on her spirit. After exhausting hours she slept, her face still in a circle of light.

After Amy was asleep, I walked to the window and studied the lights of Phoenix. I knew that Amy might be staying here for most of the remainder of her pregnancy—for however long that might be. Let it last, I asked God. Let her keep these babies long enough for them to be born.

Surprisingly, the next morning the doctors released Amy. With bed rest, they said, they hoped she would be fine. But we were back within hours. The contractions had returned with force. I couldn't understand why my wife, a woman who was always strong and healthy, reacted this way to pregnancies. It was as if her body refused to be pregnant. The doctors put her on a heavy-duty med to relax the muscles of the uterus. It was administered through a pump into her arm. Amy was stoic. The medication made her feel jumpy, and I watched her eyelids twitch as she lay on the hospital bed, watching television. Still, the contractions continued. They broke right through the muscle relaxant. The doctors increased the dose. The contractions continued even more.

"If we don't get the contractions stopped, she will miscarry soon," one of the doctors said forcefully. I counted the weeks. If the twins were born now, they would die.

I knew Amy was nowhere near the weight she needed to be. I was overwhelmed with anxiety. My wife was in premature labor and might miscarry at any moment, and there was nothing I could do. It was a sense of helplessness that made me want to wring my hands and pace.

"What do we try next?" Amy asked, her eyes twitching.

"A high dose of magnesium," the doctor said. "It may stop the contractions." She explained the risks. "But such high doses can also lead to many other muscles of the body relaxing. This means the facial muscles may droop, and weakness can set in. And it means Amy stays here. If she is on the magnesium, we need to monitor her."

Amy waved her hand in consent. Whatever works, her hand said.

"Randy, can you spend the night?"

"Of course."

The nurse wheeled in a chair that unfolded into an uncomfortable bed. I reclined next to Amy and held her hand. The magnesium carried her into sleep. When she was deeply asleep, I took my hand back. I was up most of the night, thinking about Amy. It didn't seem fair that this would happen to a woman who wanted children so much. All the time I saw kids on the van who had parents who didn't seem to care at all. The injustice of it stung. In the morning I rinsed my face and mouth in the sink, kissed Amy, and went to work. Luckily, I was scheduled for shifts inside the hospital.

I returned to find Amy looking comatose. Her wrists lay limply across the crumpled white sheet. Her head was turned toward the television. I wiped drool from her chin. Half of her face didn't seem to be working anymore. I called the doctor, telling her she needed to come right away.

"Is this normal?" I asked.

"Yes," she said. "Amy's contractions are unusually strong. We had to up the dose. We've reduced the contractions somewhat, but I don't think we'll be able to eradicate them entirely." She sounded apologetic.

I sat with Amy. "Can you eat?" I asked. She shook her head no. I felt strained with turmoil. The anxiety was only getting worse. I knew Amy could be in this hospital for the next few months, and each day would be high risk. I was glad the hospital had a lot of experience in multiple births. The doctors would know about retaining a pregnancy. But even under that assurance I still felt insecure. I didn't know how to help my wife. As a doctor I wanted to fix her, make it all better. I had the irrational feeling that I was failing by not fixing it.

"Stay here again tonight," she whispered.

While I was in the hospital, I checked on her throughout the day. But I had a responsibility to the van too. I tended to seemingly endless lines of needy kids. For the first time I saw them and later couldn't recall their faces. I felt as if I were splintering into a thousand pieces. It was not the physical exhaustion but the stress that made my body hurt. I drove home only to feed and walk Ginger.

The house smelled empty and lonely. I packed an overnight bag. Then I drove directly to the hospital, where I changed my clothes. I sat with Amy until she fell asleep, and then I unfolded the cot.

One week of this seemed excruciating. The next seemed impossible. Still, it went on until I could taste the exhaustion in my mouth and feel it in my skin.

After over a month of hospitalization Amy was back home. The doctors said it was a trial run. If she could stay in bed, she might finish the pregnancy at home. She lay in our bedroom, buried in a sea of craft projects and magazines, bored out of her mind. I was gone all day, and she had nothing but the walls and television to look at. Amy hated bed rest.

I was coming in from working all day. So far we had made it to day two of the home bed rest. I was starting to hope it might work.

"Randy?" Amy called. "I'm hungry."

"What would you like?"

"Pancakes and bacon."

"I'm not so good at bacon. It always burns. How about just the pancakes?"

"I really want bacon," she said, looking up from her pillow while I stood in the doorway. I hadn't even unloaded the codebooks from my pockets yet or walked Ginger.

"Honey, I just got home from work. It's been a long day. I'm tired. And seriously, you *know* I always burn bacon."

She gave me an even sadder look with her big brown eyes. I started to argue but quickly gave up. She wants bacon, I thought. Fine. I went into the kitchen, got the pancake mix out, and started heating the griddle. I put the bacon on and then started making pancakes—very ineptly. They were too dark, too big, and too messy. When I turned around, the grease from the bacon was smoking. She knows I'm not good at this, I thought. I was looking for the tongs. Where were the tongs? Not in the drawer. Not in the cabinets. Were they outside by the barbecue? I went to check. No tongs.

I came back in to see a jet of bright yellow and red flame shooting from the bacon pan. The smoke alarm went off with a screech. "Randy, what's wrong?" Amy yelled from the bedroom. "Nothing!" I grabbed the smoking pan and threw it out back, onto the patio. Instead of being extinguished, the grease fire simply spread across the tiles. I ran and turned the hose on it. The water only seemed to spread the flames until they were lapping at the edges of the patio. Eventually I got it under control.

"Randy!" Amy was screaming.

The doorbell rang. The firefighters were here.

"I got it under control," I told them.

The young man in the helmet looked disbelievingly at my disheveled shirt and smoke-stained face. "Can we come in and check?"

"Sure." I opened the door. "I'm making pancakes."

He sniffed. "I think they're burning too."

"Shoot!" I remembered the griddle.

He smiled at something behind me. "Howdy, miss."

I turned around, and there was Amy. She was completely dressed. She had her overnight bag in one hand.

"What are you doing up?" I sputtered.

"We need to go to the hospital. I'm having contractions again." Just like that, we were out the door once again. I felt guilty. I couldn't even make bacon, and after less than two days at home my wife was back in the hospital.

The summer dragged on, and Amy was just barely holding on to the twins. She spent weeks in the hospital, and every effort to go home failed. The contractions simply never stopped, not even with high doses of medications. I knew that sooner or later the contractions would lead to dilation, and when that happened, birth was imminent. The key was to try to hold on as long as she could. Each day more increased the chance the babies might live.

On the van the homeless kids continued to come by, day after day, an unrelenting stream of broken bones and infections and stories of abuse that tore at my heart. The world seemed full of stress and sadness and despair. Yet in the middle of this sadness there was the miracle of life growing inside my wife and the miracle of kids finally getting help. I prayed quietly next to Amy's bed while she slept. My sense of purpose and faith remained. I felt sure all would be well. At the same time I had a pressing sense of worry. Maybe all would not be well.

The morning of September 11 I had gone home to shower and change. My phone rang. It was Amy. "Turn on the news," she said quietly. That day I sat silently by Amy's bed, watching the news with her. Nine-eleven, people were already calling it, as if we could pick up the phone and say, "Stop, we have an emergency." We held hands.

The next day at the office, Jan was uncharacteristically quiet. We spoke softly about what had happened. "A lot of teenagers are talking about enlisting," Jan said. There was strain in her eyes. It hit me that Jan had teenagers. Maybe she was worried they would enlist.

"I think about my babies being born in such a sad time," I said.

"You have no idea what love really is until you have children," she said.

I took the van out alone to downtown Phoenix. The kids I treated looked as distraught as everyone else. One of them was carrying a large roll of paper he'd gotten from an art store. He crouched down and unrolled it. Other kids helped him.

"What have you got there?" I asked.

"It's for the firefighters." The kids pulled markers and pens out of their backpacks to write notes and draw pictures. I returned from the van with a Dixie cup full of extra pens.

"Want to help?" they asked me.

I sat down and started putting my thoughts on the paper.

"What are you writing, Dr. Randy?" one of the girls asked. She had finished a beautiful free-form horse galloping over the desert. The red hills were in the background, with tall cacti. "This horse makes me feel free," she had written underneath. "I am sorry about what happened." I was touched. This girl had survived a childhood of severe neglect.

"It's about how thankful I am for everything in my life," I told her.

"Including us?" she asked.

"Including you."

She looked back down at the paper. "I'm going to make another horse."

⌐⌐⌐⌐⌐⌐

Only four days had passed since September 11. It was six-thirty in the morning, and I had spent a quiet but lonely night at home. I was putting a load of laundry into the washer. My phone rang.

"The babies are coming," my wife said with a gasp. I could barely catch my breath. She handed the phone to her doctor.

"The babies are coming now," the doctor said.

I was already climbing into my truck. I made it to the hospital in minutes. Amy's cervix had dilated overnight to the point where birth would happen quickly. Part of my mind went into hyperdrive. I counted the weeks. The twins were only thirty weeks. At thirty weeks, I knew, they probably wouldn't be able to breathe on their own. They ran risks of such disabilities as cerebral palsy. I thought of Donald on the van, smiling at the pastor. I prayed they would be OK. I ran to Amy's room and almost went running past her as she was being whisked down the hall on her back, her feet elevated higher than her head. The position was to keep the pressure off the cervix. Everything was happening so fast. The room was in controlled chaos, prepared with two warming Isolettes ready for the twins, my wife on the table, the doctors ready for surgery. I knew they could deliver in seconds if need be.

I felt myself split into separate people: the husband comforting his wife; the doctor paying attention to medical issues; the regular human being completely panicked about the health of his newborns and wife. Everything was happening so quickly. The tent went up between Amy's belly and her face, so she wouldn't have to watch the C-section. There was the incision, with the soft burring sound I knew so well. The doctor reached in and brought out the tiniest human creature I had ever seen. She was so small she might have been a tiny doll. But then I heard the word *girl*, and with joy we all heard my daughter's tiny, life-affirming gasp. She was breathing. The nurse showed her to Amy and then quickly placed her in an Isolette, the incubator for premature infants that would offer controlled humidity and heat.

My son is next, I thought, watching as they reached in and brought him out. Only this tiny froglike figure was limp and a terrible blue-black-gray color, like the bottom of a sick pond. The limp figure made no sound. I felt a horrible rushing sensation, and the room moved around me. The nurse carried him rapidly away from my wife. Without a word she shoved a tube down his throat and ran him out of the room.

Only a few moments had passed. The doctor had blood on her gloves. Her eyes were grave. Amy was barely coherent. She turned around and called for me. She looked confused. "What happened?" she asked, and I remembered that she couldn't feel anything and, with the tent, probably had no idea what had happened.

"Your daughter is breathing," the doctor said. No one said anything about our son.

I ran down to the neonatal intensive care unit. It was a place I had spent many call nights as a physician. I knew all the complications and tragedies that could occur with premature birth. Only now it was different because it was my children. The unit was one gigantic room with close to ninety babies, all lined up in Isolettes. They were wheeling our girl in and showed me where our son was. There was barely room in between each Isolette for the medical equipment. At the far end of the room were movable plastic privacy screens that could be set up around each domed Isolette. There was a hive of activity around my son's incubator.

"He's going to be OK," the nurse said as I ran up. She had a falsely reassuring tone that I was sure I had used as a doctor too. My son was lying on his back on a cloud of white cotton, still gray in color but with the coming red blossoming on his skin. He was so small he would fit in my palm. An oxygen tube snaked out of his mouth. His body seemed covered with wires. His tiny frog hands looked smaller than my thumb.

"Reed Coleman," I whispered, amazed.

I went to see my daughter. She had been placed clear across the huge room. Her color was better than her brother's, but she was also so unbelievably small, her thin legs no bigger than bird bones. She was breathing on her own, the rise and fall of her tiny chest barely perceptible.

"Janie Marie," I named her.

I ran back and forth between them in a daze. Their rounded, purpled, button eyes were closed, their red lips pursed. I wondered if preemies continued to dream the silent moving dreams they had in the womb. Would they awaken dreaming? Reed coughed, and his face turned purple. I turned to yell for a nurse, but she was there, gently adjusting his tubes. I could only croak a thank-you in response. All that night I walked among my wife, my son, and my daughter. My life seemed confined to this triangle. I hung over the Isolettes, another parent worrying, and through the long night I heard the murmuring of other parents, the whisper of their shoes on the floors, and the quiet advice of the doctors. I stared at my babies, willing them to stay alive. I had planned high schools, colleges, and their entire futures. Now all I cared about was that they might live. In the hours before dawn I bowed my head, and I talked to God. I prayed for Reed and Janie and all the kids on the van.

As night turned to morning, I found out what those plastic privacy screens were for. Quietly a nurse brought one out to put around the baby next to Reed. I watched as the doctors brought in the mother. Her preemie was getting ready to die. I could hear her sitting inside the screen, talking to her baby. Finally they let her take it out and hold it for the first and last time. She wept as she said good-bye.

That could be me, I thought, and worse, that could be Amy.

As the day passed, I felt vastly off center. The outside world was in chaos after 9/11 and our world on the inside was not much better the first few days after the birth. I went and looked at my babies a dozen times a day, but I felt helpless. I was allowed to hold only Janie. I knew I wasn't thinking rationally. When the nurses sat down to talk to Amy and me about our expectations, one of the questions was how long we thought the twins would have to stay in the neonatal unit. "Oh, they'll only be here a week or two," I responded blithely. I saw one nurse blink. I had to know that such preemies might stay for months. Yet I shut out this fact from myself.

I was deeply concerned about my wife. Her health was bad. The months of forced bed rest, the heavy medications to stop the contractions, the nausea, and the birth all had served to sap her vitality. She was bone thin; her eyes were hollowed. She had gained only twenty pounds out of the fifty she was supposed to gain, and most of this was probably water weight. Her arms and legs were far too thin; her skin tone was flaccid. She had no muscle tone left, from all the bed rest, and was so tired that even raising her hands was hard. All I could do was encourage her to eat.

It took her days to recover her sense of self. She sat up in her bed, sometimes disoriented. I took pictures of the babies and showed them to her. Her father had been in New York when the twins were born and, after 9/11, couldn't get a flight. He drove all the way to Phoenix and arrived about five days later. My parents came, bearing flowers and cards. For her first visit to see her children, Amy went down the hall in a wheelchair. She looked at her babies. That was when I saw the spark come back.

Finally, in November, Reed and Janie were allowed to come home. Their two months in the neonatal unit were a memory both Amy and I wanted to put behind us as quickly as possible. Amy had spent every day there after her discharge, from morning until eight or nine at night, and I had stopped in frequently, coming back in the evenings. It was a routine that we were desperate to leave.

But if I thought it would get easier at home, I was wrong. I was blown away by the constant medical care the twins required. Our living room looked like a hospital ward, with apnea monitors and a massive five-foot-tall oxygen tank for Reed. Janie had severe apnea spells, during which she would stop breathing and turn different shades of purple. The episodes were terrifying to watch. Every time I thought about her brain cells dying. Even getting the right clothes was a hassle. It irked Amy's frugal nature to buy expensive preemie clothes. My aunt Margie came to help out. She was fantastic with the babies, but we couldn't let many others visit. The risk of infection in preemies was just too high, and we didn't want them exposed to RSV, an illness sweeping the city that winter. Outings with the babies were not going to be possible for some time, a fact that left Amy isolated.

And I was back on the van. I had taken two weeks off following the birth, but that time was long gone. I was still working more than eighty hours a week. I often came home late to find Amy feeding one of the twins. They took food so slowly that an hour could pass for one feeding.

I invited my parents to babysit early one Sunday morning in December, a few weeks after the twins had come home. They had met the babies in the hospital and had spent time with them, but I was still surprised at how gentle and yet confident my dad was with them. Mom and Dad showed up excited to finally get to babysit. My dad was dressed in pressed casual trousers and a short-sleeve shirt. My mother was wearing a long-skirted dress and her favorite golden cross, which I had given her for Christmas one year when I was a teenager and working at the Golf n' Stuff. Her shiny brown hair was brushed into a short bob, and she wore a touch of lipstick. I looked like a train wreck, from too much work, junk food, and lack of sleep. Amy had at least brushed her hair. I was losing mine so fast I had started joking about not needing to brush it at all.

"So, you two, off to church," my father said. Amy and I had made plans to try a nearby church. One of the things I liked about

Amy was that her Quaker faith shared many traits with my Lutheran upbringing. We both were private about our faith and felt communication with God was a personal matter.

"We're going to the one down the street, Shepherd of the Valley," I told him.

"I really like the female pastor." Amy spoke up. "She had twins of her own."

Amy went into our bedroom to change. She soon came out, with nice loafers and fresh pants. She immediately looked presentable. Mom gave me a jaundiced eye.

"Aren't you changing?" she asked me pointedly. "You can't go to church in sweats. At least put on a nice shirt."

I ran off to hustle into a fresh shirt and clean cargo pants.

Moments later, as Amy and I were shutting the front door behind us, I heard my mom remark, "A tie wouldn't kill you either." I heard my dad cooing to Janie and Reed as Amy and I went down our walk. My mom was saying something about breakfast.

Amy giggled. There was a lift in her walk, and she turned her face toward the sun. "Your dad is really good with the babies," she commented.

"It's weird because I never would have thought he'd be comfortable with their being so delicate."

"They won't be delicate forever," she said with assurance. I was looking forward to the day we could take the twins out to church as a family.

It was two months after 9/11, and the community was still reeling. It was comforting to hear the female pastor talk about the need for strength and community while around us I saw our neighbors' faces, still bleak with tragedy. We all were still feeling such a sense of shock, disbelief, and fear that life was beyond our control. I knew that my sense of shock was compounded by the grueling ordeal of the hospital stays and the round-the-clock care the twins required.

But I was glad to see Amy out and about. She was taking care of two preemies all day and night every day. I thought this was a time when she probably missed her mother. She didn't have a lot of female relatives or friends nearby. That night I called her mother's cousin Jo Ann in Virginia. She was in her late sixties and had known Amy's mother well. "Can you call Amy? Offer some support for a new mother?"

Amy was overjoyed to hear from Jo Ann. "We talked on and on about the babies. Sometimes I think being a doctor and a mom makes other women afraid to give me advice, but Jo Ann wasn't at all."

"How great to hear from her," I said.

Amy gave me a big hug. "Jo Ann told me it was you."

"Does that bother you?"

"No. It's the nicest thing you've ever done. OK, except for Janie and Reed."

The drive to Mesa took longer than I had hoped. "This is our busiest yet," I told Wendy. Dozens of kids were waiting to be seen soon after we pulled up in front of the shelter. There was a line out the door and more waiting in groups. Even the Mesa police were bringing them in. An eighteen-year-old Navajo girl brought her baby sister for medical care, carrying her in a sling around her waist. "My name is Rebecca," she said softly, "but my Navajo name is Nizhoni."

"What does that mean?" I asked gently.

She laughed shyly. "Some say 'beautiful one,' some just say 'beautiful.' "

I noted that her long black hair was clean. She had the smooth, regular features of a Navajo, with golden skin and dark eyes. She was dressed in jeans and a clean top. She wore small turquoise studs in her ears. The baby's sling was freshly washed, and the little feet poking out were covered in clean socks. Nizhoni was evasive when I asked her where their parents lived.

I took the baby gently from the sling. I studied her for a moment. "Did you know your sister is albino?" I asked quietly. The condition led to a complete lack of pigmentation. The baby looked up at me dreamily. Her pale eyes were like the reflection of a light blue stream. She had white lashes and, though she had the same strong Navajo features as her big sister, white hair and white skin. She was less than a year old, and she kicked her fat little legs as I examined her. Albinism in infants can be very dangerous; the pigment serves a protective purpose.

"The doctor told my parents that she was an albino when she was born."

"Where *are* your mom and dad?" I asked. Nizhoni didn't answer, looking at her fingers. It crossed my mind that she might be the mom. Maybe there was a reason she was denying it "Are you the only one taking care of her?"

Again she made a murmuring answer, half yes, half no. I suspected they had a home of sorts. But I wondered why she was playing mother to a little baby. She wasn't equipped to take care of a medical condition like albinism.

"Does she have protective eye wear?" I asked. She shook her head, confused. I explained that if the baby didn't wear protective glasses, her eyes would let in too much light and she would go blind.

"My mom and dad—" She started to answer and then stopped.

"What?"

She didn't answer. Something in the way she picked up the baby, with long practice, gave me answer enough. For whatever reason—maybe her parents had alcoholism, AIDS, cancer—this teenage girl was the only mother this baby had ever had. I gave her everything I could and set her up with appointments for a specialist for her sister. I weighed the baby and gave her a good exam. Nizhoni left with her sister cooing in her sling. After she was gone, I realized I had spent all my time on the baby sister. The big sister needed our help just as much, maybe more. I had foolishly ignored her.

It was more than a month later that we were back in Mesa and saw Nizhoni again. Looking distraught, she came in carrying her little sister in the sling.

"My parents," she whispered. "They took the baby in the sun. I was at school, I couldn't stop them." The baby swung silently. I lifted her out of the sling and held her up to my face under the exam room lights. She looked back with pale eyes.

"It's extremely important we get her to the ophthalmologist immediately," I told Nizhoni. "The exposure is already causing permanent damage. If it keeps happening, your sister will go blind." I set up the appointment for her, gave her explicit directions and bus passes, but when I called the center later, it said Nizhoni had never arrived.

Another month passed. Jan and I were told that our trips to Mesa had to be canceled because the local shelter was closing. There would be no safe place to park. Hoping to see Nizhoni, I took the van out one last time. I couldn't find her, and no one I asked seemed to have heard of her. I wanted to think she had gotten help. I kept seeing the baby's pale eyes, under my lights. Another one lost, I thought. If only I had had more time. Regret filled me. I wished I had driven her myself to the appointment. I wished I could find her and continue to see her and help her and her sister. I reminded myself of the old saying: You can only affect the future. But I still ached.

This was the hardest part, I thought. There were going to be times I couldn't help everyone. I knew if I dwelled on these losses, I could become incapable of helping the next child. At least that is what I told myself. And then something would trigger the memory of the two of them, and I would see Nizhoni in my mind, standing next to me as I lifted her sister to the lights, and in my fears the baby was looking through me with forever sightless eyes.

Several of the local residency programs wanted to send their residents to us. The experience on the van would broaden their experience as well as give them some valuable medical education. Many times the programs would send a resident for just a day or two, to give him or her a taste of real-life medicine.

This day the resident was a young, gawky-looking doctor with unfortunate jug ears. The kids reacted to him with suspicion. I soon learned why. He was sitting in the lawn chairs, cussing up a storm, and trying to sound streetwise. "Dude, I know just what you're talking about," he told one kid, along with a string of colorful cusswords.

I immediately called him over. "Listen, that's unprofessional behavior."

"What is?"

"Swearing."

"Oh, I was just trying to build rapport," he said.

"We're running a mobile hospital, not a locker room," I said. "If Jan had heard you, trust me, you would feel the hurt."

"Yeah? That nurse? Well, the kids need someone to relate to them," he said smugly.

My frustration was building. It had been a long, hot, sweaty day, and sometimes I felt that with the developing recession, the needs of the kids got worse and worse. More and more kids seemed to be on the streets because their families had been destroyed by unemployment and poverty. "*That* nurse is a hundred times more popular with the kids than either of us will ever be, believe me. You know why? It's because she's not afraid to be an adult. These kids don't want children pretending to be cool. They can get that a hundred times a day on the street. They want adults they can trust."

I softened my voice and asked him a question. "What's your background?"

"My background? I was at Harvard. Top of my class."

"Harvard. Were you a homeless kid?"

"You've got to be kidding." He laughed.

"Then you don't need to pretend you are."

He looked disbelieving. "They need rapport," he replied, looking at me as if I were unbelievably dense.

I now felt I was cradling my temper with both hands. "Rapport doesn't happen because you are trying to be cool. Trust me on that. I am so not cool." I had learned that from Jan, I reflected. The best way to develop a connection was to be a positive authority figure.

Jan had walked up behind me. "That's right," she said with a smile. "You are so not cool."

I stomped off and went back in the van. I was upset. How we presented ourselves to the kids was vitally important, and unprofessional help tarnished our image, not to mention impeded our ability to help the kids. If there is one thing that is not romantic, I told our volunteers, it's the life of a homeless child. There was nothing cool about being homeless. I began pacing the van. Jan called me for another patient.

"You take this last patient," she said soothingly, knowing I needed to cool off. "I'll shut down the van with Mr. Rapport." She pointed a thumb at the intern, who was now standing alone at the edge of the van. The homeless kids had shut him out. Maybe, in the long run, I thought, this would be a learning experience.

I dashed into the office the next morning, my stethoscope flying. I had been up much of the night, helping Amy feed two cranky babies.

"Randy, we're in trouble." Jan met me immediately at the door. "The Flinn Foundation just changed their mission."

"Oh, no." The Flinn Foundation had generously funded our first few years. The foundation was a wonderful nonprofit organization. Like most nonprofits, it had a mission statement about what it wanted to support. Before, its mission statement had been to improve health care in Arizona. We had applied for grants, and it had been extremely generous. Now Jan told me the foundation was moving into supporting programs that enhanced biosciences. Obviously the van had nothing to do with the biosciences. Changing its mission meant a huge source of our budget had just vanished. "We're in crisis," Jan said.

"How long until we run out of money?" I asked her.

She hedged. "Soon enough. The medications alone are a huge bill. Our overhead is a monster, with everything from gas to gowns. You know how it is," she said, pointing at the stained and buckling ceiling above us. "We're always living on the edge. But now this— we can't make it long."

"What do you think is the answer?" I asked.

She thought carefully. "My opinion is we are relying too much on a few big donors. As great as they are, they're hard to find. What will really keep us afloat are the smaller donors and the smaller grants. They're the ones that add up."

"How do we get those?"

She smiled and poked me in the chest. "You're the boss."

When I had a brief break from the van that day, I called Dr. Irwin Redlener, who had founded the Children's Health Fund, along with Paul Simon. I felt a bit bowled over by him. He was such an animated person, so passionate, so confident.

"Randy, this is your element," he said right away after I had told him our predicament. His rough voice was reassuring. "It is up to you to tell the story of these kids."

"And funding?"

"That's what I was just talking about. You need to get out there and tell the stories of these kids."

I didn't think I would be a good public speaker. I was worried about my stutter. It always got worse onstage. I told Irwin, but he didn't care. He gently pushed back. "You can do it," he said. "People won't care if you are polished. Matter of fact, they'd rather you not be. Just tell the story from your heart. When you're talking to me, I can hear in your voice how much you care. No one is going to help if you don't ask for help."

I thought about it over the next few days, which were as hectic as ever. My experiences with the Old Timers had been so positive, even if I felt I had goofed my speech, but I still wasn't sure I could do a big event. Still, I saw I needed to give it a try—I wasn't about to let the van fail because I was stage shy. So I made some calls.

My first fund-raising event was at a Lions Club annual dinner. I had picked the Lions because their mission, which was to help people with disabilities, encouraged me. Their annual dinner was being held at a McCormick & Schmick's seafood restaurant, and while the food looked and smelled delicious, I was too nervous to eat my Dover sole. I took the small stage and looked over the faces, turned up to me. Many of the members were elderly; quite a few were blue collar, and most were wearing their well-washed best, the men in bow ties and the ladies in flowing dresses, and there were more than a few military medals and pins thrown in. As always it amazed me how people from different walks of life spent so much time trying to help others. Few of these people probably had a reason to care about homeless kids. Yet they did.

I talked about some of the kids I had seen, taking care not to violate their confidentiality. The further I got into their stories, the more my voice choked up. I felt rather than heard the silence in the room. Finally there was applause. My shirt was soaked under my jacket, and when I opened my eyes, I saw everyone was standing. They were standing for the kids.

Afterward a man came up to me with a check for two thousand dollars. I guessed from looking at him that this was money he had worked hard for, and tears of gratitude filled my eyes.

8

ROULETTE

G o see who's in the exam room," Jan said.

Sugar. It had been many months since I had seen her. She was sitting on the table, her hands between her legs. Her curly hair was long. It hung limply by her cheeks. Her face was down, pointing at her knees, which were clad in scuffed, torn jeans. I felt a surge of relief just that she was alive.

"I can't stomach calling you Sugar," I said, going in. "I think it is time you told me your real name."

She turned her face up. She had been badly beaten. Her jawline was purple and swollen. Her lips were bruised and split. Her left eye was a purple mass. I felt myself gasp. "What happened?" I asked, my voice calm, despite my horror. "Who did this to you?"

She spoke through bruised lips. "John." She said the word in a monotone. It took me a moment. His name wasn't John. He was a customer.

"Someone you know? A regular?"

She shook her head. She trembled a little and pressed her legs together. I suspected then that it had been more than a beating. "It was a white guy in a van." She gave a desperate little cough.

"Were you raped?"

She nodded, and the tears spilled. She tried to wipe them away. "Stupid."

"You're not stupid. You're hurt," I said, passing her a Kleenex. She wiped her face. When she leaned over, I picked up the stale, rank smell of fear, the kind of sweat that comes only when people are in terror.

"We'll need to examine you. Would you rather have Jan?"

She nodded. The tears were flowing now. Her shoulders began to shake.

"Good, that's good. I'm glad you're thinking of yourself. When Jan's done, I'm going to look at your other injuries, OK? But only after you're dressed."

She nodded. I had never seen Sugar cry, and something about it was more heartrending than anything I had experienced with her before. This incredibly strong girl, I thought, this strong girl.

A few minutes later, after Jan had examined her and taken some cultures, we talked in private. Jan's face was sad but calm. I was suddenly so glad to have Jan here on this particular day, with all her experience and wisdom.

"There was vaginal and rectal tearing. It was a violent rape. He hurt her. He was *trying* to hurt her. But she refuses to let us call the police."

"Why?"

"She says they won't believe her."

The idea was appalling. "Do you think that's true?"

"She said they'd say there is no such thing as raping a prostitute."

"But she didn't ask to be a prostitute."

"Maybe that's not how they would see it. I don't know. That's not how she sees it. This is a girl with extremely low self-esteem," Jan said. "Whatever happens to her she thinks she deserves it. Plus, she's eighteen. We have to respect her choice."

"Amy said something like that once too," I said.

"Well, maybe it's time you listened," Jan said. Her smile wobbled a little around the edges. I could tell the exam had gotten to her. I thanked her and went back to the exam room.

I wished there were a way Sugar could be taught to love herself. I wished there were a way she could see that she deserved better. Jan had given her a box of apple juice. She was carefully sipping from the straw. I put on fresh gloves and began checking her facial injuries. There were a lot of small cuts.

"Was he wearing a ring?" I asked, looking at the inside of her mouth.

"Wedding ring," she mumbled.

"Your teeth look OK. No eye damage." I finished the exam. "It should all heal." At least the outside, I thought.

"I should have known better," she whispered. "A white guy in a van."

"Don't blame yourself. Blame him."

"Stupid."

"If you report this to the police, you can save another girl from going through the same thing." I felt as if everything I was saying were falling on deaf ears.

"It's all the same."

"It's not," I said.

I saw her becoming resistant and defensive. I was not going to badger her, especially not now.

"I'm going to give you a shot of Rocephin, a dose of Zithromax, and a dose of metronidazole," I told her. "Those are in case you were exposed to anything. We'll be testing for hepatitis, HIV, syphilis, chlamydia, and gonorrhea. I'm going to assume there was no condom."

She wiped a stray tear. "No."

After she had left, I went and sat down up front. I rubbed my face with my hands, smelling the powder smell the gloves had left. Jan came and joined me. I was glad there were no other patients for the moment. "Of all the days for you to be here, Jan, well, I'm glad," I said.

"I've been nursing for a long time," Jan said after a long pause. "I've seen a lot of rapes."

I looked at my hands. "I feel like I'm going to dream about bruises. Why won't she see a counselor?"

"You have to give it time," Jan said softly.

"What do you mean?"

Her eyes were distant. "Sometimes it takes a few months. Then the symptoms start: the nightmares, the flashbacks, and the insomnia. That's when she might be ready for help."

"I'm not sure I understand."

"Understanding rape is part of our job, Randy. Please try to recognize why a woman would want to try to forget it."

"OK."

"This is hard work, Randy. Make sure you take care of yourself." She paused. "Let other people take care of you too."

I knew Jan was right. More than two years had passed since we started the van, and I had spent all my time trying to help others all by myself. I left out my own wife far too often, and in trying to do everything maybe I wasn't doing it right at all. But it was easier to recognize this than to change it.

At home that night I took Ginger for a long walk. Soon we had covered over two miles. I was cutting through an extremely wealthy neighborhood where houses were hidden behind high walls. The sun was setting. I thought about how some people might feel frustration with Sugar. Why wouldn't she go to the cops? they would ask. I didn't feel that frustration. Instead I felt a huge burden. Here was a child who had been neglected her whole life, raped into prostitution, and then left to make decisions all by herself. Of course they were not the right decisions. But they were her decisions. I had to support them.

I knew as a doctor that people made self-destructive choices. They ate too much even when they had serious complications from obesity. They kept smoking when they knew they could die of cancer. They didn't exercise or eat right or take their medications. I had seen adults die because they refused to take simple steps to save their own lives. Even some doctors, like me, were guilty. I ate too much junk food and didn't sleep enough. That Sugar had survived this long was like surviving a game of Russian roulette with HIV and violence.

I thought that for Sugar even to come to our van was an act of courage. For some kids that alone was a huge step. Someplace inside her there was a voice that was telling her that she did deserve help. Someplace inside her was a fighter who had decided that even for just a few minutes she deserved care. I felt hope entwining with darker emotions. Sugar had a chance. I didn't care how slim it was. I was going to fight for that chance. If it took years, I would keep trying to save her.

When I walked back in, both the twins were crying. They were now almost a year old and getting into everything. Time seemed to be flying by. There were times I still veered around the oxygen tank in the living room, but it was long gone. Amy handed me one of the twins as soon as I came in. I knew instantly from the weight in my arms it was Janie. "You were right, Amy," I said.

"Right? About what?" Amy held Reed while she pulled forks out of the drawer. I noticed how gangly he was getting. He kicked his legs in dismay. He wanted down, so Amy put him on the kitchen floor. There was a delighted look of freedom on his face, as if he had just discovered the magical world of drawers and knives and electric sockets.

"Reed!" I said as he reached for the stove. It was way too high, but still, I worried. He grinned at me, his new teeth coming in. Janie babbled in twin sympathy to him. Our dad, she was saying, is a mean old man.

Amy was saying something over the din of my thoughts.

"What was that?" I asked again. "What?"

"I'm pregnant again," Amy said, stepping toward me. I froze. "Pregnant."

I felt the same wave of excitement I had felt before. Only this time it was tempered with more notes of caution. The miscarriage; the endless months in the hospital; the exhausting nights spent feeding preemies: it all came back to me.

We both had wanted large families and from the early days of our marriage had made plans to have many children. Four or five or even more kids were what we had dreamed. In those early talks we had never considered we might have a problem with pregnancies. Amy was so healthy; why would we think there would be a problem? I knew it was so important to her to have children that she would try again and again. I saw how happy Amy was, and I was happy too. But I didn't see the same worries in her eyes that I felt in my heart.

In only a few weeks we were back in the hospital for an early ultrasound, receiving the brutally familiar news, a cruel déjà vu. I felt as if I had stepped into a time tunnel. Waves crashed in my ears. Once more our baby was dead.

"There is no heartbeat," said the doctor. How could this happen again? We had told each other the first miscarriage was random. We had told each other that Amy's illness with the twins was bad luck. But a pattern was emerging. Our efforts to have babies seemed to come with terrible risks. Amy and I touched hands. Her face was calm.

"We have two options," the doctor told us. "We can do a D and C right now to remove the dead tissue." I envisioned our dead child being taken from Amy's womb. I knew how Amy would react to this. "Or we can wait a week or two. The chances are your body will expel the dead tissue." Like last time, I thought.

I remembered waking to the sound of Amy crying in our bed. We would have to go through that again. I wasn't sure I could do it.

"We'll wait," Amy said.

I had expected the miscarriage to happen quickly, like the last time. I thought it might be that night or the next day, maybe a few days at most. But weeks passed. Amy became quieter. I thought it was a mistake to have waited. She was walking around with a dead baby inside her. Still, she went to work. Her own practice was in a small family clinic. I wondered how she felt, holding those babies in her hands while we waited for ours to leave. Both of us had immersed ourselves in the lives of children, at home and at work.

As the weeks passed, we both went back to work, with Amy caring for the twins as well. She had made an appointment with her doctor to get the D & C. She was on a part-time schedule and was able to arrange her hours around day care.

I took the van out by myself. Jan was off for the day. I had parked in outer Phoenix. It was a fine, sunny day, and the blue sky seemed to stretch forever without a single cloud.

A Phoenix police car pulled up in the dusty lot. The kids waiting under the awning fell silent. A young police officer jumped out. He looked to be of Native American descent, with bronzed skin and shiny black hair cut into a military crew cut. He opened the back door of his car. The teenage boy who got out was what we call in medical terminology *cachectic*, or extremely emaciated. His hipbones jutted out of his jeans. Skin was stretched tautly over his cheekbones and jaw. I could see the shadow of his teeth through the thin membrane of his skin. He looked like the survivor of a death march. If I'd had to estimate his fat percentages, I'd have guessed in the single digits. He had lost much of his muscle mass as well. Right away I thought he must have a terminal illness or be anorexic. Rarely had I seen such emaciation, even among addicts.

The police officer shook my hand. "I found this boy here sleeping in an alley. You'll see why I got concerned. I'd heard about this Big Blue van, so I thought you should check him out. He hasn't done anything wrong, by the way," he quickly added. "He just needs help."

I thanked the officer and watched him leave, his car tires crunching in the dry sand. I led the boy inside. The kids waiting outside started playing a game of hockey with two sticks and a ball of wadded-up newspaper.

"How come you're so thin?" I asked the boy once we got in the exam room. I had discovered sometimes it was best to be direct. Without saying a word he lifted his baggy shirt. There was a hole in his stomach. I recognized it as a G-tube site for tube feeding.

"I was a preemie," he said. "I guess my intestines never developed or something. If I eat, I get really sick and bad diarrhea. I'm supposed to get fed with a tube." He shrugged as if it were hopeless. I thought of my own preemies, now thriving because Amy and

I had insurance and could afford the astronomical cost of their extremely expensive specialized formula and the medical equipment and the months in the hospital. Had we been poor, would they be doing as well today? I doubted it.

"Where have you been living?" I asked.

"I was in foster care. But I turned eighteen, so they kicked me out." This was common, I was discovering. Once kids turned eighteen in foster care they were on their own, with no home to return to for emergencies or holidays. "I ran out of tubes," he said. "I haven't had a feeding in a long time."

He yawned and, once he started yawning, couldn't seem to stop. The exhaustion was probably the result of his malnourishment. I decided to call the children's hospital. I wanted to get him a supply of G-tube feeds and some high-octane formula nourishment. We had a protocol for feeding infants and children on tubes. He would not be much different.

My phone rang. It was Amy. "Randy, you need to come home."

"What for?" I asked.

She stopped. "I'm sick," she said. "Please come." I felt a tug of frustration. I was out by myself. I didn't want to make this kid leave and then drive the van back to the dock to get my truck.

"Excuse me," I told the boy.

I stepped outside the room. "Can it wait?" I asked.

There was a huge silence. "Just come."

I apologized to the boy and made a call to HomeBase to let it know he was on his way. He would need to get the G-tube feeds and be seen by a doctor. He was uninsured. My phone rang. It was Amy, her voice querulous.

"Randy, are you coming?"

"I'm taking the van in right now."

I walked into our house. Sun slanted in the living room window. Ginger greeted me, whining in the back of her throat. There was a dripping sound. The faucet, I thought. I walked into the kitchen. Amy was sitting in one of our wicker kitchen chairs. Her face was pale. She had a wad of towels between her legs. They were saturated with blood. Oblivious, the twins were toddling around.

Janie had blood smeared on her cheek. It was the miscarriage, finally arriving.

A wave of guilt and anger swept over me, yet at the same time, I wasn't really tuned in.

"I'm OK," Amy gasped. "I just need to get cleaned up."

"Cleaned up?"

"Before we leave. I'll take a shower."

"Really, Amy . . ." I said, and didn't finish the sentence. This is madness, I thought. And then my phone rang. It was another doctor. He was someone who I knew would call only with a medical emergency.

"What about the twins?" I asked her, holding the phone out.

"We'll take them after I get cleaned up."

I answered the call, and she staggered off to the shower. I could hear the water running. I didn't want the doctor on the call to know I had a family emergency, so I tried to talk as normally as possible. I knocked on the door.

"Amy, we really should leave," I said, cupping my hand over the phone.

There was silence. The water stopped. I waited for her to get dressed while I finished the consultation. Then I calmly loaded the babies into our van. My wife came out of the shower, already bleeding through her pants. Her cheeks were white.

All of a sudden it was as if I had snapped to life. "You should have called nine-one-one," I said, helping her into the van and jumping in.

"You should have come when I called," she said, gasping. "I'm getting blood on the seats, Randy." I felt a rush of fear. What had I been thinking? How could I be so attentive to my patients yet so out of it when it came to my own wife? I was realizing that I was completely in control and clear-eyed only when I was working as a doctor. When it came to my own loved ones, I suddenly became flustered and had a hard time making decisions. It was as if my love for them were a barrier to my taking care of them as a doctor or even, I worried, as a husband and father.

The houses raced past. I called my friend Ron and my parents and asked them to meet us at the hospital to help with the twins. I held Amy's arm as she stepped from the van. The doctors at her small clinic tried to do one procedure and then said the words *emergency room*. I led her outside to drive the few blocks from the clinic to the hospital down the street. She swayed on her feet. Blood streaked down her legs.

She's bleeding out, I thought. I'm going to lose my wife in a parking lot because she wouldn't call 911. Another voice intruded: Because you didn't come when she called, and when you did come, you took a damn phone call rather than attend to your wife. In minutes she was being rushed into surgery for an emergency D & C. She was hemorrhaging so badly, the doctor said, that if they didn't remove the dead tissue immediately, she would die.

Two weeks later Amy was still weak. We talked.

"You could have died," I said, still traumatized. Amy was on the couch while the twins toddled around. She just looked at me calmly.

"You seem to be handling this better than I am," I told her. She picked up Reed and grabbed a children's book from the edge of the couch. It was *Brown Bear, Brown Bear, What Do You See?* I saw. She cuddled Reed in her lap and opened the book. Janie toddled closer and swayed while holding on to the edge of the couch. Amy turned a page and began to read out loud to the kids.

I scooped Janie into my lap and curled up close. The twins were healthy babies now, fifteen months old and chubby, with no signs of special needs from their past. There was no reason to think of them as preemies. But the shadow of the past was still on them, at least in my mind. I still touched them like a gentle doctor, not like an assured, rough-and-tumble father. They were cutting their first teeth. The magnesium that Amy had had to take in such high doses before had affected their baby teeth, which were discolored, striped with pale marks.

I listened to Amy read. Her strength frightened me. It was as if she were capable of handling far more stress than I could ever handle. I thought we should talk about the miscarriage, about our children, about the kids on the van. But I was afraid to say anything because I knew Amy wanted to try again. I could see it in her face, in her eyes. I knew she would want to keep trying to have children even after this.

I didn't want to confront my own fears, my own incapability of dealing with these losses. There might have been a part of me that sensed she was furious with me for how I handled the miscarriage. But Amy, I thought, was the kind to let things go. If she were angry, she probably wouldn't tell me. She would do anything, and perhaps put up with anything, to have a family and keep us intact.

⬜⬜⬜⬜⬜⬜

I had just gotten back from speaking at a conference, and Jan and I were in the office, trying to work on a new grant. Jan grimaced at the dreary office surroundings. There was a fresh water stain on the ceiling. Sometimes we heard mysterious bumps from the condemned floor above. Jan joked that there were giant monster rats.

"Guess where I was last night?" she said.

"Where?" I was clearing a stack of books I had left on her desk.

"The HomeBase graduation. They had a ceremony for all the kids who had passed either their general equivalency or work program."

"I'm sorry I was at the conference."

"Do you know who was there?" Jan said. Her old smile was back. "Donald. Graduating with a modified GED."

"Donald! How is he?"

"You almost wouldn't recognize him. His hair was nicely cut, and he was wearing trousers and a white shirt. A lot of girls were looking at him, I'll tell you that much. He can read and write now. And you know the best part?"

"What?"

"I swear the pastor's entire congregation was there. I talked to him and his wife afterward. They said Donald is still with them.

He works in the church and does construction." Jan also filled me in with the news of the other kids she had caught up with. Matthew, the skinny boy with the glasses who loved motorbikes, had also gotten his high school diploma and was moving into his own apartment. I felt that I was seeing success now with our programs. These kids hadn't had a chance before. Now they were moving out into the world.

A couple of months after Jan told me about the graduation celebration I was driving through Chandler, having been to Tucson to visit old friends. I decided to stop at a Subway off I-10 and have a footlong sandwich. On second thought, I told myself, looking down at my growing paunch, maybe I should make it a six-inch. I had gone from not eating at all because of stress to noshing mindlessly on whatever got in front of me. The result was obvious. I stepped up to the counter, still looking at the menu, trying to decide between a turkey or ham sub.

"Dr. Randy!"

I was startled and looked down. "Mary!" I couldn't believe it.

"I'm working here now," she said. "Saving for college."

It felt so good just to look at her. "I was just thinking of how I used to get subs all the time when I was a kid in Tucson," I said. "I used to sit in a corner booth with my friend Danny after our shift at the Golf n' Stuff."

"*You* worked at the Golf n' Stuff?"

"Sure. I got paid two dollars and ninety cents an hour to wade after golf balls in a pondful of duck poop. I think for the better part of a year it was permanently plastered to my legs."

She giggled. "I went to the Golf n' Stuff with my friends. We drove there with my aunt. We were trying to hit the balls into the duck pond. Sorry." She smiled and smoothed the apron down over her midsection, and I thought, there is no way anyone would know how far she has come. How many other girls I saw in daily life, working behind counters or even in business suits, had a past like hers? Maybe not as extreme, but it was a revelation to me how people can overcome such hardship.

"I thought you were, like, raised rich," she said.

"I never even got on a plane until I was in college," I said. "I grew up in an area like this, just regular houses and regular people."

"How is Jan doing? Is she still racing?" she asked.

"Well, that got to be a bit much for her," I said, waiting my turn to order. "But you know what? She took this welding class. She made a huge art installation for her lawn. It's like ten feet tall and made of this scary dark bronze metal. I keep telling her it scares the neighbors." Mary giggled again.

"Jan is so cool," she said.

I became aware that someone had stepped behind me. I gave Mary my order. She made my sandwich and then handed me my change, her hand briefly touching mine. There was nothing on her wrists. She had taken off the bracelet. I wondered what she had done with it. Had she kept it, or had she ceremoniously thrown it away? But then I realized that I was warmly reassured not to know. Other people in Mary's life, like her aunt, or her friends, or her counselor, would know. I suddenly was deeply consoled to know that Mary had found others to help her.

I sat down to eat my sandwich in the hard booth and thought about Danny, who had encouraged me to go into medicine. I looked out the window into Chandler, and I could have been back in Tucson, both of us looking out for our dream car. I drank my Diet Coke and remembered my mom's taking me to Kmart for school clothes. I remembered how once a month my parents would load up their dirt bikes on the trailer that Dad had made himself and take us riding out in the desert. I remembered my first day with Dr. Copeland. I remembered what it was like to be Mary's age. I had felt so nervous and excited, as if my life were blooming in Technicolor. I remembered it all, and I wanted to tell Mary, "It is your turn now. Dream big."

I finished my meal and threw away my garbage. Mary was standing at the counter.

"Good-bye, Mary," I said, stepping closer. "I want to say that I'm proud of you. I know you're going to accomplish a lot in life. I hope to see you again."

She blinked, as if in perfect, calm agreement.

⌐⌐⌐⌐⌐⌐

It was now Christmas 2003, and I was attempting to write the yearly letter we sent out to family and friends. The twins were two. I was thirty-seven, and Amy was thirty-six. Three years had passed since I had started the van.

I was trying to sound chatty and funny, but what really seemed to come out was chaos. How could this much have happened in such a short amount of time? Other families seemed to have placid years punctuated by rare moments of upheaval. We seemed to live not in the eye of the storm but in the storm itself. And I wasn't even writing about all the kids on the van I had seen that year.

I wrote about how in the last year alone we had just moved, from the house with burned tiles on the back porch to an older house in a good neighborhood with decent schools. I wrote about how Reed and Janie were potty training and how they liked to decorate the bathroom mirrors with Amy's face cream. I wrote how my cousin Annette had lived with us for a while. I wrote about how we had had a flood when we remodeled the new house, and how Amy had changed offices, and how we had taken the twins to Sea World, the Wild Animal Park, LEGOLAND, Disneyland, and California Adventure. All this had been done in some sort of mad dash in one short year in a way I really couldn't remember.

I also wrote about how Amy was pregnant again. This time the ultrasound had confirmed a girl, alive and well, in her womb. We had decided to name the new baby Charlotte, after my father, whose name was Richard Charles but whom everyone called Charlie. We had already told my dad the name.

I wrote in the letter that Charlotte would be our last child. Was there a note of relief in this statement? I didn't think so. I was terrified and didn't want to admit it. It was our fourth pregnancy in only three years. Amy was already on bed rest with severe nausea and premature contractions, and the pregnancy felt frighteningly like a dark replay of the twins'. I was fighting all the time to keep Amy in bed, waging a battle between her and two needy toddlers who wanted their mommy. I had called my aunt Rose to come help, and I knew I was bossy with her, giving strict instructions she was to keep the kids away from Amy and let her rest. But Amy wanted to get up to attend to their needs. The twins were lucky, I thought. They had no permanent damage from being preemies. I couldn't say we would be so lucky again. Maybe we had already used up our luck, I thought, putting the pen down. I was afraid of losing Amy, afraid of losing another child, afraid of having to spend more months in the neonatal intensive care unit, all fears to which Amy seemed immune.

As these stresses stacked up, I took odd comfort in Ginger. As she had with the twins, the dog had begun sleeping on Amy's side of the bed long before we knew she was pregnant. Sometimes when I was anxious, Ginger would come to me and put her head in my lap and look at me with her large brown eyes, and it seemed she knew more than any dog.

9

ANGIE

Another year and a half passed by in a stressful but joyous blur. It was August 2005. The twins were now almost four. After another difficult pregnancy, Charlotte had been born a bit prematurely but had gone home at thirty-six hours old, much to our relief and surprise. She now toddled after the twins, her wide eyes following their every move.

When I stopped at the hospital, the other doctors and nurses were glued to the television screens. Hurricane Katrina was coming. The talk was about levees and flooding. Then the storm hit, and it was worse than anything we had imagined. I watched as the news showed waves battering the coast of Louisiana. Floodwaters rose, and frantic people begged for help on national television.

"We're talking injured people with no food or clean water," a man was yelling on the television news. "The situation is desperate."

That night I could tell Amy knew what I was thinking as we sat down to dinner. She had been watching television too. We talked as she cut quesadillas for the kids and I spooned out some applesauce for Charlotte. I expressed my desire to help. Amy, as always, encouraged me. In fact she said she had been thinking about it all day.

"You are the perfect person to direct a team," she said with assurance. "You have all the experience on the van. You can deal with lines of patients with all sorts of traumas—minor infections to major emergencies," she said.

"You're sure?"

"Of course I'm sure. I feel the same need to help." She paused. "I'm a doctor too, honey. If I could be there, I would."

"You'll be OK with the kids and everything?" I asked again.

A line of irritation knitted her forehead. "I'll be fine," Amy said.

I almost rushed to the phone to call Dr. Redlener at the Children's Health Fund. He was just as quick to ask if I would lead a team. It was easy to see we all were on the same page and that the situation in New Orleans was dire.

The first step was making sure it was OK with Jan. During the past few years I had been able to hire on Wendy Speck and Michelle Ray as our employees, after HomeBase had announced budget cuts. Without them I wouldn't have been able to consider the trip to Louisiana. They could help Jan with the van while I was gone.

The next day was spent in meetings with the Phoenix Children's Hospital. The hospital administrators were more than supportive. They asked only if our plans were in line with response efforts already in place. I told them that Dr. Redlener from the Children's Health Fund was in close contact with high-level administrations in Louisiana and Mississippi. The Children's Health Fund had already started working on our temporary medical licenses, and it seemed way ahead of other organizations that were pitching in across the country. The hospital committed itself to a couple of thousand dollars in IV supplies and got ready to send us on our way.

We were expecting a lot of diarrhea and dehydration. Because of the sewage, we also expected hepatitis and waterborne diseases. Thinking about how many infections we would encounter, I decided to call Dr. Mark Rudinsky, a friend of mine in pediatric infectious diseases.

"Keep your cell phone on twenty-four hours a day," I said, "because I'm planning on calling for advice."

I formed the team quickly. The first to say yes was a senior resident at the children's hospital, Dr. Jonathan Lee-Melk. The residency program said it was fine for him to go if the infectious disease team approved him. I approached Mark Rudinsky, the head of the infectious disease team, to ask if I could steal Jonathan. "I'll let Jonathan go only if I can go," he said. I was unbelievably relieved and appreciative. Having Mark would be hugely beneficial. Dr. Michelle Wang, who had recently been a resident on the van and was now a fully trained doctor, also joined us. I rounded out the team with Catherine Fogerlie, a nurse and the head of the triage call-in center at Phoenix Children's. I had never worked with her but got the thumbs-up from lots of people at the hospital.

In the days leading up to our departure, there were dozens of reports of guns and looters. Stories abounded of girls being raped in makeshift shelters and bands of thugs roaming and terrorizing at will. I was having second thoughts. I had three young children. Was it fair to them for me to take these risks?

"This will be one of the more important things you do," Amy said that night, while I held a sleepy Charlotte in my arms. "Remember we love you and believe in you." I felt she was giving me courage. "This is one way I can help too," she said quietly, taking Charlotte from my arms.

I felt especially bad leaving Charlotte. She was just a toddler now, so young to leave for what we estimated to be a three-week trip. I wondered if my baby girl would remember me when I returned. And despite her reassurances, I wondered how Amy would fare.

As much as I wanted to take the van, I knew it wouldn't make the trip. We had retired our original Winnebago in 2004. Our new van had been acquired from a church health outreach program on the east coast. Like the first, it came needing many repairs. The costs were much lower this time because we were able to move medical equipment from the old van to the new one. But it turned out the second was just as plagued with problems as the first. There was no way it could make the thousand-mile trip.

Fortunately, the Children's Health Fund had located a medical van in Arkansas, a brand-new thirty-eight-foot-long mobile medical clinic. It also lent support by sending a driver, Lorenzo. This was another relief. It was nice to know that the team would be able to focus on providing mobile health care without having to worry about finding our way around the blighted areas. We were told to meet the van in Alexandria, Louisiana.

By the time we drove into Alexandria on September 9, only four days after I had decided to leave, our initial excitement was already being worn down by the shock of the hurricane. The city was teeming with refugees from the storm. Everyone looked exhausted. People were sitting alongside cars loaded with belongings. I was warned that the nearby barbecue restaurant was the last one open for hundreds of miles, so we ate barbecue sandwiches and chips and drank fountain sodas under bright lights, on sterile tables. It was impossible to imagine a place without running water for fountain sodas or life without electricity for lights.

After eating and making sure the new van was all packed up, I thought, Finally we're ready. We boarded the new van, and Lorenzo took the wheel. Twenty minutes later the van broke down. Lorenzo was shocked. Mark jumped out with me at the side of the road. "Randy," he said, "you *are* cursed with vans." We called a mobile mechanic, who was able to make it out to us. The news was disastrous: serious axle problems, and we would need a big-rig mechanic to fix them. I was advised to haul it all the way to Baton Rouge.

"You say you're going to help people?" the mechanic asked with concern. "Let me call a friend at the tow yard. You're gonna need a flatbed truck for this van."

We waited for hours in the hot tropical sun next to the van until the tow company arrived. But the driver demanded cash. I had brought a thousand dollars for emergency funds, and now, as I paid for the van to be towed away, it was all gone. Our first view of the command center in Baton Rouge came as we followed our broken van into town. Huge mountains of garbage were piled everywhere. Garbage service had been suspended along with everything else. In the warm, sticky weather the garbage would soon create health hazards. Circling these mountains of trash were parked ambulances, military vehicles, and groups of soldiers.

Inside the command center was chaos. City workers and volunteers had poured in from all over. AFTER TOUCHING ANY WATER OR SEWAGE, WASH IMMEDIATELY, one sign read. In the middle of this deafening noise I found a woman who had somehow found herself in charge of organizing all medical help for one of the worst natural disasters ever to strike the United States. Everything was so chaotic I wasn't even sure I was told her name. She was one of the thousands of nameless civil servants who coalesced to help after Katrina, often with no pay or accolades or acknowledgment. She told us what everyone else we talked to was saying: there was no way we could get parts or big-rig mechanics to fix our van.

Later a woman named Sharon came trotting over. She was now an assistant in charge of health services. "I heard about you guys. You know, the city bus system is shut down," she said, somewhat conspiratorially. "Before all this I worked at the department of motor vehicles. Some promotion, right? Well, I got a friend who runs the mechanics team there. They take care of the entire fleet of buses. I bet they can help." Miraculously, by the end of the day we had five mechanics swarming around our beached van. They had even brought portable welders. In hours it was fixed. I found it almost unbelievable. We had gone from certain disaster to being fully functional at the drop of a hat.

"Where do you need us?" I went back into the deafening noise to ask the administrator.

"There's a little town called Angie," she yelled back. "A radio station up there did an emergency broadcast. Turns out there are a lot of people who need care. They're about eighty miles north."

Angie, I repeated to myself.

We drove into desolation. It was as if anxiety had come in with the storm and were still in the air, pressing down on us. Town after town was darkened from lack of electricity, the flattened houses crowned with broken trees. Entire lots had been swept clean of houses and barns. Exposed basements were like gutted sores where homes had once stood. A fishing boat was perched in a tall tree. A gas station had been obliterated, with only the pumps left standing. Railroad tracks were buckled out of the ground. Massive trees had been jerked from the ground. It was as if giants had marauded the land. In front of one empty lot a handwritten sign said: MISSING: ONE RED HOUSE. PLEASE RETURN. We were close to a hundred miles inland, and still the storm had raged. The devastation was ongoing and relentless. It made me feel dizzy.

Lorenzo looked panicky. "If this van gets stuck," he said in his thick southern accent, "ain't any way to get it towed from out here."

Every new turn brought a fresh vision of devastation. It wasn't long until even the worst of it seemed usual, and every block looked the same, with crushed houses and overturned trees. I tried my cell phone. No service. It was early, but the towns had a dark pall on them, even in the sunshine. Like ghost towns, I thought. The highway stretched out, occupied only by military and emergency vehicles.

"The director said the population is only two hundred and forty," I told the crew, as we peered out our windows at Angie, Louisiana. The empty streets were littered with debris. The few stores were dark. Windows had boards over them; crushed roofs were crowned with tarps weighted with bricks. In the front yards were makeshift tents. People came wandering out to watch us. Two children sitting on the steps of a church stood up.

"Right this way," an eager volunteer firefighter shouted, leading us to his station. He was wearing jeans and a T-shirt with a logo that said "Angie Volunteer Fire Department." There was a baseball cap over his shorn hair, and his young face looked drawn and worried. The fire station was a modest tan building with a sign that read: WASHINGTON PARISH, DISTRICT # 5 FIRE DEPARTMENT.

An aluminum folding door covered the truck. Spindly rails held up the porch. The roof was metal. We parked the van in front of the small building. Our windshield was spotted with the biggest bugs I had ever seen.

Mark jumped from the van. He was relieved that it hadn't been raining. As an infectious disease specialist he worried about that. Rain would spread contamination and flood sewage into water supplies. Until pumps began working again, we would pray there was no rain. But even without rain the humidity made it hard to breathe. Just stepping out of the van, I was covered in a thick sweat that attracted dirt like a magnet. Being from Arizona, I had thought I could handle the heat. But early September in Louisiana was something entirely different.

Mark gasped. "This is like eating stew," he said. Sweat immediately trickled down his face. His cheeks grew pink with trying to take a breath. Only the southern native Lorenzo seemed unaffected.

"Good old bayou weather," he commented.

"You can set up right here," the firefighter said. We ducked inside a door to find a small but clean room containing the firefighters' kitchen. Sunlight poured through a window set above a sparkling sink. A long folding table had been set up to one side. The men had arranged bottles of hand sanitizers. This folding kitchen table would be our clinic. We would see some people on the van, we decided, but could fit many more in this fire station. We began bringing supplies inside.

"There's no electricity, no running water, no Internet," the firefighter told us. "We've got the only generator in town. We've been lugging it around town every day. Some of the old folks need it to run their asthma machines."

Within minutes we had a crowd outside the door. Half the team began seeing patients while the other half hastily set up the equipment. The citizens of Angie seemed in shock. An eight-year-old boy screamed in pain as his mother brought him inside on a gurney made from a blanket. His mother explained that he had been injured before the storm. Both his arms had been crushed in an accident. When the storm hit, the staff at the nursing facility where he was being cared for had simply fled. Like many others, they had gone north, thinking that they would be out of reach of Katrina's wrath. Little did they know that the tornadoes and high winds would cause destruction hundreds of miles north of the coast. The boy's mother had been trying to care for him all by herself, and infection had set into his wounds.

Another man was out of his heart medicine. "I tried to fill it when they said the storm was coming," he told us. "But they said it was too early. Then the storm came, and I ran out. Now the pharmacy is closed." It was a story I heard often as the hours passed. When news of the storm was coming, many people tried to stock up on medications. They knew they would be stuck in town because of lack of transportation or illness. It was smart thinking on their part, but the pharmacies refused to give any advance medications, especially for the poor on Medicaid. Now the pharmacies were closed, and people had been out of their meds for days.

"I feel stupid." I groaned to Mark. "We stocked IV tubes for dehydration. They're useless. We should have brought heart meds, antidepressants, albuterol, insulin."

We worked for twelve straight hours the first day. Aware I was courting dehydration from all the caffeine, I fueled myself on Diet Cokes. There was no shower that night. When I stepped outside, bugs and flies, drawn by the smell of sweat, swarmed me. I felt unbearably greasy and sticky. I curled up in the back of the van to sleep. Dark fell over the town swiftly, and still, I had a hard time falling asleep. I was too aware of the unfamiliar night noises, too aware of the distance between Amy and the kids and me. I wondered what they were doing at that moment. I pictured Amy reading them stories in bed. I hoped the kids were being good for her and not keeping her up all night with demands.

Before I had even rubbed the sleep from my eyes the next morning, I was aware of the smell of swamps and moss and the fecund smell of things growing. The morning started early, before we had time to gulp instant coffee or eat a granola bar. The citizens of Angie came with chronically undertreated medical conditions that predated the storm: decayed teeth, poor nutrition, and diabetes in the young and the elderly. That morning a man came biking into town. He was so exhausted that the bike was swaying side to side as he rode. His hair was matted with thorns. He looked completely out of it.

"Biked from way down south," was all he said, out of breath. He collapsed on a couch. He held out an arm, and I whistled at a huge septic wound. "Doctor, a few days ago this was just a bug bite, believe it or not," he said. In the heat, without proper water or sanitation, simple bug bites were turning into a major medical issue. The similarities between these people and the kids I treated on the van were striking. I thought how tragedy always hits the poor the hardest and how misfortune multiplies when left untreated.

Later that day an elderly Cajun man appeared. He had a cloud of yellowing white hair above a liver-spotted face. He began telling me about his fishing that morning in the local swamp. "Fish are all spooked by the storm. Threw the line out and felt a tug. Turned out to be an alligator," he said.

"What did you do?" I asked. He looked at me as if that were the silliest question he had ever heard.

"Hit that sucker on the head. Then I took it home, and the wife and I ate it. Best meal we had all week." I was quiet as I took his blood pressure. His breath whistled. "Asthma," he said after a while. "Ran out of my puffer."

༼ ༽ ༽ ༼ ༽ ༽ ༽

The next day a troop of national guardsmen showed up. "We were given orders to come protect your team," one of the men told me. I told him I wasn't sure we needed protecting. "We've been trained to keep order," he said, shifting his rifle awkwardly. The troop unpacked boxes of MREs, meal replacements, carrying them into the fire station. Famished, we crowded around. Without refrigeration or clean water, we hadn't wanted to eat or drink anything local. Besides, food was in short supply, and the last thing we wanted to do was take it away from the townspeople.

"Check this out," Mark said, reading a label. "This puppy has over three thousand calories."

"How did they get that many calories in one meal?" I asked, disbelieving. "That's enough calories for an entire day."

The guardsman laughed, peeling back his own lid. "Lots of cheese and pasta. And cookies. They made them for soldiers who are working all day."

I opened one and tasted it. It was ravioli. Before I knew it, I had eaten the entire dish. Great, I thought. Three of these a day, and they will roll me home.

"Have you heard about the locals eating alligators?" I asked the man. He was digging into a grayish stew.

"Sure," he said, gulping. "They're eating whatever they can get. I would too. There's no food down here, besides what they can forage." He took a sip from his bottled water.

"We've been sharing our food with the kids," he said quietly.

He squinted up at the hot sun. "I sure wish they would send real help soon. These people are hurting."

"You're here," Mark said, opening his meal.

"Yeah, but they need people to help fix their roofs and the electricity and get the water running. None of that is stuff we're trained to do." He hefted his rifle. "This is what I'm trained to do, and trust me, I don't want to."

The days moved at lightning, crackling speed. We worked fourteen and sixteen hours a day in Angie. Once we had Angie under control we drove our van into nearby towns, expanding our coverage area to include Bogalusa and Pine. In the town of Pine a police officer came gasping in, and sat down in a waiting chair. "I think I had a heart attack during the storm," he said.

I was shocked. "Why do you think that? Do you have any pain right now?" I said, reaching for my stethoscope.

"Pain in my chest," he gasped. "And it's been worse the last few days. Right now I can barely breathe it hurts so bad."

I turned to yell at the others, "Anyone got any nitro?" As I turned, the police officer collapsed, nearly falling out of his chair. In seconds we had the paddles out and were administering CPR. Then he was sent by ambulance on to Bogalusa, where he was stabilized.

After about a week of our trip, we moved our temporary sleeping quarters to the empty beds at the LSU Bogalusa Medical Center. It was a spooky setting. The emergency room was functioning at a skeleton level. The rest of the hospital was abandoned and empty, with IV bags left dangling from hooks. I wondered what had happened to all the patients. Had their families simply taken them? I thought about the months our twins, hooked to respirators, were in the neonatal unit. I wondered how they would have fared if we had been here, during the storm, and the electricity had gone out. We took over the third floor as our temporary sleeping quarters, choosing rooms at random along the echoing hallways. Just looking at my plain hospital bed, capped with white sheets, made me feel depressed. This would be my home for another two and a half weeks. Though we had been in the area for only a week, it felt like months.

To lighten the mood, the team wrote our room numbers on the dry-erase board in the nurses' station. Soon the board was covered with extra comments. Next to Catherine's room someone had written that she needed four-point restraints. Michelle Wang's notes warned she had bird flu. Mine made reference to a bad case of food poisoning I was recovering from. Desperate for something different from the canned meals, I had gone into the first restaurant to reopen in Bogalusa, even though Mark had warned me it was a bad idea. He was right. I got violently sick from tainted food or dirty water. Despite the calorie-heavy army meals, I was dropping weight like crazy.

It had been several weeks since the storm, but we still had only sporadic cell phone coverage. The only places that had electricity were those approved as priority by the military, such as the hospital emergency room. The citizens still had no power to heat water for cleaning, cooking, or boiling drinking water. They were living in darkness at night, with no fans to cool their days. Weeks after the storm, and there were still no Internet connections. Illnesses were rampant. I wondered just what our government was doing. People were getting sicker. How long would they be expected to live under collapsed roofs, with no sanitation or ways to get clean? I longed to open my laptop and communicate with Amy or call her on my cell phone. I was allotted only two minutes every other day to call her on our clunky satellite phone.

The sense of dislocation was profound. I felt I was in another country, another world. Volunteers were now flooding the towns and cities, bringing trucks filled with donated clothing. Empty lots took on the appearance of bazaars, with folding tables piled high with everything from Pampers to candleholders. Like the National Guard, the church missions and volunteers brought good intentions, but they weren't able to provide the essentials that the citizens really needed. So many used clothes were being brought in that the surplus was piled into high mountains and left to rot in the sun. Mountains of clothes, I thought, and the citizens still couldn't cook food or flush their toilets. "What is wrong with our system?" I blurted out to Mark as we tended lines of people with completely preventable food poisonings and other illnesses. "Help should be here by now."

Toward the end of our first week in Bogalusa, a volunteer told us to go check out this family he'd heard was living on an isolated farm outside town. It hadn't occurred to me that there would be people on farms outside town who would need our help.

When we pulled down the drive to the farm, two kids emerged from an old red pickup truck parked in the front yard. The small house had been crushed by the storm. Around it was a halo of mossy green trees. There were two children, a boy and a girl, about seven or eight. The father came out, and from his tired face I knew not to ask too many questions. The mother looked as if she was in a shocked daze. I caught a brief but strong distinct odor of decay on the warm breeze.

The children were lean with work, their eyes calm with experience. Before the storm their lives had probably been happy and whole. They probably had favorite animals on the farm and pets they cared about. As a child I had spent many weeks on farms, both that of my father's family and that of my mother's Mexican family in Las Cruces. For me the memories of the farm came back in smells: the smell of hot cotton fields and the sweat of the men laboring beside us, their sweat clean and pure; the smell of my mother, her lavender soap; and the warm skin smell of my sister, Stephanie, as we took turns stepping in the way of our mother's hot washcloth after a day spent picking cotton or playing outdoors. The life of a farm child was hard, with work from sunup to sundown, but it was also a life lived in bright tastes and experiences.

But this storm had ravaged these children. They were covered in excoriated bug bites, scratched so hard that they bled. Mark and I began cleaning and treating their wounds. Mark talked to the parents about going into the makeshift tent city. At least there they would have food and water and medical care. It was clear from their response that they didn't want to leave their farm. I realized if they left, they probably would not return. They might end up one of the thousands left completely homeless by Katrina.

"What are you doing for water?" Mark asked.

The mother looked off in the distance and didn't answer. The little boy piped up. "We ran out of water, sir."

What that meant on a farm I hadn't considered. I noticed then how quiet the farm was. Birds sang in the grass, and there was the hum of insects, but that was it. There was no lowing of cows, no bleating of sheep. I had spent enough time on farms to know how noisy they were. This farm was quiet. Dead quiet. The father rubbed his face with both hands, as if scrubbing it. The little boy looked at him forlornly.

"We tried to make the water last," the boy told us, his eyes wide. "We had to be careful not to spill it. Every day we gave them each a drink, isn't that right, Dad? We carried it in a cup. They each got one cup every morning."

I smelled the decay again. I stared out in the fields. A barn stood empty. The silence was ominous. From afar I heard the screech of a crow.

"It wasn't enough," the father said abruptly.

"The sheep cried at us," the boy said, his eyes as blue as the sky above him. "My sister and me brought them a drink every day, and they cried and cried."

"What happened?" Mark asked, his voice low. He had crouched down to talk to them, and his wrists dangled between his knees.

"The water ran out. They died," the boy said.

The little girl went and sat by the fence. The mother sat wearily next to her and started braiding her hair. I thought about what it must have been like for those children, carrying cups of water every day to give the animals a drink, realizing it was not enough, and watching them weaken and die one by one, until the field was no more than huddles of damp wool. I didn't want to go out in the field and look. I knew that they had probably lost not just their entire income but dear and loved animal friends.

Mark and I had tears in our eyes. We talked to them again about staying in the tent city. The father didn't want to leave. They had lost all their sheep, their home was ruined, they had no water, and no help was coming. He didn't want the shame of living in a tent city and the finality it suggested: that there was no going back. Finally, though, he agreed to let his wife and kids go stay in the shelter. He would stay on the farm, seeing what he could do.

"We should check on them later," Lorenzo said when the three of us got back in the van. It was the kind of thing you say when you know it isn't going to happen.

"Amy?" I held the clunky satellite phone well away from any trees. I had exactly two minutes allotted for my call. "How are you holding up? How are the kids?" My questions came out in a rush. I saw her hair, the sides of her cheeks, the glasses she wore for distance. I saw her hand resting on my thigh in a restaurant. I saw her teeth, her lips, heard her laugh. I was desperately homesick.

"The kids miss you," she said. Her voice sounded far away.

I listened hungrily to every word she said. This was the only time I was connected back to what was increasingly feeling like the real world. Katrina was another reality altogether; I could have been orbiting the moon. I had been here for only three weeks, and it felt like forever. Everything had changed around me, and I was engulfed by a new reality. The days of pulling cockroaches out of ears and dealing with terrible abuse on the van were now my norm. That was the reality I hungered to return to. My phone calls to my wife seemed like my only chance of rescue. There was a part of me that wanted Amy to order me home. I knew the rest of the team felt the same way. We had been traumatized, not just by the vast need for medical care but by what felt like complete government disorganization or even indifference.

"I've been thinking about my grandparents," Amy said, startling me.

"What do you mean?" I asked. Static interfered.

"Everything they went through."

"How so?"

"Well . . . I don't know if I ever told you about my grandpa."

"No, you didn't." I listened carefully.

"It was in the Depression. My grandmother had passed away not long after giving birth to her twins. So my grandpa had three kids, including the toddler they already had." Her voice was distant. "Everyone tried to help. They brought covered plates; they pitched in with the child care. Some even offered to adopt the kids. But Grandpa wanted to keep his babies. But he had to work."

"What happened?" I asked.

"At first he hired help. That didn't work well at all. This was in a bad time, and he couldn't afford help. No one wanted to deal with three little babies and a man who didn't know what he was up against."

"No kidding." Just the sound of her voice was soothing.

"So my grandpa built a pen in the backyard. They even called it the cage. It was a sort of playpen before they had playpens. He made it out of chicken wire. He plopped those babies in there. Every now and then he moved it to a fresh spot of grass."

She laughed. It was a tired laugh. I thought of Amy all alone with our three kids. They were also twins and a toddler. She had done her part.

"Amy, I don't want you to have to build a cage," I said.

"That's good, because I don't have any chicken wire." And then she said what I wanted most to hear: "Randy, it's time to come home."

In Angie the mayor's wife insisted on hand washing our clothes before we left. We had stayed nineteen days, but it felt like months, which had often been spent wearing the same clothes. She brought us our laundry in clean stacks, as stiff as boards and smelling like the sun. I walked the empty halls of the medical center. I stopped to take a photograph of the wallboard with our room numbers. My feet echoed on the stairs. Downstairs a group of bright-eyed people came toward me. They were from FEMA, and they were ready to take over. I heard their titles, "firefighter," "paramedic," "nurse." It seemed like a good omen. Help was coming and with luck would keep coming.

On the drive back we stopped in a brew pub that had just opened. The team teased me about taking my chances with food poisoning again. But this time we all took the risk. The electricity was back on, and people could boil water. Anything, we joked, was better than those army meal replacements. Our spirits were high. We were going home.

The waitress who took our order looked curious. "Are you that medical team that's been around?" she asked. Without a word she pulled up an empty chair and sat at our table. We waited, not knowing what to expect. Mark cleared his throat in a friendly way. In a flat, emotionless voice she started talking. "I was east of New Orleans when the floods came," she said. "All I remember is being on the street when a huge wave just came riding down on me. It seemed twenty feet high. I got up to the top, spitting water. Everything was a swirl, and I was riding by the tops of houses. I saw this tree." She stopped. I felt she needed to tell this story, to make it a reality for us too. "It was the top of a tree. I grabbed ahold of it best I could. I was out there holding that tree for the whole day. The water was brown and cold. You wouldn't believe how powerful it was, all cold on your legs and pulling so hard. It kept trying to pull me down. All these snakes were swimming by. I never saw so many snakes. Cottonmouths. They all were stirred up by the storm. Other animals came by too. There were bodies of dead dogs. Cows. This one little gray kitty was trying to swim, and she just went under, and I never saw her again. And there was this baby, I think. It was a little baby in a dressing gown. A real baby."

She looked relieved as she talked. I thought about how beneficial it is to survivors to tell their stories, only if to see that someone else cares. She got up as if her story were finished. No one said anything. She tucked the notepad in her apron.

"What finally happened to you?" Lorenzo asked.

"I held on that tree all day. Evening came, and I thought I would die. I don't remember the boat coming to rescue me. I guess they had to unpeel my fingers from the tree. The sun had burned my face so bad it made blisters, and when they pulled me into the boat, I fainted. That's what they told me later. I woke up being carried into a shelter. Now I'm here."

She walked away. In a moment she was back with our drinks,

smiling. I drank a cold bottled Budweiser and ate my food when it came. I saw the waitress later, standing by the counter. She raised a hand to wave good-bye.

I was back home, but nothing felt the same. Nothing was the same. I picked up Charlotte and felt her featherlight bones against my body. Her wide rosy mouth turned toward mine for a kiss. Even her hair smelled different.

Amy had postponed the birthday party for the twins until I got home. I had missed their birthday on September 15. I had missed our wedding anniversary on September 19. I had hungered to come home, and now I felt out of place. I needed some time, I told myself, to adjust. It would have to wait until we had the party for the twins, I thought. Amy had asked me if I wanted to cancel, and I had automatically said no. There was nothing I wanted more than to return to normalcy, I thought, and the party represented normalcy.

I stepped out of a long, hot shower. I stepped on the scale. I had lost fifteen pounds. Cleaning the fog off the mirror, marked with the palm marks of our children, I saw the weight had melted off all the wrong places. I looked drawn, my temples hollowed, my cheeks drooping. There were dark shadows under my eyes. In the living room the children played quietly. They were subdued as if playing in the presence of a stranger. Since I had come home, the kids had been whiny, difficult, and tantrumy. Amy looked more exhausted than I had ever seen her before, even after the birth of the twins. She had lost weight too. Her slender frame looked gaunt.

"Do you really want to do the party?" I kept asking her. My voice sounded funny even to me. I wondered if it was culture shock, from returning. She nodded. We had talked about the party while I was gone. It was like a thread leading me back home.

"They need to know you are back," she said. "The party is something they looked forward to doing with their dad."

The twins were mad for snakes and reptiles, so Amy had decided the theme would be all about reptiles. She had even hired the Phoenix Herpetological Society, which brings real live creatures to children's parties. As the guests arrived, I walked around feeling like an outsider. I felt as if I were living under a dome. I watched the kids and their friends play but had a hard time focusing on them. Normally I would have been gregarious and outspoken, but now I felt like one apart. I had a hard time following the conversations of the adults. As bright and hot as the sky was that day, it seemed dark, and the shapes of my own wife and children were indistinct. When others talked, I watched their lips move, and I heard them, but nothing really made sense. A few of the parents asked about Katrina. I jerked back from their questions, looking at their flushed, happy faces. My answers sounded incoherent and awkward, and I watched their faces cloud with confusion. I walked away. Kids were walking around with pythons draped around their necks. A staff member of the Herpetological Society let a small alligator swim in the pool. Its dark scales splashed in the blue water. Amy walked with the kids in the yard. I saw them as if in a snapshot: the twins holding hands, toddler Charlotte trying to keep up. The sun was darkly burnished on Amy's hair.

All through Katrina I had dreamed of coming home safe and sound. What's more, I had dreamed of coming home with a feeling of accomplishment, of a job well done. Well, I had made it home safely. But how sound was I? And how much had I really accomplished? I had left thousands of people still suffering. What was more, they would continue to suffer. I had come home, but part of me was still back there. I'm suffering, I realized with a shock. The tragedy I had witnessed was too vast, too shattering, and too poorly handled to understand. Like the kids on the van, I thought. Their pain was often too vast to understand as well. For the first time in my life I felt overwhelmed. There is too much suffering in the world, I thought. You can't fix it all. You have to choose what you can do. You know you can help many children on the van. That's what you need to do. No more trips.

I sat by the pool in one of our lawn chairs. Amy came and sat next to me. For once in my life I had nothing to say. I saw trees bending in the wind; I saw them scattered over roads. I saw cottonmouth snakes, angry at the storm, writhing in swamps. I heard people talking about eating alligator. I saw a landscape that looked as if the force of the earth had exploded it outward, rupturing the world, as we knew it. The lives of the homeless children I tried to reach were like this. The lives of my own family could be like this.

Amy put her hand on my knee. "I'm sorry," I said. I turned to my wife and buried my face in her neck.

10

NICOLE

I had thought it would help to be back on the van. I thought it
would be good to be back with familiar voices and the nostalgic
smells of gasoline and disinfectant. But for weeks the sense of dislocation following Katrina remained. I felt as if I were swimming
in the bottom of the ocean. I knew rationally that the kids I was
seeing were no different from before. But the world felt harder.

I spent the day in downtown Phoenix with Wendy. A boy came
up to the van carrying a broken bicycle. It was missing its front
tire. He had carried it for miles, he told us, intending to fix it. It
was old and rusty and worthless. I had seen kids lug around all
sorts of crazy items. Sometimes they had computer parts in their
backpacks or old toys or teddy bears from home. One girl had a
broken laptop she had found in the trash. She was convinced she
was going to learn how to repair it, and when she did, she could
find work as a computer expert. These items represented hope,
I realized. After I examined him, the boy sat down outside next
to his bike and idly spun the working back wheel. I sat down in
the chair next to him, and he told me how he would fix the bike
and then ride it around town, and from the tone in his voice, it
sounded as if the bike were a magic talisman that would fix his

life—if only he could fix it. I looked at the rusted, bent bike and wished this could be true.

The next patient was a huffer, an addict who sniffs glue, paint, or other noxious substances to get high. Huffing is among the worst of drug addictions, because it can cause horrific, irreversible brain damage. Huffing was making a resurgence in the area, and Jan and I had seen dozens of kids with permanent neurological damage, some of them no more than thirteen or fourteen.

This boy was tall and praying mantis–thin with long arms and stick-thin legs in skinny jeans. The area around his mouth was stained with the gold spray paint he had been inhaling. He held his plastic bag clutched in his hand, as if he had forgotten it was there. The bottom of the bag was stiff with the residue of the spray. He looked at me with empty eyes. When he tried to speak, nonsense words came out. It was the garbled sound of brain damage, a television set to a broken transmission. "Wab-ottle," he kept repeating.

"What is it you need?" I asked patiently in the front of the van.

There was no flicker of light in his eyes. "Wab-ottle," he said.

"Oh. You want a water bottle." I gave him one. He was still holding his paint bag, the insides flecked with dots of dried shiny gold. It looked like Christmas glitter.

He couldn't get the top of the bottle up. He pulled at it with numb hands. I gave him a hand. He spilled water all over himself, trying to drink. His empty dead eyes looked right through me. "Wab-ottle," he said.

I wondered what I could do for a boy like this. His circuits were fried. I wished I could help him, but I didn't know how. If I called the police, they would tell me they couldn't arrest him unless they caught him huffing. If they did catch him, they might take him in for public intoxication. He would be booked and released right back onto the streets. There was little chance of finding any programs that offered the intensive treatment he needed. They just didn't exist. In all likelihood his brain damage was permanent. If there was help for him, I didn't know what it was or how to find it. He went to sit in a chair outside the van, spilling water down his front. Watching him go, I pulled off my gloves and rubbed my face with my hands. I felt the overwhelming despair that seemed to be a constant in the background of my mind since Katrina.

Wendy called me for the next patient. I pulled on a fresh pair of gloves and went to see him. The boy had a rugged nose and perfect blue eyes. He could have looked like a movie star if his blond hair hadn't been matted with grime. His eyes had dark circles. Almost every visible part of his body, from the sides of his face to his neck and arms, was covered with red sores. Each sore was hotly inflamed.

I almost involuntarily stepped backward. "Do you remember how you got these sores?" I asked him immediately. He looked at one arm and, as if remembering, scratched it.

"I don't know," he said. "It keeps happening at night, and then the bites like get infected or something."

"Please don't scratch." I surmised he had been bitten all over by bedbugs. They had become epidemic in squats and shelters. Now, because this boy was in poor health and living in dirty conditions, a staph infection had set into the bite wounds. I closely examined his arm. A tiny circle of soft, damp, dead skin surrounded many of the bites. I rubbed a cotton-tipped swab over the wound to collect material for a culture. I suspected the infection was MRSA, methicillin-resistant *Staphylococcus aureus,* the drug-resistant staph infection commonly called the flesh-eating bacteria.

"Where are you sleeping?" I asked as I carefully swabbed the area.

"I was staying in this shelter downtown. I got beat up outside by these guys, so me and my friends have been crashing in an empty house."

I stopped. "We should get your friends in here and take a look at them. Sometimes this infection spreads to others in the same household."

"Yeah? I think some of them left for the train yards." This was how illnesses got spread, I thought. MRSA was spread easily in places where people came into close contact, like prisons and squats.

MRSA wasn't called drug resistant for no reason. Only a few antibiotics are effective against this particular staph species. Sometimes even they were not enough, and the only cure was a surgical debridement to remove the infected flesh. This meant actually scraping off the flesh; amputations were not uncommon. Though it was in the beginning stages, this case seemed particularly bad because the infection seemed to be all over the boy's body. I called Wendy in. She was wearing a white hospital smock over clean trousers, her name tag on the smock, her long hair shining and clean.

"Have you heard about diluted bleach baths in conjunction with other treatments for MRSA?" I asked her.

"Yeah, something like that. Weren't you saying they were used at the hospital?"

"That's right." I remembered. "I heard it in the dermatology department. They said it works. The bleach water kills the staph on the skin better than a lot of antibiotics. The problem is it needs to be done pretty regularly."

"Does it sting?" the boy asked curiously.

"Probably not if it is diluted."

"OK. But where am I going to take a bath?"

He was right. "Do you have any place to take a bath?" I asked him.

"No." He thought carefully. "I don't think so."

"The shelters only have showers," Wendy said.

We all were silent for a moment. "I don't think there is any place for a homeless person to take a tub bath in the entire city of Phoenix," Wendy said.

I sighed. "I'm going to give you a nose antibiotic instead," I told the boy. This was a topical gel that was placed inside the nostrils for the first four or five days of each month for six months. I hoped that along with oral antibiotics it would kill the staph organism. "The problem is you are going to keep getting infected as long as you squat in that house. The place is probably crawling with infection. We need to get you to a shelter."

"I'm already on all wait lists," he said. "None of them have room."

In the van bathroom I scrubbed my wrists and hands. I didn't want to take the staph home to Amy and the kids. In my mind I saw one of the twins or Charlotte in the hospital, hooked up to an IV, being treated for MRSA. I looked in the little mirror. I wished I felt better, but I didn't. "I'm fine," I told myself, knowing I wasn't fine at all.

"Randy?" It was Wendy, calling me to the front. "You'd better come here now." Her voice was calm, but the tone told me it was important.

When I stepped out of the van that moment and first saw her, I thought of broken toys. She was as tall and slender as a wand, and as she came swaying up to the van, people fell silent and stopped to stare at the heart-shaped face, at her wide, beautiful eyes, at the wavy hair that caressed her shoulders. Her blank eyes turned this way and that, seeing nothing. There was something mechanical about the way she moved her head.

A tough-looking blond girl named Lisa was leading her. Lisa was a street-savvy girl who often took a mothering attitude toward the more vulnerable kids. Wendy stepped out of the way as I came down the steps.

"Dr. Randy?" Lisa's clear voice called. "Can you help this girl? We call her Nicole."

"What's wrong?" I asked.

"She's really messed up in the head." Lisa paused. She lowered her voice, though the girl didn't seem to be aware of her surroundings. "Lots of times she acts like different people."

I took Nicole inside to an exam room. I didn't get far in questioning her. She simply stared off in the distance. She sat on the edge of the table. Her long arms were limp. There was something yellow, dried mustard perhaps, smeared around her mouth.

"I'm Dr. Christensen," I said. "What's your name?"

She didn't respond. I was not a psychiatrist, but I thought I was looking at psychosis. Then all of a sudden a light flashed in her eyes. She smiled and giggled behind a dirty closed fist. "My name's Rebecca."

"Rebecca. Pleased to meet you."

She held her hand out briefly and then snapped it back. The giggle came again. She looked coyly up from under her lashes. She pulled a lock of her hair.

"My stepdaddy calls me Becca." There was another twirl of hair.

"That's nice."

"Sometimes he calls me Cupcake."

She made a quick, girlish gesture by folding her legs up, so her feet were almost tucked under her. I was about to ask her what had brought her to the van when the gesture caught my eye. I knew what I wanted to ask first, her age. She smiled a smile that almost made me believe she was gap-toothed and in second grade, though I knew she had adult teeth.

"I'm eight," she said proudly. "I just had my birthday too."

"What can I do for you, Becca?"

"I got an owie." She showed me a tiny mark on her wrist.

"Would you like a Band-Aid?"

She gave the same little-girl smile. There was dried food on her chin and mats in her hair. I pulled out a box of Band-Aids. We kept Disney ones for the little babies we saw at the domestic violence shelter. She looked delighted. She patted the Band-Aid on her wrist.

"Do you have any medicine?" she asked.

"Like aspirin?"

"I'm too young for aspirin, silly."

"How about some Tylenol?" The conversation was surreal. The longer I talked, the more convinced I became that Nicole was eight. If it was an act, it was pitch perfect.

I got out a sample of Tylenol pills. She shook her head, her eyes wide. "I don't like pills." Without saying anything I put it away and found some liquid baby Tylenol. Now her face split into a smile. I poured the red liquid in the measuring cup for her. She drank it daintily. When she was done, I gently cleaned the dried food off her chin with a wet wipe.

"Where are you from, Becca?"

Suddenly the blank look returned. I waited for a long time. She just looked vacant.

"How did you get to Phoenix? Do you live around here?"

Then she smiled at me, again a little girl.

"I'd like to give you an exam," I said. She shook her head rapidly. The little girl was back.

"Oh, no. My mommy told me not to take my clothes off for strangers."

"She honestly seemed to believe she is eight years old," I told the team at our next-morning meeting at our HomeBase offices. We were now regularly meeting to go over our patients, and budget and other issues, though we all still dashed out to the van as soon as the meetings were over. Wendy and Michelle said the smell of the offices made them sick, and I knew the air aggravated Michelle's asthma.

"What happened when you asked for her history?" Wendy asked.

"All of a sudden she lapsed back into that nearly catatonic character," I said. "I wasn't able to get any information from her at all."

"Do you think she is really multiple personality?" Jan interrupted.

"I don't know enough to say," I replied slowly. I tapped my hand on her file. "Only a psychiatrist can tell us that. Which is why we really could use one on board."

Jan pointed out that we'd never be able to afford it.

"I know. But the longer we do this, the more I think it's what we really need. We see so many kids with depression, bipolar, or the onset of schizophrenia. We are not equipped to diagnose or treat them. Heck, we can't even afford to keep medications for them on board." Jan nodded in understanding. We had realized early on that we simply could not afford to stock medications for the mentally ill youth. A month's supply of a common medication for schizophrenia could cost nine hundred dollars. Often teens came to us with empty bottles, pleading for their psychiatric meds. We had none, and if they had no insurance, there was no way they could get their prescriptions filled. It was a situation that made me angry every time we dealt with it, which was sometimes several times a day. We had a few pills for emergency use only, and that was for kids with existing diagnoses.

"Can we even get her to a psychiatrist for an evaluation?" Jan asked.

"You can try," I said hopefully.

"I'm on it," Wendy said.

"In the meantime what do we call her?"

Wendy spoke up. "The other kids called her Nicole."

"Good enough for now," I said.

The next morning I stopped again at the HomeBase offices. My own desk was a mess. Jan's desk was surrounded by a huge collection of training manuals and medical documents. I swore she kept every training manual from every conference she had ever attended. Michelle's desk was quiet and orderly just like her. Wendy's desk was surrounded by empty water bottles. Wendy was the queen of recycling and would even scout our trashcans for water bottles. I was sometimes tempted to leave some in my trash with notes just to tease her.

I could hear Wendy on the phone. "How do I get her to see a psychiatrist?" There was a silence. "No, I understand you won't do that. I just want to understand how it works. . . . OK." There was a scratch of a pen. "So you're saying first we have to get her on the state Medicaid insurance. . . . I know she needs valid identification." There was another scratch of the pen. "I understand. But here's the problem. This girl is too delusional to even tell us her name. Obviously I need to get her evaluated and medicated. But I can't get her evaluated without identification. You see the catch-22."

Wendy was quiet for a moment, listening. I heard her lower her voice. "I know you didn't invent the system. . . . OK. But what if the child is too delusional or psychotic to cooperate?" There was a pause. "I understand you can't help until she has identification. Once she gets the identification she still has to sign up in person. Then what happens? She has to request the provider? . . . OK. Which one offers mental health services?" Another scratch. "So you are saying that none of the providers offers mental health. So even if she gets on the insurance, how can she see a psychiatrist then?"

The pen scratched. "OK. So you're saying that *after* she gets on the insurance, she needs to enroll in the mental health program. Then she needs an intake assessment. Then can she see someone? . . . Oh. She has to find a psychiatrist who will accept the insurance. Can you give me an idea of how many do? . . . Oh, my. No, I understand. So from start to finish, how long will it honestly take before she sees a psychiatrist, provided we can get her identification?" The pen wrote and then paused. "Wow. No, I understand. . . . OK." I heard the phone go back in its cradle. Wendy sighed. "Six months to a year." I heard her whisper to herself. There was the sound of phone keys being punched. "On hold," I heard her mutter to herself. Twenty minutes later she was still on hold. I heard her tapping her pen.

I left for a meeting and returned an hour later. I walked by Wendy's cubicle to check in. She was still on the phone. Her face was a tight, frustrated mask. She had a notepad filled with angry doodles. I left to take the van out for a quick visit to the domestic violence shelter. When I came back that night, I found a note on my computer. "Sorry, Randy, still working on it."

꒰ ꒱꒰ ꒱꒰ ꒱

Driving home that night, I decided to call my sister. The truck had turned into my de facto time to make calls. With the kids at home to take care of, it was becoming harder to keep on top of

Stephanie's medical issues. I felt guilty because I knew she was having more trouble with her MS. It had been flaring up. "I'm using a walker now," she said. "But no way am I going to be in a wheelchair. I've got two crazy boys to keep up with." Stephanie and Curtis had two beautiful boys named Matthew and Trevor, both blond-haired, bright-eyed, and full of happy intelligence.

"That's the spirit," I said. It was hard to think of her limited mobility when I remembered how carefree and energetic she had been as a child.

"Have you talked to Mom lately?" she asked.

"Yesterday. I was planning on calling her tonight."

"Dad says she's not feeling very good." I opened the front door to the sound of shouting and crying. Amy had one crying child, Charlotte, in her arms, and the twins were wrestling on the living room floor. Charlotte was now eighteen months old, and the twins were four years old and in preschool. Amy turned to me and saw I was on the phone. She looked tired.

"I know," I said. Both Stephanie and I were in close touch with our parents, often speaking to them daily.

"Her pains are getting worse."

My mother had started having symptoms of colon cancer when I was in the third year of my residency. Then, two weeks before my wedding, I got a call from her doctor. He told me that Mom had colon cancer. I was floored when her doctor asked me to be the one to give her the news; his request was incredibly unprofessional. If he is this inept, I thought, I *should* be the one to tell Mom. The news was devastating. I knew as a doctor that her prognosis was not good. She needed surgery and chemotherapy if she was going to have a shot at remission. I vowed to keep this knowledge to myself. The first thing my mom said was, "I don't want to miss your wedding." She insisted on waiting until the wedding was over for her surgery and treatment.

A few weeks later Amy and I went on our honeymoon. We kept telling each other how wonderful it was not to hear anything about the surgery, because no news was good news. I even expressed the naive hope that my mom would be one of the "lucky ones." It didn't occur to me that my dad and she would wait with the news. For the first time my parents hid information from me. The cancer had metastasized. For six months she did chemotherapy and eventually seemed to be in remission. But there were complications wrought by the radiation. Mom was often weak and in severe pain. We all had learned to live with her illness as a family, just as we were learning to cope with Stephanie's MS. But it was never easy.

"Dad says her intestines are having trouble absorbing nutrients," Stephanie said.

"She had a lot of chemo," I said. I had been hoping this alone was the cause of the increased pain. "That can lead to scarring and kidney damage."

"Are you going for Sunday supper?"

"We're planning on it. When is your next doctor visit?"

When I finally got off the phone, I glanced at my watch. I was surprised to see it was past ten. I checked on the kids. Charlotte was conked out in her little bed, but Reed and Janie were still awake in their beds. I quietly encouraged them to go to sleep. I walked back out, and Amy was at the counter, making a shopping list. I reminded myself she was putting in her own long hours, as well as doing most of the child rearing, and we had three children under age five.

"Do you mind going to visit my parents this Sunday?" I asked.

"No. That's what we usually do," she said, crossing out "pot roast" and writing "chicken" with a question mark after it.

"My mom's stomach pain is getting worse."

"I don't want your mom to feel she has to cook. We'll make a casserole."

That Sunday Mom looked drawn. I didn't want her to think I was worried, but in truth I was. Maybe the cancer was back. Her face had the tight look of someone in pain, and she walked slowly. Dad spoke to me quietly. "We'll have to just keep trying to figure out why the pain is getting worse. We've got another appointment in a few weeks."

◻️◻️◻️◻️◻️

On Monday my week started with an early-morning team meeting. I left the house while Amy and the kids were still sleeping. After the meeting I took the van to downtown Phoenix for the day. We treated dozens of kids, including Nicole, who had shown up with mysterious bruises all over her thin legs and arms. She was out of it and seemed unable to explain anything. As soon as we docked, I ran off for more meetings at the hospital. By the time I got home it was 8:30 P.M. I had been gone for thirteen hours. When I left, the kids were still asleep. Now they were back in their pajamas, bouncing off the walls, with Amy trying to wheedle them into bed. Bedtimes had turned into epic marathons for the four-year-old twins, and I blamed the fact that we had coddled them so much when they were young. They had not learned to self-soothe. Amy looked frazzled, trying to clean up the toy room while Charlotte whined for soy milk. I filled her sippy cup and went into the home office. I had a million e-mails to catch up on and a speech I needed to draft. By the time I came out the kids were asleep and Amy was in bed, watching television. We went to sleep in silence.

Tuesday was no better. I had another morning meeting, another trip out with Jan on the van, this time to where the kids squatted in the abandoned house, only to find them gone. I rushed out of the hospital office to an evening meeting. This time it was for the American Diabetes Association. I got home after 8:00 P.M. I came home to more pajamas, more bedtime meltdowns, and more tired Amy. The house was a mess. Ginger needed to be walked. She stared at me with reproachful brown eyes, her body trembling in anticipation. Dishes were piled in the sink, and a part of me wondered why Amy hadn't done them already. She had got off work earlier after all. She could have at least done the dishes, I found myself thinking. Janie and Reed, usually so compatible, picked a fight with each other and started screaming. Amy swooped in, separating the kids. I grabbed the leash and took Ginger for a walk.

When I got back, Amy was bathing the kids. I didn't know why she insisted on bathing all of them every night. I had argued with her about it. When I was growing up, a bath every few days was good enough for a growing child. I turned on my home computer and found an avalanche of e-mails. By the time I crawled into bed Amy was asleep.

Wednesday morning I woke to hear Janie singing through the house. "Daddy's taking us to breakfast, Daddy's taking us to breakfast." Amy was up early, sitting at the counter with her head in her hands.

"Daddy isn't taking us to breakfast," I said, walking in.

"Why not?" Janie asked.

"Because he's going to work," I told her.

"You're going to work?" Janie asked me. She looked crushed. Tears formed in her eyes.

"It's a workday," I said, bewildered.

I raced to the hospital for my work there while Jan took the van out. Amy worked late on Wednesdays, and it was my day to get the twins and Charlotte from day care. We were blessed to have them all attending day care at the Shepherd of the Valley church, where we went for services. As soon as she got in the van, Janie began chattering about an art project she was supposed to do at home. Homework in preschool? I thought. The world is getting crazier all the time. "Sure, I can help, honey," I said idly while buckling Charlotte into her seat

"I'm hungry," Reed said from the backseat.

Charlotte was babbling something about horses. "Later, honey," I told her.

I herded them in the house and opened a box of crackers for a snack. I cut oranges and pulled string cheese from the fridge. I looked at my watch. It was close to 6:00 P.M. I dashed into the bedroom. By the time I came out Amy was coming in from work, dropping her purse with exhaustion. I was buttoning a fresh shirt.

"What did you make for dinner?" she asked. She frowned. "Why are you putting on a tie?"

"I have a diabetes camp meeting tonight," I said.

"I thought that was yesterday."

"That was for the diabetes association. This is for Camp AZDA."

"When?" she asked, plaintive.

"Now. I'll be home later." I kissed her.

Ginger followed me to the door, wagging her tail and whining.

Thursday. I woke after less than five hours' sleep. It had been weeks, probably months, I realized, since I had gotten a full eight hours of sleep. Thursday brought yet another morning meeting, this time with the children's hospital. I took the van out with an intern. We saw a suicidal boy who had slashed his wrists. That evening I had a fund-raiser to attend. I called Amy. I didn't have time to go home. I would eat on the road. I stopped at an Arby's and wolfed a large roast beef sandwich, curly fries, and a Coke. There goes fifteen hundred calories, I thought, and once again, no exercise. I got to the fund-raiser just in time to give my speech. It was after ten by the time I managed to shake hands on the way out. As I walked in the house, I heard kids screaming. Reed and Janie were having a water fight in the bathroom. Amy was shoving a batch of laundry into the dryer. There were clothes all over the floor and dishes over the counters. Amy didn't say anything to me. She slammed the dryer door.

It was midnight before I made it to bed. My eyes burned with exhaustion, and my body ached. Amy had the television blaring in the bedroom. I hated having the television on while I was trying to sleep. My legs burned with stress. I buried my head under the pillow. I thought about the next day. It would be Friday. I was scheduled to receive an award that night. I had been voted Outstanding Young Arizonan by the Arizona Jaycees. I was proud I had won, but it would mean another late night. I knew there was something I had forgotten too. I groaned to myself. It was Janie's art project.

"Honey, did Janie get her art project done?"

"I helped her." Amy's voice was remote.

I tried to remember what we had to do that weekend. We had to go shopping and clean the house, and then there was church and Sunday night supper with my folks. How was I going to fit all that in? I still had to drop off the dry cleaning and a million other things. My mind began to race. Suddenly sleep seemed like a distant proposition. I was wide awake with adrenaline.

"Randy."

I had felt the argument brewing all week. Amy and I rarely fought, but when we did, our arguments were emotional and intense. Neither of us liked to raise our voices, but somehow, even if we talked in low voices, there would be incredible amounts of feelings. Both of us, I thought, avoided issues until they were pent up. Here it comes, I thought.

She took a deep breath. "I feel like I'm doing all my stuff and I'm doing your stuff too."

That was true. I felt an instant rush of guilt. But what was I supposed to change? I took my head out from under the pillows. I tried to apologize. I wanted to fix it. Right then. Whenever we argued, this was my response.

"Let's hire a nanny," I said immediately. "We can get someone to help with the housework—"

"That is *not* the issue," Amy said heatedly.

"Then what is the issue? You're saying you have to do everything. I'm not arguing. You do have to do too much. If we get some help—"

"I don't want any help."

"Well, what do you want then? Do you want me to cut back on the extra stuff I do? Like Camp AZDA?" I would have given up the extra things I did for Amy and the kids. But I also knew that Amy really didn't want that.

She sighed, exasperated. I felt my temper rise.

"If we got a nanny, then it would be easier on you," I said, trying to keep my tone even. I remembered when Amy had had Jo Ann come stay for a month after Charlotte was born.

She stared at me. Her eyes were rimmed with red from exhaustion. From the set of her mouth I could tell she was furious. "I don't care if you work sixty hours a week," she said, her voice tight with tears. "I don't care if you do all that extra stuff. I want you to help homeless kids. I *want* you to work the van." The tears were getting closer. "But when you are *here*, I want you *here*. Not in your office answering e-mails. Not someplace far away while you think of the next thing you are going to do." She paused and swallowed. She wiped her eyes. "I don't care if it is only ten minutes a day. You need to find time for us. You need to *talk* to *me*."

It hit me then. In the very beginning I had talked to Amy, but that had quickly ended. For years now I had not talked to her about the stresses in the van or the other issues in my life, thinking I was protecting her or perhaps protecting my image of myself with her. But what Amy wanted was closeness. She was probably the most understanding and supportive person about my commitment to the van. All she wanted was to share it, and I had kept that sharing from her.

It's my emotional distance that she is angry about, I realized, not the hours. It's me and how I handle stress.

"You're right," I said in a muted voice.

Her voice was sad. "Right when you started the van, we talked all the time. Remember how I suggested the paper gowns? But that disappeared so quickly. You stopped asking me for advice."

"I'd like to get back to that. Please."

She wiped her eyes. "Me too."

I went to splash water on my face. When I came back, Amy was curled on her side. I curled against her and apologized. She took my hand in acceptance, and I told my wife how much I loved her.

"She's getting a little strong-smelling," Jan whispered to me. "I'd really like to at least change her socks."

Whenever we stopped the van in downtown Phoenix, Nicole had been coming in with Lisa, who usually led her by the hand. Sometimes she was Becca, the eight-year-old girl. She did childish things. Once she came in with one of her ears packed with tissue paper. I carefully pulled it all out to find a pencil eraser stuck deep in the canal. She denied knowing how it got there. Other times she was a very friendly, outgoing young man. A few times she was a rough, sexual older woman. That woman rarely appeared at our van. Sometimes she was a silent, very dark person who refused to answer any questions at all. When she was this person, whoever he or she was, she stared at us from under a curtain of dark hair. The other kids told me that the rough, mean personalities appeared more often on the streets. Our van was a safe place for Nicole, I figured. It was where her childlike personalities came out. But try as we did, we could not get any meaningful history out of her, not even a former address, a name, or a sense of where she had come from. She was so deep in her psychosis that for the moment the information simply didn't exist.

As the days passed, she still refused to get an exam. Sometimes, when she was the little girl called Becca, she would consent to let me listen to her heart. She would giggle. But her jeans and shirt stayed on, and so did her shoes. "Oh, no," she would say as Becca when we asked to give her a full examination.

I did what I could. When the bug bites on her arms got infected, I washed them and medicated the sores. When her hair developed a large mat in the back from never being combed, I talked her into letting me comb it. She was Becca for the combing. She held very still while I combed her hair. The mat was too large to comb, so I cut it out, talking quietly to her as I snipped. She wanted to hold the clump I had cut out. She petted it like an animal.

The next time we parked downtown Nicole was back, still carrying the magic talisman of hair. Holding it, she sat on the exam table. Jan entered the room. As always, her eyes softened when she saw Nicole. "Hi there," she said, waiting to see who Nicole would identify as being. "Who are you today?"

Nicole looked confused. "I'm Becca, silly. You know me."

Jan and I exchanged a glance. "Of course, honey," Jan said. "Of course."

〔〕〔〕〔〕〔〕〔〕〕

Things seemed better with Amy after our talk, but the pall of Katrina continued, or maybe it was my relentless schedule. It seemed that as soon as I had come back I was back on the same roller coaster. More happened on the van in one day than happened in months or even years in another medical practice. Sometimes a single day passed and I looked back in shock at the number of kids I had treated—dozens—and the horror they presented. One intern made the comment that a week on the van had more drama than the entire *Sopranos* series.

I had been back only a few weeks, and we were parked in downtown Phoenix, in the lots where I had met Donald in what, I realized, had been an amazing five years since. I had just finished taking care of three different urgent cases, including a troubling head injury, when I was distracted by the sudden sound of kids making a racket. It was a rough area of town we were in, and shouting and yelling had erupted outside the van. The first thing I thought was: fight. The second was that someone was going to get hurt. I was ahead of Jan and out the door in a flash.

I landed in the middle of a large group of kids. They were dustier than usual but loud and laughing, slapping one another's backs and dropping loaded backpacks.

"What's up?" I asked, bewildered.

"We just got back from camping," Lisa said, not sounding quite as tough as usual.

"Camping?"

"Yeah," one boy said. His brown hair was tangled, and his face dirty, but he was happy. He was weighted down with a big pack. "Fall is the best time of year to go camping."

"Where did you all go?" I asked, mystified.

"Up in Dreamy Draw Gulf," the boy said. He dumped his backpack with a sigh, stretching his back.

"We had a campfire. Marshmallows and everything."

"It was awesome." The boy chimed in. "Lisa sang. She sounded like a dying crow." This earned him a punch on the shoulder.

Jan had joined me, her hands on her hips. We exchanged a delighted look. I was amazed. Here these kids were, homeless and on the streets. Despite all fear and hunger and stress, they had decided to go camping. There were no holidays on the street, no birthday parties, or trick-or-treating. But they're still kids, I thought. Despite everything, they are still children who want to have fun.

ロワワワワロ

That night Reed wanted to show me something. He had come out of the messy toy room with a plastic spider in his hand, talking nonstop about how he wanted a tarantula. I was trying to pay attention, though I was distracted by having to get ready to go out. Only this time it wasn't for an evening meeting: Amy and I were planning to go out to dinner once the sitter arrived. It had been a long time since we had had a romantic night out together. I was trying to take what she had said to heart. I picked Reed up to wrestle with the spider in his hand, but he didn't want to wrestle. He wanted to tell me about tarantulas and what awesome pets they would make.

I watched Reed, and I remembered my own father, who had endless time and limitless patience for me. Whenever we needed to fix the truck on the farm, he would make a day of it. We would spend a leisurely morning driving to town to pick up the parts and then stop for lunch. I always insisted on Burger King. I would order a Yumbo, a ham and cheese sandwich it had for a time on the menu when I was a kid. Dad thought it was so funny I would insist on a hamburger place to order a ham and cheese sandwich. While we ate, Dad would share with me all sorts of advice. He was a big believer in the right tool for the right job. We would take home the bag of parts to fix the truck, and by the time we were done it would be supper, and Mom would be calling us inside. She and Stephanie would have also been spending the day together, and I would see Stephanie at the stove while Mom gave a cooking lesson.

I didn't have that time for my own son, I thought sadly. I could tell myself I spent more time with him than some dads. I could say it was quality time. I could bring up all the little rushed trips we had taken and the time at the diabetes camp when Amy brought them for the day. But that was being dishonest with myself. The daily time counted too.

"How about we take the kids camping?" I asked Amy that night as we ate under candlelight at the Parlor. We both liked the pizza place for its casual but romantic setting. From where we were sitting we could look up through the skylights and see the stars. Amy had ordered one of her usual crazy combinations, with wild mushrooms and goat cheese, while I had my typical ham and pineapple.

"Camping?" The look of happy surprise on her face was answer enough. When we were dating, Amy and I loved camping. It was one of the special things we liked to do together. I found out soon enough that she liked to rough it. No trailers or cabins. I suspected she thought tents were a little sissy and would have been fine with a blanket in the woods. When I was a kid, my family saw the country by car: Mount Rushmore, Old Faithful, the Grand Canyon. Dad got a little camper shell. We stayed at Motel 6's, but I thought we were kings of the road. There wasn't a famous site that my parents didn't want to drive to, watching America pass outside our dust-spotted windows. Each morning Stephanie and I would eagerly pile into the back of the car, ready to play with our toys. We never minded the long hours of driving, because we knew at the end we would peg the family tent out somewhere, and Mom would put her pot of water above the fire to boil. If there was a lake nearby, Dad would take me to catch trout, and Mom would cook them above the fire. But since the twins had been born, Amy and I had forgotten about camping. I hadn't taken the kids fishing yet either.

As soon as we got home, Amy was online, making plans. "How about a trailer?" I asked. "When I was younger, my parents eventually got this little trailer—"

"Pffft." She made a derisive noise. "Why not just tie a mattress to your back? Let's see . . . a national park would be nice. Randy, honey, when can you promise a weekend off?"

"Let me make some calls. I know we can do it."

Within a few weeks we were in a state park in New Mexico for a long-overdue weekend camping trip. I watched the twins run around the tent, while little Charlotte pointed at the trees and the squirrels. Fall and winter in Arizona were the best times to go camping. Amy was crouched in front of the fire, threading marshmallows onto sticks. She had a plate with graham crackers and pieces of Hershey bars all ready. I sat on a log, and Reed came and leaned against me. We didn't say anything. We watched the smoke drift up to the sky a bit. I should take Reed fishing, I thought. And Janie, and Charlotte.

For me, the times I spent fishing with my dad were some of my most precious memories. I remembered how he had packed up a tackle box specially for me. I should do that for Reed too, I thought, and the girls as well. I wanted them to have the same wonderful experiences I had had as a child. I know what is important, I thought. My family is as important as the kids on the van—more important. I can't let their needs be forgotten next to what seems the more pressing needs of the homeless kids. Or I will be repeating the same neglect of the parents I condemn.

Amy came and sat next to me, handing me a marshmallow to roast. "Ready?" she asked.

◻◻◻◻◻◻

Jan and I had learned over time that we had to focus our efforts on the here and now. If we worried over what had happened to so many of the kids we saw, we would be bogged down in constant stress. So we tried not to play the game of Have You Heard. Too often it came with depressing results. *Have you heard what happened to that albino baby girl and her sister Nizhoni?* No, I haven't seen her or heard anything. I hope she and her sister are OK. *What about that blond girl who came in from the squat with the mastoiditis? Remember her?* She died. When she got to the hospital, she went into acute respiratory distress. She went under before they could save her. Her heart was weak from the infection, they said. *Did her friends make it to see her before she died?* I don't know.

We had learned that asking "Have your heard" came with too many questions unanswered and too much heartache. Most of the time we didn't know what happened to the kids after we saw them. It could mean they were now successful, having moved on to a better life once we referred them to shelters. Or it could mean they had disappeared, were in prison, or were dead. We often never knew.

Sometimes the question didn't need to be asked. Sugar still appeared occasionally. I imagined a chart showing the dissipation and decline of her spirit over the years since I had first met her. Her eyes became haunted. Her cheeks narrowed. Her hair was no longer thick and full. Sometimes she had venereal diseases; often she was sick with one ailment or another. Always she refused help. She rarely joked anymore, and when she got on the table, it was never with the energy she had once had. Her one sign of hope was she always asked after our dog, Ginger. I kept pictures of the puppy as she grew into an adult dog, and I always shared these with Sugar. But eventually she would leave, grimly clutching the white bag of her STD meds. Each time I checked her eyes I felt I could still see light of survival in them. But it was diminishing over time, like the dot on a television when you turn it off.

A year after my return from Katrina she came in, having been badly beaten again. She denied she had been raped, though I suspected she had been. I cleaned her facial wounds. A new intern was helping out, and I passed him the bloodstained cotton, which he disposed of. I applied a butterfly patch to a cut on her cheek. I could still see the faint scars from ring marks from the last time I had treated her wounds. Eventually, I realized, her pretty face would be covered with scars.

"Remember when you first came to me?" I asked softly. "That was a long time ago, wasn't it?"

"I guess."

"Several years."

She looked reflective. "I remember that first day. I'm older now." She cracked a little smile. "And I don't look a day over forty." She batted her eyelashes at me.

"You're not supposed to make me laugh in this situation." I gently wiped the rest of her face.

Her battered eyes lifted. "I've done a lot of bad things."

"No," I said. "A lot of bad things have been done to you."

"Do you still think there is hope for me?" she asked, her voice breaking.

"Yes, I do."

"How's Ginger?" she asked suddenly.

"She's doing great. I tried to shave her for the heat, and she looks awful." I waited a moment. "You know, if you can care about a dog, you can care about yourself. Let me help you."

She was thoughtful. Maybe this will be it, I thought. Maybe this will be the miracle. Her lips moved. Numbers. She was counting. I could see the abacus in her head. I had a sudden wild hope she was counting something good. Maybe she was counting future birthdays. Maybe it was the hours until she found shelter. "Are you counting the years?" I asked. But I should have known better.

"No. I was counting how many johns I had this week." She painfully slid off the table. "Time to go."

The intern was furious with both her and me. "I can't believe you let her get away with that," he said angrily once she had left.

"Let her get away with what?"

"Not going into a shelter."

"She said no," I said, realizing I sounded curt.

"That's what I can't believe. I mean she has a chance to go in a shelter. Who would chose prostitution over that?"

"The person who has known no other life. Who knows what she fears? Maybe she thinks people will judge her. Maybe she thinks there is no way she can succeed in life. Maybe she even tried a shelter once and something happened that convinced her it won't work."

The intern followed me up front. "That doesn't make any sense," he said.

"You should try living in a shelter for a night. Kids get hurt in some of them. Besides, giving someone a cot and an army blanket for the night is not a cure. The next day they wake up and the reasons they became homeless in the first place are still there. Sugar has to wake up every day with pain you and I could never understand. That kind of pain might make her feel that life is hopeless."

"Then cut her loose," the intern said.

"What do you mean?" I asked, appalled.

"Tell her she can't come back unless she accepts help."

I wanted to give some passionate speech on how all our patients deserved a chance. But I was too tired. "We're doctors," I said. "We are here to treat, not judge. If you plan on denying treatment to patients you don't like, then it is time to find another career."

Time flew by, as fast as ever, and soon it had been two years since Katrina and Christmas was fast approaching. "Hey, Randy." It was Bob Sarnecki, the vice president of our IT program at Phoenix Children's. He came walking down the hospital corridor after me. "A computer and video company would like to donate a bunch of gift cards to hand out for the homeless kids at Christmas this year," he said.

I was elated. Jan and I had been handing out sleeping bags and sweatshirts for years during the holidays. Every year we got more, and every year we ran out.

"They also suggested we transmit a video signal from the hospital here to a videophone on the van. We could have somebody dress up as Santa at the North Pole."

"That's an even better idea!" I exclaimed. "Who could we get to be Santa?"

"Me." He gave a shy, goofy grin.

The days before Christmas Jan and I carried boxes of ten-dollar gift cards out to the streets. For many of the kids, I knew, it would be the only gift they would get. They ran off in packs and soon returned, showing what they had bought. One girl got herself a pad of paper and a collection of colored pencils. She sat down in a lawn chair to spend the day coloring. A boy got himself a new pair of cheap shoes. Another got a belt. I was struck at the kids' practicality. Several bought phone cards to call relatives far away. A few purchased gifts for others, like the boys who brought small presents and cards to Jan, their mother figure. She took them, thanking each boy sincerely.

On Christmas Eve we drove to a busy location. We had the videophone all set up in the front of the van. I invited Amy and the kids along to help. I had doubted that teenagers would want to talk to Santa, but I was wrong. The kids clamored, eager to have their turn. One by one they stepped in front of the videophone. Santa was there, dressed in his red suit and white beard, sitting in a chair in front of a white background that I knew was butcher paper. The amount of fuzzy static was perfect. I could almost hear the cold winds at the North Pole howling. We had suggested that Santa not promise the homeless kids anything, but just listen to their wishes.

"Hey, Santa," one boy said. "I want to get clean."

The girl behind him stepped nervously up to the video. "Hey, Santa," she whispered. "Long time no see."

For four hours the vice president of the Phoenix Children's Hospital sat in his office, talking to the kids on the van on the video. As each child filed past, Charlotte and Janie and Reed greeted them, handing out candy canes and cookies that Amy had brought. Younger kids got a toy or stuffed animal. For the older teens we had the gift cards. The word spread on the streets, and more and more kids showed up. Santa's voice got hoarse, but he continued, stopping only every few hours for a bathroom break.

It was 8:30 P.M. when we took the kids home. Charlotte was crashed out, sleeping hard against her car seat. Janie and Reed were in the backseat. They were six now and often surprised me with their knowledge and insights. I found their different reactions to that evening fascinating. Janie took it all in stride. Like Amy, she figured helping others was her job and felt no internal conflicts about doing it. She rode with a pleased expression on her face. She has Amy's strength, I thought. Reed seemed to wrestle more with the what-could-have-been questions. He had a strong sense of empathy and, as we drove, asked a million questions from the backseat. "How did the kids get homeless?" he asked. "How come they can't find jobs? Can I help them go back to school?"

Amy and I fielded the questions as patiently as we could. We had decided that it was important the kids know about my work— but not in ways that would frighten them. "Not everyone is lucky to have a family like our family," Amy replied.

"Mom," Reed finally asked from the back seat.

"Yeah?"

He waited for a moment, looking out the car window. "How about I give them my toys?"

Amy and I exchanged a look. "You don't need to," she replied. "But if you want to, you can."

A few days later Donald was standing before me, his face thinner, eyes blue as ever. New muscles filled out his shirt. He was now a mature young man in his early twenties. He came up to the van while I was showing it to a reporter from a magazine. Pastor Richardson was behind him. He too looked much older, as if he had crossed that invisible line from being late middle aged to elderly. His hair was now entirely gray, and he walked with a bit of a stoop. His eyes were a little cloudy.

I left the reporter for a minute to talk to Donald. His hands were dusty, just the way the pastor's hands had been when I first met them both. "We wanted to deliver you some good news," Pastor Richardson said. I could swear Donald seemed brighter, more mentally adept. He had an assurance now, maybe an understanding of who he was, and a gift that surely comes from being loved.

Donald handed me a small envelope. The paper was creamy, and I saw my name engraved on the front. "A card, how nice," I said. I was thinking vaguely it must be a birthday, a retirement, or a church event. I opened the envelope. Donald waited expectantly.

I read the announcement with awe. "You've gotten married!" I exclaimed. He grinned and showed me the ring. I saw his name in fancy print: Donald Richardson. I was astounded again. Pastor Richardson had given Donald his last name.

Donald shyly handed me some photos of the wedding. His new wife was the plain-faced girl from HomeBase, the one who had had her eye on him. She wore a dress bright with satin, and for shoes she had bright red heels. Her brown hair was pulled back into a simple ponytail, and next to her Donald had a huge grin. Surrounding them were the pastor, his wife, and his congregation. They all were standing on a stage next to a podium draped with a faded cloth.

"The wedding was in Pastor Richardson's church," I said.

"Of course," he said.

I felt a trembling of emotion that threatened to break through me. It all came crashing in: the van, the kids, the schedule, the worries, Nicole and her pet of hair, Amy and my ongoing struggles to let her be my support, my own children and my guilt at not being the father I'd always wanted to be. And now here was Donald, smiling at me more brightly than any stained glass window. There was a reason for it all, I realized. Good things could happen. I lifted my head and looked into the clear blue sky. It was as if I could see right through it into the heavens.

11

UMOM

The girl was pregnant. She was pretty far along, at least six months. Her belly was distended, and her ankles were so swollen they lapped over the tops of her sneakers. She was seventeen. She wore dirty gray socks with tiny pink pom-poms. I examined her carefully. She had all the complications of a homeless pregnancy. Her throat was swollen. Her tonsils were infected. Her gums were radiant with gingivitis, which was particularly worrisome because oral decay can send a cocktail of bacteria into the bloodstream toward the developing baby. She had signs of anemia and low calcium. She, and her baby, had received no vitamins, no tests, and no prenatal care.

"What sort of foods have you been eating?" I asked.

"I've been drinking milk," she said defensively.

"We buy the white kind, not just chocolate," the boy standing next to her said. "When we panhandle enough, I buy her a whole quart." She had insisted the boy join her for the exam. He was only fifteen. He had lank brown hair and sleepy green eyes. Cat's eyes, I thought.

"Are you the father?" I asked.

He looked at her for help. The two exchanged a glance. "I was gang-raped," she told me. "It was a bunch of guys. I was sleeping in the park. I woke up, and they were on top of me. I don't want to talk about it."

"Would you like counseling? I could refer you—"

"No," she said.

"When you're ready," I told her, "I can get you help. OK?"

"I'm going to be the dad," the boy said. He covered her hand with his. "I'm going to take care of her and the baby."

I looked at them. He was fifteen and homeless. She was seventeen. She was also homeless. "Raising a baby is hard," I replied.

"It's my baby," she said stubbornly. "I don't care if I got it because of rape."

"Me either," said the boy.

"I'm not an OB," I told them. "I can try to make sure you are healthy. And I can see about finding you shelter. But I need to get you more help if you are serious about having the baby. Number one, we need to finish the exam."

"Can I get vitamins?" the girl asked. She touched her belly. "I want the baby to be healthy."

"Of course."

"I'll take care of her," the fifteen-year-old boy repeated. "I'm going to be a good daddy. Not like my parents. We're going to take good care of our baby."

When the two left, they were holding hands. They had waited several hours while we tried to find them shelter, but there were no openings. She was on a waiting list. In her hand she carried a bag containing prenatal vitamins. Vitamins and nowhere to sleep, I thought.

I remembered when I was fifteen. I could never have imagined myself as a father. I didn't think I could have even imagined anyone else as a father. The idea that this boy would think he was capable of fatherhood should have been appalling. Yet at the same time I understood. The boy was reaching out for one thing in his life that had meaning. So was the girl. Since the beginning of time people have had babies, I reminded myself. Sometimes they were younger than these two and facing harder odds. People had survived much worse. Maybe these two could make it work. But still, I thought, they were children having children.

"Jan, do you ever think about the odds these kids have?" I asked her as she labeled the girl's blood work. Her eyes were sunburned around where she had worn sunglasses.

"Like those kids, two teenagers having a baby," I added.

"If it was one of my kids, I'd hit the roof."

"I know you would."

"But I'd still love them." Her face got softer. "I guess I'm always just hopeful for the best." She looked over to the sunlight rectangle of the door. More kids were approaching.

"Me too," I said.

⌐⌐⌐⌐⌐⌐

Life on the van hurtled forward as always. I found it hard to believe that January 2008 was here. Eight years had passed since we started the van. In 2007 I had been able to hire a new nurse, Julie Watson. She was an outstanding nurse, and Wendy and Michelle were over the moon that they could now do case management duties without having to cover medical issues.

All the same, I could tell that Wendy was beginning to dread our team meetings. She was still profusely apologetic for not being able to get Nicole help. We had been seeing Nicole now for two years, a lifetime for someone of her needs to survive on the streets, and every effort to get her help had been fruitless. During this time we had watched helplessly as she slid more and more into psychosis. Wendy had called the local inpatient psychiatric unit. She had called everyone, from social workers to the courthouse. They had told her what everyone else had said. Nicole couldn't be committed against her will unless she went through extensive court proceedings and was found to be a danger. And she couldn't get voluntary help without identification, which, of course, wouldn't happen as long as she was psychotic. She was trapped in a system that punished her for her own mental illness. Wendy refused to accept this, and I understood how she felt.

I felt the familiar stab of helplessness. "You can't blame yourself for the system," I told Wendy. "The system is not set up for the mentally ill, whether they are adults or children."

Wendy's blond head dipped. "I just wish there were *something*."

"I know," I told her, wishing I could offer more.

"More requests," Jan said, and we all groaned. Jan was always answering the van's phone and hearing requests from agencies that wanted us to bring the van around: adult shelters, schools, soup kitchens, and alcohol and drug treatment centers. The problem was we had only one van and one team. We were limited by our budget and by our staff numbers. Every day we took out the van it cost a few thousand dollars in overhead for upkeep, salaries, supplies, and medications. That meant every new site we added came with costs. I tried to weigh the number of kids we served at each site against the chance that we could get funding, which mostly came from grants. My big dream, spoken to no one, was to get another doctor on board. Then we could split shifts and reach twice as many kids. But that also meant somehow coming up with thousands in extra funding. The way the economy was heading, I didn't think that would happen.

"This Darlene Newsom just won't stop," she said. "Do you know her? She told me yesterday you did."

"I've met her. She's a total dynamo." I had met Darlene at a task force on homelessness. She was a bright, grandmotherly-looking woman with a cap of silver hair and boundless energy. She walked with a slight limp, but I had heard she loved to go hiking in the mountains.

"She calls at least once a week and tells me to tell you one word: UMOM. What is that anyhow?"

I laughed at her persistence. "UMOM is her family shelter. It stands for United Methodist Outreach Ministries. I haven't been there, but I understand they serve homeless families."

"We go to domestic violence shelters. Why not them also?" Jan argued.

"It's a matter of time and staff. We're already working overtime."

"She did say they had a lot of babies."

"OK, OK. I'll head out there today and check it out."

UMOM turned out to be in a run-down area outside the city. I turned in past a high fence with a gate to find an old Motel 8, with peeling paint and concrete stairs up to each row of rooms. As I pulled into the parking lot, I noticed a fleet of gleaming RVs parked at one end. A beaming Darlene stood outside to greet me and to give me the grand tour.

She started by showing me the shelter's catering business. I was impressed. What had been an old kitchen had been converted into a shining, well-run professional kitchen. Darlene explained that the homeless parents who stayed at UMOM could work in the catering kitchen. They not only got job experience but also passed their food permit tests. The company's catering was in high demand. It catered a lot of weddings and business meetings. It also fed the residents, and it was all done under the supervision of a professional chef.

Darlene moved on to the next room, the career and educational center. It was small, with rows of computers on tables and folding chairs. She explained how she had volunteer tutors come in. Most of the parents who came to the shelter had no high school diplomas, and some were illiterate. The tutors educated the parents, helping them study for their high school diplomas and, in some cases, helping them get scholarships for colleges.

"We have strict rules here," Darlene said over her shoulder. She was walking so fast I had to trot to keep up. "Each parent gets a room for herself and her kids. No drugs, no criminal activity, no violence. I have way too many parents waiting to get in here to put up with nonsense. They all know that.

"Did you see all the RVs parked outside?" Darlene asked as she went past a day care room. "Those are mission volunteers. They travel the country in their RVs. They contacted me and asked if they could stop here for the winter. They've been doing everything from painting tables to helping in the kitchen."

She led me up a flight of stairs. "I do wish the rooms themselves were bigger," Darlene said apologetically while knocking politely on a door. "But that's what you get for taking over an old Motel 8." A young black woman answered, balancing an adorable baby on her hip. "This is LaShondra," Darlene said. "And this is her baby, Chantel." LaShondra gave Darlene a big sideways hug.

"I got my food handler's license!" she exclaimed.

"Do you mind if I show Dr. Christensen here your room?" Darlene asked. "He's going to be helping us." I shot her a wry glance.

The room LaShondra called her home was really a small square box. There was no kitchen, no bedroom. On one side, crammed against the wall, she had her bed and a crib. In the middle was perhaps two feet of free space, and then on the other wall was a bookshelf crammed with children's books. A television was perched on the end of a table. Food supplies were stacked in neat boxes on the floor. I saw cereal, bread, peanut butter, and powdered milk. It was all food that could either be eaten without cooking or made on the little hot plate resting on the bookshelf. We peeked in a dime-size bathroom with a faded shower curtain. There was a clean saucepan sitting in a drain on top of the back of the toilet, along with a scrub brush. This tiny sink was where LaShondra did her dishes.

Despite her humble surroundings, LaShondra wouldn't stop telling me how wonderful UMOM was and how much Darlene had helped her. "I was sleeping with my baby in a bus shelter before I came here," she said, scooping up her little girl for a big hug.

"If you don't mind my asking, how come you were homeless?"

"My whole family is in gangs. They were shooting each other. I don't want that for my baby."

"How old are you?" I asked.

"Eighteen. But now that I have my food handler's card, I'm getting a job. I've been applying everywhere."

After we left LaShondra's room, I began to tell Darlene how

impressed I was with UMOM. It had surpassed any expectations I had for a family shelter. She stopped me. "You know what we don't have, Randy? Medical care for babies like Chantel. Did you know that sweet little baby has yet to have all her shots? Just think of that."

"You're guilt-tripping me."

"Of course I am."

"Look," I told her, "I'd love to stop here. But the van is already fully booked as it is, and we have a waiting list of places that would like us to visit. I just don't have the funds to add UMOM as a stop." In 2006 we had expanded our staff and the number of clinics—stops—we made with the van. The CEO of the children's hospital, Bob Meyer, had asked me to think about having teams staff not just the van but a fixed clinic at the HomeBase center too. It had been a time of big, risky growth, and we were swamped with requests. It would be impossible for me to go back to the administration and ask for more money.

"What if you had your own little clinic here? With a nurse? She could have her own little space, and you could supervise it, since you're the doctor."

"That would be a dream." I smiled, thinking Darlene probably had no idea of the start-up costs of creating a clinic, let alone hiring a nurse. "But again, I just don't have any money to do something like that."

She looked unfazed, "We'll see about that."

❑⠶❑❑❑❑

"Hi, Becca." I had to remind myself this was Nicole, a teenager of perhaps nineteen. She was so convincing in her personalities I sometimes felt I should keep separate files. Today Becca was in a bubbly, fun mood. She let me check her ears and take her blood pressure. She was acting goofy.

"Knock-knock," she said.

"Who's there?" I asked.

"I forgot." She giggled. It was strange hearing a knock-knock joke come out of the mouth of a teenage girl with tangled hair.

"I'd still like to give you an exam," I told her. I expected her to say no. This time little Becca smiled.

"Sure," she said.

I was caught by surprise. "I'd like to do what we call a pelvic exam as well," I said.

"Okey-dokey," she said, giving me that gap-toothed grin.

I called in Jan. I had never approached a pelvic exam with more trepidation. I wished I could explain to the real Nicole, whoever she was, what was happening. But instead I was talking to a little child. Jan got out a gown and asked her to change. We waited a bit and knocked. Jan went in first, talking quietly. I gently explained what I was doing as I came back in the room and pulled on the gloves. I rolled the stool closer to her. I reached for the speculum. And then I stopped.

Where Nicole's genitals had been there was something else. I felt my eyes blink. Outside my doctor's demeanor was calm. My doctor's voice and eyes stayed even. But inside my heart was breaking open and weeping its own tears. I didn't want to think about how or why this had happened. I didn't want to think about the nature of these scars. What I wanted to say was, "Oh, you poor baby." But doctors can't talk like that.

I cleared my throat. "Becca—"

"You're probably wondering about my owies," she said in a crystal-clear little voice.

"Yes," I said.

"My stepdaddy did that. When he was punishing me."

Jan and I stared at each other. I didn't know how to continue. But I did. I took the Pap smears. I dropped the swabs into vials. I finished the exam and pulled off the gloves. I gave the vials to Jan. I told Becca she could get dressed. The little girl in the grown woman's body bubbled.

"Am I healthy?" she asked, sitting up.

"Healthy as a horse," I said.

"See? I knew I was brave enough to do it."

Afterward I went in the bathroom and washed my hands. I splashed water on my face, feeling the hotness of my eyes. I felt so sad my heart ached inside my chest, and the tears threatened to burst out. I wanted to cry for Nicole and all the hurt children, but I knew that if I did start crying, I would never stop. How could life treat this child this way? I asked myself. How could people *do* such things? The horror of it hit me. I looked in the mirror. The face that looked back at me looked bleak. When I came out, Jan was leaning against the wall. For the first time I saw her weeping. Her shoulders were shaking. She wiped her eyes when she saw me and walked back up front.

At home that night I pulled Charlotte into my lap. It was hard to believe she was almost four. She kicked her legs and nestled her face against my chest. She smelled like fresh-baked bread; she always had, since she was born. She babbled. Charlotte had the cutest little voice, with just a touch of a lisp. Just like Becca, I thought involuntarily. All the memories of the day flooded back: seeing Becca's scars, seeing what could be done to a girl, seeing with my own eyes the travesties and pains of the world. I held my own little girl in my lap. For a moment a dizzy sick wave came at me.

"Are you OK, Randy?" It was Amy; bless her, Amy who seemed to know intuitively when any of us needed her.

"I'm fine," I said without thinking.

Charlotte was still babbling. She was just a baby, I thought, and then corrected myself. She was a three-year-old little girl. What if what had happened to Becca happened to her? What if it happened to Janie or Reed? It wasn't just the girls. So many of the boys I saw reported they had been molested. It could be a neighbor, a coach. Amy and I could die in a car accident. One of us could fall ill. Our children could be molested without our knowledge. I wanted to push the thought aside, but it kept intruding. You do everything in your power to prevent the unthinkable, I told myself. I remembered when the twins were in the hospital after they were born and how I had considered the impossible, that they might die. Now all the other what-ifs came rushing at me. My babies could get hurt in unspeakable ways. I knew nothing could be ruled out for good. And now this thought included molestation. I held my baby girl in my lap, our beautiful moment tainted.

Amy caught me that night. "Randy, you've been quiet for hours. Something is bothering you. You *promised* me that you would start talking to me."

"I thought I was doing better," I said.

She smiled. "You have been. You just still need a little reminding."

I sat next to her on the couch, holding her hand. "It is the badness that is so bad I don't even want to think about it."

I told her about Nicole. It was cathartic to talk. Her face was calm, that was a relief. "It was never so real to me before," I said. "I mean, it was real before. But it was real for the kids I treat, not real for my own children. Now all of a sudden I feel like it could happen to them. How do we prevent that from happening to our kids? What if we can't prevent it?"

"We do our best," she replied calmly. "What happened to Nicole was because no one knew or intervened. We have each other, and we have extended family. We can teach our children how to come to us for help."

"I don't know how to help her," I said. "That's the really hard part. She's been coming to the van longer than I want to admit. It's been two years. *Two years,* I haven't been able to help her."

"Maybe you can't," she said.

"When she is Becca, I feel like I am letting an eight-year-old wander the streets." I felt close to breaking down. I remembered the rage and frustration I had felt in Katrina at how the government had failed all those people. Now I felt the same rage at how our country was failing this mentally ill, sexually abused child.

"I feel like there is something wrong with this world." For a moment my emotions overwhelmed me, and I couldn't explain the depth of what I was feeling.

"You're trying to help," she said.

"I wish I had talked to you before. I was afraid you'd think less of me, for getting in over my head."

She rubbed my head with her knuckles and gave me that sweet, teasing smile. "Honey, you're always in over your head. That's what I love about you."

After six years our morning meetings at the HomeBase office had finally smoothed into a pattern. It usually involved Jan and the rest of the team bossing me around, or so I complained. Often Jan had some new procedure she wanted to implement, and Wendy, Michelle, and Julie had lots of energetic ideas and opinions too.

Today Wendy had news. "Nicole is in jail."

"What?"

"I guess she went into a Circle K and starting trashing the place. The clerk called the cops. They took her to jail. But it might not be as bad as it sounds. I called over there, and they said they have her in their psychiatric unit. She's getting evaluated and treated. The jail staff that I talked to said that she seemed to be doing really well."

"Well, I guess it's not terrible news," I said. "But how sad that she has to end up in jail to get help." I had a lot of respect for law enforcement, and from my interactions with jail staffs, I knew they agreed that jails were not the place to treat mentally ill people. But with all the program closures they often ended up doing exactly that.

"At least she is safe in there," Wendy said.

"So she's getting medicated?" I asked.

"That's what they said," Wendy said. "I'm eager to see what she is like once they get her stabilized. Won't it be something to meet the real Nicole?"

It was with a slight feeling of optimism for Nicole that we moved on to the next item on our agenda. I made the announcement. To my surprise, Darlene at UMOM had wrangled together enough funds from private donors to hire a nurse. "I think it would be fantastic if you guys could have your own little clinic here," she had told me, almost sanguine about the huge coup she had accomplished. "The nurse could see the parents and their babies. And maybe teach some basic parenting and health skills while she is at it."

I knew from hiring Julie Watson, the new nurse, in 2007, that the addition of one nurse could treble our efforts; strong nurses were like a force unto themselves. I told the team that I knew whom I wanted to hire. She was a great nurse who had climbed the ladder at the Phoenix Children's Hospital from floor nurse to educational manager for the emergency department. Kim Williams-Smith was the perfect person for the job. The problem was Kim made good money. And what we were going to offer her was not half as good.

That day, after the meeting, I approached Kim at the hospital.

"Are you kidding?" she said. "I'm in."

I tried to make sure she understood she would be giving up a lot of financial security, but she was adamant. "I went into pediatric nursing because I like to take care of children. I especially like to deal with emergency and difficult situations. If I wanted to get rich, I would not have picked this field." She smiled at me, glowing.

Within a few weeks I was helping Kim carry extra supplies up to her new nursing office at UMOM. She had turned one old room of the motel into her clinic. This permanent setup would be much easier than bringing the van. Suddenly I envisioned the van's ability to expand from mobile care to creating little clinics like this one, right where homeless women and their children needed help.

"Ta-da," she said, opening the splintered door. I carried a box into a warm, cheerful room snuggled with pillows and places for little kids to rest. Kim had hung bright posters on the walls. "Brush Your Teeth," advised one. "Helmets for Safety," said another, showing a wide-grinning boy on a bike. In orange crates she had an assortment of books.

"I needed something to hide the cracks in the walls," she said happily when she saw me looking at the posters.

"Kim, were you a cheerleader in high school?" I asked. "You've got to be the most positive person I know." I dropped the box.

She skipped down the stairs after me. "In a week my office will be crammed," she said.

"I wouldn't give it that long," I said. When we got back upstairs, there was a mother waiting for us. It was LaShondra. Her baby had been crying, her little face screwed tight with misery.

"I think she got an earache," LaShondra said apologetically. "I've been putting a warm washcloth on it."

Kim smiled reassuringly and offered her hands to the toddler. "You're a good mom to bring her right away."

My own mom was in and out of the hospital again, having tests. The doctors had found large masses in her abdomen. They hoped it was scar tissue. When we visited her, she had done her hair before we came in, applied lipstick, and was wearing her favorite earrings. She talked about her pain a lot, to me a sign that it had become more pronounced. The pain also came out in the lines around her eyes, in the misery obvious when she thought no one was watching. I thought about how sad it was when pain becomes a person's identity, and I wondered how much medical progress we were making in pain management. The heartache of it becomes so glaring when it's your own mother who's sick.

"One of the doctors wants to do some complicated intestinal surgery," she told me one day, sitting up in her bed. "But they said the surgery might kill me."

My dad turned to me. "There will be three surgeons," he said. "It is the only way to repair all that scarring. The problem is one of the doctors thinks it is too risky."

"It could kill me too," Mom repeated. Her mouth trembled. Dad went to her to hold her arm. My mother tucked her head, her brown hair shining under the hospital lights, under his shoulder.

"Maria," my father said softly.

Mom decided to do the surgery. Not only was she in constant

pain, but she was getting dangerous kidney and blood infections because of an opening in a kidney tube. Without the surgery she would die. But afterward she barely came through. It was touch and go for over a week, and we were by her side. I hoped this would be the end of the pain for her and a chance at health.

On the way home from visiting my mom in the hospital, the kids were unusually quiet. "Tell us about *your* mommy," Janie said to Amy when we were back at our house, climbing in her lap.

"My mother's name was Jane. When I was little, my mom did all sorts of things," Amy said, and the kids listened carefully as she began telling them stories of her own mother. She was passing on memories.

"What happened to her?" Reed asked.

"She died when I was a teenager," Amy said, hugging him.

Reed thought about this. "That's like the kids that Dad helps. They're teenagers too."

I held Charlotte in my lap. She sucked her thumb while she listened to Amy, dreaming against my chest.

"I love Grammy Jane," she said. I hugged her tight. Amy caught my look. Charlotte's thumb was still in her mouth. "I'm going to wave to her in heaven."

Nicole was sitting on the curb outside the van with Lisa, who was patiently holding her hand. Nicole was wearing the same filthy clothes she had been wearing for months, before she had gone to jail, but she had pulled an old sweater on over them. It had a reindeer on the front and looked incongruous in the Arizona heat. Her hair was a tangled mess.

"Here you go," Lisa said, turning Nicole over to us.

"Thanks, Lisa. Do you need anything?" I asked. Lisa was the kind of self-sufficient, streetwise teenager who often flew under our radar. She wasn't as needy as the others.

"I'm fine," she said nonchalantly. "When I need money, I pan-handle, and when I need a place to sleep, I find one."

"That's not much of a life," I said.

"It's cool," she said, and wandered off.

I led Nicole inside. "When did you get out of jail?" I asked.

She stared at me in her mute, catatonic personality.

"Are you OK?" There was no reply.

Once we were in the exam room I saw an ugly gash on her fore-head under her hair.

"What happened?" I asked. She didn't reply. She stared at me. Her eyes were blank.

"Do you mind if I fix that?" Again there was no reply. I began cleaning the head wound. There was dirt caked in the dried blood.

"Where's Becca?" I asked tentatively.

Suddenly she started talking in a rough, loud voice. I was star-tled. It was a new personality. "Shut up!" she yelled. "Shut your head!" She was full of malice. She looked like an angry older man. "Shut your head! Stupid!"

"It's OK," I murmured. "It's OK."

"Stupid! Shut that noise! You don't need to cry about it!" she thundered. Her voice was incredibly loud and deep and reverber-ated off the van walls.

My hands were almost shaking as I finished cleaning the wound. Nicole kept bellowing and thundering for me to shut my stupid head.

There was a soft knock. It was Jan. She poked her head in. "Is everything OK? Need anything?"

"Everything's fine," I said.

Nicole twisted her angry old man's face toward Jan. She looked at her blankly. "Shut up! Shut your stupid head."

Jan approached Nicole. She gently stroked her arm. "It's OK," she said. "It's OK."

The baleful glare diminished. "Shut up," Nicole said, her rough voice lessening. "Shut up. Don't cry about it."

"OK," Jan said, still calming her. "OK."

"What happened?" I asked at our next team meeting. "I thought she was in jail, getting help."

"She *was* in jail," Wendy said with an edge. "I called this morning. They said when she was no longer a threat to herself or others, they gave her back the old clothes and released her."

I felt appalled. "You mean they didn't even give her fresh clothes?"

"That's not their job," Wendy said. "Apparently."

"I'm more baffled by the medication issue," I said, taking a deep breath and a sip from my morning Diet Coke. "You said they stabilized her on meds."

"Yeah. They said they had her on antipsychotics. She stabilized really well. She was starting to act coherent. She was even saying something about her family. The officer said it seemed like she was really coming around."

"Then what happened?" Jan asked.

"The district attorney dropped the charges. Like we all say, the jail isn't a mental hospital. They can't keep someone against their will. They released Nicole with two days' supply of medication. And here we are. She is back to being psychotic, and we are back to ground zero."

A dozen questions ran through my mind. "Why did they give her only two days of meds? Did they at least get her on the Medicaid insurance while she was inside?"

Wendy took the last sip from her water bottle and added it carefully to the others on her desk. I thought I saw her hand shake a little with stress and anger. "They told me they have the same problem we do. They don't have the funds to supply patients with more than a few days of meds. I don't know about the insurance. Maybe they can't do that in there. You know what gets me? She had a few days when she was released when she was probably wandering the streets lucid for a change. There was a window of time when someone could have helped her, and no one did."

□□□□□

We were halfway back to the dock a few days later when smoke began curling from under the hood of the van. The needle bounced into the red zone. I steered the smoking behemoth off the side of the road.

After a hefty tow charge, the mechanics called the next day to tell me the entire engine had to be replaced. It would cost twenty-six thousand dollars. The amount boggled me. We didn't have the money. Every dime from grants and donors we had budgeted for salaries, supplies, and medications. We were already surviving month to month, always in a state of anxiety about what grants we might get. I fretted at home, on the phone, at our offices at Home-Base. For days the dead van stayed docked. I paced the halls at the hospital. At night I had anxiety dreams. I saw Nicole, alternately yelling at me to shut up and turning into Becca. She was lying on the street. Donald appeared. He was still by the Dumpster. The pastor, he told me, wasn't real; he was just a silly dream. He needed me to come get him because he was going into the hospital and he had a hole in his head. Other kids appeared, crowding up with sores on their arms. I woke up, my heart racing. I wanted desperately to get the van going again. I could not imagine returning to a time when it was not running.

"I'm counting on getting that grant we applied for," I told Jan.

"Then you won't like the news," she said, handing me a printed e-mail. "This just came in this morning. Our name is not on it."

"Great," I said, depressed.

"I refuse to give up," Jan replied.

"Maybe someone will give us a ton of money and we can live without worrying for just a few months," I said.

"Are you dreaming or being your usual Mr. Optimistic?" Jan replied.

"No, I'm trying to find a way to avoid more public speaking. You know I hate it. I always get all hot and sweaty, and my stutter still comes back."

She patted my arm. "I think you do better than you know."

I wanted to be out on the van, serving my patients. But I knew now just how crucial the speaking was—not just for getting money but also for educating people about the plight of homeless kids. So that afternoon I picked up the phone. I called agencies and groups and task forces. I asked to talk at conferences and galas and events and board meetings.

At home I made notes about what I wanted to say. I didn't just talk about homeless issues. I talked about the life of teenagers today. They were living lives of unimaginable stress, I thought. The days when a kid with a high school diploma could get a good blue-collar job, enough to raise a family and buy a home, were long over. As doctors we were seeing in children dramatic increases in adult disorders, like chronic stomach pain and fibromyalgia. Depression and mental disorders were rising rapidly. For the average teenager, I wrote, life already seemed impossible. Take all that, and then try being a teenager on the streets.

That was the speech I soon gave at a statewide conference. I had just gotten back when I got a call from Irwin Redlener, from the Children's Health Fund. "I just got off the phone with CNN," he announced. "They're starting a new segment called 'Heroes,' and it is about everyday people doing extraordinary things in their communities. Of course I suggested you. So don't be surprised if you hear from them."

Sure enough, within a week Allie Brown from CNN was on our van, the cameras trailing cords behind her. Anderson Cooper narrated the segment, and I teased Amy, knowing she had a huge crush on him. She rolled her eyes. When the show came on a few weeks later, Amy and I sat on the couch, ready with a bowl of popcorn, the kids spread across the carpet. The van appeared on-screen, and Charlotte squealed before throwing an entire box of puzzle pieces in the air to celebrate. I leaned forward to tickle her.

"Daddy's famous," Reed said.

Amy corrected him. "Almost famous." She gave me that sweet teasing smile. "We don't want you getting stuck up."

Within days the letters and donations flooded in. I was most touched by the gifts sent in from children. One little nine-year-old girl from across the country sent us a care package with important hot-weather supplies: sunscreen, caps, and bottles of water. Support came from big companies like FedEx and Metronics and Wells Fargo Bank and from various medical departments inside the Phoenix Children's Hospital. In the last several years, they told me, they had never known we needed money. I realized I had been too shy to approach other medical departments and ask for funds; it would have felt oddly like bragging. The van was getting more recognition now, and I had won humanitarian awards. Hospital staff had taken to teasingly calling me their rock star. I'd been afraid that if I approached departments for money, they would think the awards had gone to my head or that I was ignoring the contributions of my team, but now I saw how my shyness had kept us from getting the funds we needed.

I was overjoyed. I had never known how terrible I would feel if I couldn't work on the van; it was as if part of myself were missing. We had raised the money to fix the van. I was eager to get back to work. I wanted to see all the kids. As I showed up at the dock to greet Jan with a big bear hug, I thought about how much I had missed the kids, more than anything else, even the most difficult cases, like Nicole and Sugar.

□┐┌─┐┌─┐┌─┐┌─┐┌─┐

"You'll never believe who is staying here," Kim said when I stopped by the UMOM clinic. "They said they used to visit you on the van." My mind raced through the possibilities.

"I hate it when you say that," I told her. "Was it that girl with the albino sister that I told you about?"

"I wish," she said. Maybe, I hoped, Nizhoni and her sister would appear.

"It's a surprise," Kim said, opening the door to her little clinic. On the carpeted floor a toddler played, her parents sitting in the soft cushions. Sun poured through the windows. My eyes blinded by the sun outside, it took me a minute to take in the scene. The baby had soft, glossy brown hair and a pair of wide green cat eyes.

"Isn't that funny?" the mom asked, as I walked in. "She has eyes like her dad."

The parents on the cushions rose to greet me. The boy held out his hand. I recognized him immediately, the fifteen-year-old who had agreed to be the father of the unborn child conceived by rape. The girl was standing next to him, glowing and happy.

"She does have my eyes anyhow," he said. He told me how he was working in the catering business and the girl was taking her general equivalency exam.

"Where were you staying before?" I asked.

"Well, we slept for a while on the streets," the girl said. "Once we were in the hospital having the baby a social worker there called UMOM. We were lucky to get in. Darlene said as soon as we got the room, she had like ten other families apply."

"How is the baby?" I asked, and she handed her to me.

"See for yourself. Little fatty." I held the baby in my arms. She blew a big spit bubble and looked with delight at her own trick. I could tell from her skin tone and her clean, sweet breath that she was healthy. I handed her to the young man.

"A baby is always a good thing," he said. He took her with practiced ease. She stuck her fat paw in his mouth deliberately, and he laughed. "Little turkey," he said.

The girl took me aside. "Dr. Randy? You remember how you said I could always ask for help?" She acted embarrassed. "I don't know why, it's like I keep thinking about it. You know, what happened: the rape. It's weird, now that I have a place to stay. But

I keep waking up at night. I can't sleep." She hesitated. "I keep having bad dreams."

"That doesn't sound weird at all to me." I remembered how Jan had cautioned me this was what often happened with rape victims. I wrote down the name and number of a sexual assault counseling center. "This is a counselor who won't charge you. Tell her I sent you. And please, do go. It's important." As I left the young couple and their beautiful baby, I prayed that she would see the counselor. She would need help for the effects of the rape, and the two of them would need all the help they could get if they were going to be successful parents.

Outside, the sun was still bright. I smelled food cooking. A group of residents had set up old barbecues in the parking lot, and the volunteers from the RV community had joined them. Children darted here and there. "Dr. Randy, join us!" It was LaShondra and her daughter, Chantel, between her dungarees. The little girl was wearing a bright pink dress, pink shoes, and a pair of outrageous sunglasses. She gave me a huge grin as I came closer, showing even white teeth and a set of dimples.

"I really shouldn't," I said, and then spied what was cooking. "Hey, are those brats?"

LaShondra laughed and got me a plate. "Here, load up. There's potato salad too and watch out for that salsa." She watched me pile food on my plate. I thought she was hiding a smile.

"Dr. Randy needs sideboards on that plate," someone said behind me, sounding mischievous.

"Dr. Randy is getting sideboards on his tummy," I said.

12

STARFISH

I t was April Fool's Day 2008, and outside it was sheeting rain, the kind of downpour that flooded the streets and made a distant angry roaring down the dusty washes. We spent the day parked outside a family shelter. It had been an incredibly busy day, and even with Wendy and Jan with me, we were still scrambling.

More than a dozen patients showed up all at once. Three of them had to be sent directly to the hospital for serious issues. One was a pregnant fourteen-year-old with chlamydia. She had gotten pregnant, she said, from her uncle. I made the mandated phone call to the authorities, and the social worker who arrived, dashing through the rain, accompanied the girl to the hospital. She called me later. The girl had been taken into foster care, and the police had arrested her uncle for rape. Six years before, this would have thrown me for a loop. Now I just registered it with sadness.

The next boy was a long-term junkie. "I've been using since I was thirteen," he said. He was thin, with tattoos wreathing his arms, but he didn't look much like a junkie. He had friendly, narrow black eyes and an easy, self-effacing grin. He brushed his black hair out of the way with a sharp gesture.

"What do you use?" I asked.

"Black tar heroin," he said. "I like to boil it with a little coke. Then I shoot it. My arms are still pretty good, even though I've been using for six years." He held his ropy arms out. I saw the needle marks. They looked like dark chicken pox scars. Some of his veins had collapsed.

"It will kill you," I said.

"I know that. My dad died from an overdose. My whole family is junkies."

I tried to imagine. I pictured a family in a run-down apartment, the carpet stained and filthy, the windows covered with old sheets. I could see the apartment because I had been in many just like it. What I could not picture was a junkie father doing heroin with his thirteen-year-old son.

The kids were coming in soaked and coughing. A huge puddle grew outside the door. The steps malfunctioned, so I had to go out to fix them; I stepped out into a rain that turned my hair instantly into a dripping pelt. I tried to jump over the puddle and landed in three inches of water. Defeated, I went back in with my shoes drenched and my shoulders soaked. Rain ran down the back of my neck.

Along with the kids arriving in a steady flow, the health mobile phone also wouldn't stop ringing. Jan must have answered twenty-five calls in two hours. Many were from people desperate for help. But somehow, despite the organized chaos, we all were in a high good humor. When the van suddenly cleared for a few minutes, Jan had us in stitches making jokes.

"Let's play an April Fool's joke on Amy," Jan said, her eyes lighting up.

"Perfect!" I said.

I gave it a moment's thought. For Amy the joke had to be really stupid. I reached for my phone. I knew if I called her in the middle of her workday, she would not pick up. I was free to leave a voice mail. "Hi, honey? This is your dear husband," I said. Jan stifled giggles in the background. "I don't want you to worry, so I'm leaving a message. I just tripped coming out of the van. I think I hurt my arm. I don't know what to do."

Jan snickered. "The doctor doesn't know what to do."

Over the next few hours the joke escalated. I kept calling Amy back, telling her that my injury was looking worse and worse, that I had probably broken my arm.

"Help me cast it," I said at one point after getting off the phone. Jan was doubling over. A nurse we had for the day leaned against the dashboard, laughing. Some of the stress of volunteering on the van was going out of her face. I hoped she was beginning to see how necessary humor was in this work. Without it we would sail right over the edge into madness.

I made my voice as sad and plaintive as possible for the next message. "Amy? It's me. You'll have to do the dishes. And take out the trash. I'm sorry. But don't hurry home. I'll probably get there first." A few minutes later I called again. "Honey? It would be great if you picked up dinner. How about Mexican? That sounds really good. Extra sour cream for me. And we need groceries. Can you get my dry cleaning too?"

"You are *so* dead when she finds out," Jan said.

That night Amy rushed into the house. She had picked up my dry cleaning and had bags of groceries and take-out Mexican. She stopped short in the living room. By that time I had put some sort of cast on all the kids. Janie and Reed each held up a tiny cast on an arm proudly. Little Charlotte had a piece of cast over her knee. Amy's eyes followed all over our casts. Charlotte couldn't restrain herself. "April Fool's!" she shouted at the top of her lungs.

Amy's eyes narrowed, and then she smiled with recognition and embarrassment. "Dang it," she said.

Not long after, we again parked downtown, and Nicole appeared, surrounded by a group of kids. Lisa had been watching over her. I could tell she was worried. "She's really pissing people off. I saw her tell a drug dealer the other day to get off her corner. She's been shouting at people to shut up." Lisa's face was badly sunburned, as if she had fallen asleep in the open.

"How about you, Lisa?" I asked. "Have you gone to HomeBase yet?"

"Not yet."

"Why not?"

"I don't know. I'm fine by myself." I was seeing two extremes. One kid couldn't be helped because she was too crazy, while another wasn't getting help because she thought she was too smart.

Nicole was muttering and cursing in the exam room. I looked at her chart. We had been seeing her for over two years and still knew nothing about her. For someone as mentally ill as she was, to survive on the streets for so long was amazing. But it was not a triumph. She had bald spots on her scalp where she had been pulling her own hair out by the clump. The rest hung in front of her eyes. Her heart-shaped face was hollowed. There was an ugly scratch on her chin. Wendy said she thought she was decompensating, the term used when someone with a psychiatric condition begins completely deteriorating. I knew that under the madness was a beautiful girl who had been severely damaged by childhood sexual abuse. But others would not see it the same way. They would see the proverbial crazy person who sat on the street corner, shouting at people who didn't exist.

"Doctor?" A frightened little-girl voice came suddenly from under the curtain of hair.

"Becca. I'm glad to see you."

"Oh, Doctor. I'm scared."

"Scared? What scared you? How can I help?"

But the voice was mute again. Nicole stared at me through flat eyes. Becca was gone. She dug her hands through her hair and pulled out another clump of hair, and another, opening her fingers and letting the tangles of hair drop until the exam room floor was littered with them. I gently pulled down her hands, put them in her lap. I didn't know what else to do.

The front of the van was crowded with waiting kids. There was one in the intake chair, being interviewed by a volunteer, and a line down the steps. The volunteer looked up from the boy she was interviewing. The boy looked all of fourteen. As I crossed to the van steps, I could hear him saying in a monotone, depressed voice that he had been kicked out of his home. I called Amy, just to hear her voice, nothing else. From inside the exam room I could hear Nicole muttering and cursing. The noise and chaos suddenly got to me, and I stepped outside for a breath of fresh air.

We discovered a month later that Lisa had disappeared. One of the kids remarked that he had heard she had hooked up with a group of hippies passing through on their way to Mexico. Now there was no one to watch over Nicole. I began to see her less and less, only occasionally, randomly, like the day I spotted her downtown. She was rooting through a garbage can, her hair all over the place. She had found a pair of filthy baggy track shorts somewhere, and her legs were too pale and thin. I parked the van and went to her. She was sitting on the curb, eating a half muffin found in the trash. There was a new bald spot on the back of her head. It looked red and sore. "Nicole?" There was no answer. "Will you come with me?" Crumbs fell from her slack mouth. She didn't answer. I didn't think I existed to her. "Nicole?" She got up and wandered away. The tendons of her ankles stood out above scuffed shoes; she wore no socks. I called after her, but she kept walking. As I walked back to the van, I felt despair.

The next time was when a police officer brought her by the van. He had found her sleeping in an alley in nothing but panties and a shirt. With a sad look in his eyes he handed her gently over. We talked for a few moments about her; all the police in the area by now knew Nicole and tried to watch out for her. I got jeans from our supply closet in front, and Wendy helped her get changed. She had lost weight and was looking malnourished. The jeans hung off her hip bones.

And then, out of the blue, Nicole put her arms around Wendy's blond hair, leaning against her slightly. Tentatively Wendy gave her a hug. Nicole hugged her back, still voiceless, her eyes over her shoulder like a dead doll.

It was a moment that froze in perfect clarity for me. Nicole's eyes looked into me. I knew someplace behind them there was a frightened girl, hiding someplace deep in her mind, coming to us for rescue.

⃞⃞⃞⃞⃞⃞

Amy called one day while I was at work. Years had passed since her last miscarriage, but I jumped on the phone. I thought it was an emergency.

"We just got this phone call," she said.

I started to cut her off. "Amy, I am really busy."

"OK, then, Mr. Big Shot, I won't tell you it was *People* magazine."

"*People* magazine?" I echoed.

"Here, let me get some ice for that swollen head," Jan said teasingly in the background.

"The reporter said to call him when you get a chance."

He was a likable guy named Johnny Dodd, and what he wanted most was to hear what life was like for children on the streets. Soon he was flying into town. I had thought hard about what to show him. I wanted him to understand what life was really like for homeless kids. So I drove him up to Moeur Park to look at the hole that Mary had lived in. We went sliding down the shale and sand hills. He looked around at the desolate landscape. "You mean kids actually sleep out here? Yikes."

The storm drain was still there, and we crouched, looking into the fetid pit. It was still lined with old clothes and rags. I shone a flashlight down. There were rat feces scattered over the torn blankets. They could have been the same blankets as when Mary slept there. Only now another homeless kid used them. I stopped for a moment, remembering Mary looking up at me during that storm, rain like tears on her cheeks.

Johnny looked shocked. "This is one hell of a horrible place. I can't believe a girl actually lived in this hole."

"Well, it's true."

He stood up. "Hey, do you smell something?"

I did. It was warm and foul and thick. I had a flash of memory from Katrina and from visiting the farm where the sheep had died. It was a strong smell of decay. I had caught a whiff before, but the breeze had shifted, and now it was much stronger. "A dead animal, maybe," Johnny said. There was doubt in his voice. The hills stretched around us. I didn't want to go on a nature hunt for the source of the smell. I was more in mind of calling the police instead.

"Hey, look at that," Johnny said. He pointed at a hump of clothes in the bushes at the end of the wash. He walked over, and I followed, starting to argue.

"Let's call the police," I said.

Then he stopped short and recoiled. I came close enough to see why. A bloated wrist stuck out from under a dirty pale green sleeping bag. The wrist was swollen. Black insects were scrambling over a cupped palm and curled fingers. The sleeping bag covered most of the body and face. Only the wrist and a swath of reddish hair were visible lying on the hot gray rocks. While we watched, a lizard scampered over a nearby rock. The smell of death was overpowering.

"Nine-one-one," I said into my phone.

Johnny and I sat for hours in the parking lot, answering questions from the police. It was certainly unusual to find a doctor and a reporter out among the encampments of the urban homeless. A morgue van pulled up, and after some time the body, zippered into a bag, was taken out.

"Did you recognize her?" the detective asked me.

"I didn't see her face," I answered. "It was covered with that sleeping bag. I only saw her hair. It looked red. I can't say if she was a patient or not. I sure hope not." My mind rattled with thoughts of all the kids I knew with straight reddish hair.

Finally Johnny and I were allowed to go. I was going to suggest dinner, but now I wasn't sure. Johnny was quiet for a while, making notes in his little white notebook. Was everything that happened today going into *People* magazine?

"You know what I was thinking?" he asked, putting the notebook in his pocket. "That body could have been the girl you told me about, the one who slept in the hole."

A few months later Johnny's article came out. There was no mention of the body, which I had learned had been identified as an older homeless woman who had died of heat exposure. I marveled at the article. So much in a few hundred words, I thought, and I remembered his saying it could have been Mary.

I was running late. The sun, already a yellow stone in the sky, shone over a world flashing from glittering metal from car roofs. I ate trail mix by the handful as I drove to the van.

My cell phone rang.

"Randy? It's me, Jan."

"I know, I know. I'm running late," I said around a mouthful of trail mix.

"That's not it."

"Well, what is it then?" I shifted my hand on the wheel.

"It's Nicole."

"Yeah, what about Nicole?" I wasn't paying attention. I was driving.

Jan's voice was low, serious. "Randy, are you driving?"

"Yeah." Something about her voice made me catch. Was there a problem with Nicole? Was she hurt? Or was it more serious?

"What is it, Jan?"

"She was found dead. This morning."

"Dead?" The word caught in my throat. *Dead.* How could Nicole be dead? No, I thought.

"I'm sorry, Randy."

The sun flashed over the metal roofs.

"How did she die?" I heard myself ask.

"They found her body in a parking lot. They aren't sure yet, but they think it might have been a homicide."

Hearing my pulse in my ears, I saw nothing until the next exit. I pulled off the freeway into a McDonald's parking lot and saw the nose of my truck as I parked. My mind a blank, I watched people pull into the drive-through. *Dead,* I thought. I saw a woman ordering food. She had a full carload of kids, with a baby screaming in the back. Her blond hair was plastered to her cheek with sweat, and she looked harried. As I watched, an older boy leaned his cheek against his fist and looked out the window at me. I thought of Nicole. I thought of her being Becca, the child she always was for me. I looked at the red stone hills in the distance, and I imagined Nicole in a parking lot, dying. Who was Nicole, in those final minutes? Was she that little girl who would have been terrified and all alone? Was she the young brash man? Was she the dark, closed person? Would it make a difference for me to know?

I put my head in my hands, and I cried. The tears felt as if they had been pent up for years. I cried for Nicole and I cried for her scars and I cried for all the other kids I had seen who had been hurt and those who had died. I cried for the people of Katrina and the kids I wasn't able to reach. I cried for our country and the fact that despite our greatness in so many ways, we had failed this child and many others. More than anything, I cried for the realization that this precious girl was gone and would never return. Our chances had run out.

I pictured her sitting up on my exam table, asking in that childlike voice, "Am I healthy, Doctor?" And what had I said in response? "Healthy as a horse." She had said, "See? I knew I was brave enough to do it."

Yes, Nicole, I thought, you were brave enough to do it.

By the time I drove to the van I had a handle on myself. Jan met me, wiping her eyes. I spent the day in silence, helping new kids but haunted by remorse, plagued by thoughts of what I could have done for Nicole. Why hadn't I done more? I should have pressed for mental health care. I should have called members of Congress. I should have yelled from the rooftops. I had done none of those things, and the guilt pressed on me. I was sickened at how our system had failed Nicole. If only for a piece of identification she might have gotten help. But I was also angry with myself. Maybe I could have done more too.

My thoughts were interrupted when Jan poked her head into the exam room where I was finishing with a girl with diabetes. I was explaining to her how difficult it is to manage diabetes while homeless.

"Randy? There is a detective here that would like to see you."

I met him outside the van. He was a short man with red hair and very fair skin that had been damaged by the Arizona sun. Red spots of damage showed across his forehead. "Are you Dr. Christensen?"

"Yes."

"We're investigating the death of a young Jane Doe. I've spoken with some police who suggested she might be a patient of yours." He described her briefly.

I nodded. "She was our patient." I took a deep breath. "We never knew who she really was. We called her Nicole."

"No last name?"

"No last name. No real name," I answered. "No identification, nothing. The jail had her for a few days. Maybe they have a better idea. She was disturbed. Deeply disturbed . . ."

He made a few marks in his notebook, more doodles than anything. "I was there when the medical examiner was examining her." He paused delicately. He raised his red eyebrows to me. "There were scars."

"Yes," I said. "There were scars."

The detective and I held eyes for a moment longer. I wondered if he had children. I saw a wedding band on his hand. "I don't think there will be any next of kin," I said. "If you find them, let me know."

He nodded. He put his notebook away.

"So that's it?"

He gave me a look of compassion. "No one wants a girl like this to get hurt," he said softly. "We will do our best. But you probably already know that cases like this are hard." He paused. "There are some people who target homeless victims. They're easy targets. And there is no family to see that justice is done. But I will."

"I hope you can," I said. Before he left, he gave me his card in case I heard anything more.

That evening, when I walked through the door, Amy enveloped me in her arms. I had called her in advance to tell her what happened. I was doing better, I hoped, at sharing with Amy.

"What happened, Daddy?" Janie asked, running up to hug my legs. I had recently remarked to Amy that as the kids got older, it was harder for me to keep things to myself; they were like emotional sight dogs, wired into my every emotion. Amy had told me it was a good thing. I wiped my eyes.

"I lost a kid today, from the van."

Amy nodded to them. She looked as sick and sad as I felt. She herded the kids into the living room to watch a movie.

"Daddy's sad," Janie said with worry.

"Daddy will be OK," Amy told her.

We sat down to a late dinner, Amy pulling lasagna and garlic bread out of the oven while Janie told me fascinating facts about animals, trying to comfort me. Charlotte looked around. "Daddy had a bad day!" she exclaimed.

"Do you guys know why Daddy does his work?" Amy asked them, sitting down at the table.

Reed hesitated. "Because he's a doctor." He sounded older than seven.

"That's right. And what do doctors do?"

This time Charlotte spoke up. "They give people shots."

Amy smiled at her. "They do that. They also try to help people get better."

Reed looked at her. "But Daddy said one of them died. On his Big Blue van."

"She didn't die on the van," I told him. "But, yes, she died."

"How come she died?"

"We don't know yet," I said.

Charlotte looked at me. "How come you didn't save her, Daddy?"

I swallowed my milk. "I tried, honey."

"Your daddy tried because he is a doctor," Amy said in her calm, reassuring voice. "He tried because he cares about people and wants to help them. But sometimes it doesn't work. The hardest part of being a doctor is knowing you can't help everyone."

The kids were silent. Reed was staring at me with intensity. Finally Charlotte piped up. "It's OK, Daddy."

I rubbed my face with my hands. I tried to protect my kids as much as possible from the sadness of my work. On the other hand, I also wanted them to live a life of courage. Death and loss were part of being a doctor. Risk and pain were part of helping others. The dilemma was how to teach courage without traumatizing them.

We finished eating. I got up to help with the dishes, and as soon as I was done, Reed sidled up next to me. "Daddy, do you want to play with me?" he asked. "I got a cool new game called Cat in the Hat."

I dried my hands. "Sure. That sounds like fun."

He held my hand as we walked together into the living room. Amy, Janie, and Charlotte looked up at us. They all smiled. Reed sat down and set up the game. It required pulling cards that instructed us to take turns dancing around with a tiny cardboard hat and crawling under spindly canes or balancing pretend cakes on our head. Soon the whole family was playing. The kids laughed, and while the weight of Nicole's death was still a stone in my heart, somehow I felt closer to them than I ever had. That night I kissed the children as I tucked them in, murmuring my innermost feelings for them, and when I went to bed, Amy was waiting for me.

$$\sqcup \Box \sqcup \Box \sqcup \Box \sqcap$$

A few days later we held a little sunset service for Nicole. The whole team lit a candle for her outside the van. We had parked in the downtown area where we so often saw her. It was getting dark, and the sound of the freeway could be heard in the distance. We were alone, standing outside the van. It seemed like a small gesture for the end of a real person. Is this all? I thought. A girl has died at the end of years of torment and *this is it?* No one will ever know her. No justice will probably ever be done. There would be no headlines, no eulogies, no public record or memory that this was a missing child. Nicole had died and it was as if she had never existed. In our country some kids are lost forever.

I felt I had to say something. Jan passed me the candle. "I keep thinking about who Nicole was when she died," I said to the stars. "I keep wondering if she was Becca, or the young man, or one of her other personalities." I took a breath and continued. "All those people were pieces of Nicole she had to splinter apart just to survive. But now I'm thinking it doesn't matter who Nicole was when she died in that parking lot. Because now she's in a place where she can be whole."

I passed the candle to Jan. Tears were streaming down her face. She passed it to Wendy. Wendy took the candle and blew it out. We watched the wisp of smoke float up into the scarlet sky.

"Good-bye, Nicole," we said.

☐☐☐☐☐☐

"Jan, what do you think of this letter?" I asked a month later. "It's to the governor."

"The who?" She was immediately interested.

"I'm asking for change with the Medicaid insurance," I said. "I'm telling the governor we are saving the state money by taking care of these kids for free. I've shown with these statistics how much money we are saving them. But we need to revamp the system. We need to make it easier for homeless kids to get help, especially the ones with mental health problems." There was insistence in my voice. "We need to make it easier for kids like Nicole to get help."

Jan looked up from the letter. Her eyes were somber. "You're taking this pretty seriously."

"I'm mad."

She cocked her red hair to one side. The sun coming through the van's windshield showed the freckles on her face. "Usually you preach patience, at least with administrations," she told me.

"You've rubbed off on me. There's a time to fight too."

"Good luck. You'll probably get a form letter in reply."

"The voice of experience."

Later I ran into my boss at the hospital, Jeff Weiss. I told him about the letter and Jan's comment. "Oh, I've seen you get mad," he said. "Usually it isn't with governors, though. Other doctors, maybe. Come to think of it, I haven't seen an angry e-mail from you in ages," he said.

"I guess I'm learning to channel my passions," I said.

He stared at me. "This one is really bothering you."

"Yes. This is one of the ones."

"OK." He nodded. "That's good you're learning to talk about it."

"Was I bottling it before?" I asked, surprised.

"Oh, Randy, you are the *king* of bottling. All these years you've been so worried we'd think you weren't up to the job you never complained once. Let it out."

❑⌐❑⌐❑⌐

A few weeks later the FBI appeared. The agent waited patiently for the van to clear before he stepped aboard, showing me his identification. "We are investigating prostitution and sex rings in the area. The local police suggested I pay you a visit." He had brought photographs. "I'd like to see if you recognize any of these girls. We suspect they were kidnapped or sold into the sex trade."

I thumbed through the photographs. Young faces stared out at me. Brown faces, white faces, plain faces, pretty faces. Some were very young, while others were teenagers. "We're getting a lot of reports in the area," he said. "We busted one house last month. The girls had been locked up for months." He had deep brown eyes that looked as if they had seen far too much. His hair was receding, and lines were etched in his forehead.

"Where do they get the girls?" I asked.

"A lot of them are from Mexico. They're illegal, they're scared, and they don't know where they are. It's easier to keep them in a state of fear that way. But we've had plenty from around here too. Phoenix is turning into a hot spot. Some might have been homeless. No one notices they are missing."

I nodded. I had many girls tell me about being prostituted even as toddlers and young children. By the time they came on the van some had been in the sex trade for a decade, and they were only teenagers. Beyond getting them in shelters, I felt there was little I could do for them. They needed intensive, specialized counseling and a safe place to stay, and such places didn't seem to exist.

I thought about Nicole as I thumbed through the pictures. Some of the photographs were blurry. Others were grainy reproductions, many years old. Part of me was hoping, if only for a sense of closure, that I would see her in one. But a larger part of me dreaded it. None looked like Nicole. I handed them back. "We see hundreds of kids a week on this van," I said. "Thousands over the years."

"I'll be back in touch." He looked around the antiseptic walls of the van. "This is a nice outfit you got going. There are some people who work with child sex victims, in case some of your patients need help. There are a few safe houses opening up."

"Please. That would be nice."

"I'll be in touch then," he said.

13

SUGAR

In the fall of 2009 UMOM was in the process of moving its shelter from the old motel to a new and bigger facility. It was a huge improvement over the last shelter. Happy children played in a courtyard on renovated playground equipment. There was staff to guard the front. The shelter took in domestic violence victims as well as homeless families. The catering business was being reconstituted into a restaurant that would serve the public. I peeked through a dusty window. I saw leather booths and neon signs.

"This is going to be a fantastic restaurant," I told Darlene. "I can already taste the milk shakes."

Inside the main building there was a beautiful new clinic. I marveled at its size. Before, Kim had had one tiny room. This time there were four beautiful exam rooms and an office, all tucked inside the main floor. Already Kim was taping up posters and gleefully stocking cabinets. Once again the community had helped. Wal-Mart had donated sixty thousand dollars. A group of Boy Scouts was inside, trying to earn their Eagle Scout badges by stuffing fifteen hundred hygiene bags to hand out to the children.

"I can't tell you how amazing your nurse Kim has been," Darlene said as we walked the grounds. "Did you know that she's now gotten sixteen of our moms into nursing school? I don't know what strings that woman pulls, but she pulls them."

"What do you mean, she got them into nursing school?" I asked. Since I was often on the van, and Kim was at the shelter, I wasn't able to follow her achievements as much as I wished. I knew Kim was extremely competent; I just wanted to share in the challenges and successes she seemed to be experiencing in the shelter.

"You didn't know? From homeless to nursing, I can't believe it myself."

One thing I admired about Darlene was that she saw the big picture. As wonderful as UMOM was, it was not meant to be a permanent home. The goal was to move the families on to self-sustained stability. I thought of all the benefits I had had growing up. We didn't have a ton of money, but we had stability, and so much of that stability was rooted in my parents' owning a house. It was because we had a home that Stephanie and I were able to stay in the same schools, get good grades, make lifelong friends, and experience success in life. These children and their moms deserved the same stability.

I found Kim in the back, unpacking books. Her short hair was pulled back, and her tanned arms glistened with sweat. I helped lift a box.

"Kim, are you really getting these moms into nursing school?"

"Sure deal."

"How do you pay for their tuitions?"

"Oh, you know. I asked around and got some scholarships." She made it sound as if it were easy, and I realized once more how lucky I was to be surrounded by such dynamic, driven people. I listened to Kim chatter about her plans for the clinic and how this one baby was dealing with an eye infection and another mom also wanted to be a nurse, as I helped her put away books and thumbtack up new posters.

That afternoon I parked in the rough area of town. A slender blond woman was standing at the top of the van steps, blinking and readjusting her sight, having just come into the shade from the sun. I know this woman, I thought.

I thought about the first time Sugar had come swinging up into the van, so many years before. The false sexuality was gone now, burned out by the hard life she had lived. Her curly blond hair had been hacked off into a rough cut. But despite the facial scars, she was still pretty.

My heart warmed to see her. "It's good to see you," I said sincerely. It had been so long, and I had worried over her.

"Can you see me right now?" she asked.

"I'd be happy to." I led her to an exam room. She was unusually subdued. I wondered how old she was now. She had to be in her mid-twenties. Her eyes looked much older and sadder. I would have to tell her she was too old for the van. Our funding allowed us to treat children and young adults under age twenty-five. In the early days we were limited to age twenty-one, but this had changed. Soon I'd have to tell Sugar that she would need to find other medical care. I doubted she would do this. I didn't want to tell her that she couldn't return. I knew I would miss her and worry about her.

"What can I do for you today?" I asked.

She sat on the edge of the exam table she knew so well. How many times had she sat there, getting tested for STDs? More than I wanted to count. But there was something different about her this time. The dissipation had gone out of her face. It had been replaced by something new. I wasn't sure what. She placed her palms on her legs.

"I think I'm pregnant," she said.

I wasn't surprised. It was a risk of what she did to survive. "How long has it been?"

"Since I missed my period? I'm not always regular anymore. I think like three months." The lack of consistency in her cycle also didn't surprise me. It was common with women who had suffered from poor nutrition, repeated STDs, and repeated sexual violence.

"Would you like a pregnancy test?" I asked.

"I'm pretty sure I'm pregnant."

"How can you tell if you often miss a cycle?" I asked, curious.

"I don't know. I can just feel it. And I want a full STD screening."

"OK." I opened the cabinet for a disposable gown.

"Where's Jan?" she asked. She was so calm.

"She usually takes the van out on other days," I said. "It's not as often anymore we get to go out together, though I miss it. Would you like to wait for her another day?"

"No. You can do the exam. No other helpers today?"

"There's a volunteer outside." I pulled out the tray and took out a folded paper gown and handed it to her. I got ready to leave the room so she could change. "I can bring her in if you like."

She hesitated. "What if I am pregnant?"

I paused. "Would you like to discuss your options?"

Her face was still calm. "I think I know my options."

"OK. Why don't you tell me what you would like to do?" I asked gently. I was expecting her to say she wanted an abortion. I was expecting to have her ask for a referral to a clinic, since that was not a service we provided. What I didn't expect was what she said and the calm, beautiful way she delivered it, after so many years.

"I want you to help me."

I heard a clock ticking. I heard my heart beating, slowly and firmly. Some moments are too profound to be loud. She suddenly looked at the floor, vulnerable emotion sweeping her face for the first time. The real person that was Sugar, lying under all those years of pain, was finally surfacing. The emotions gave a transparency to her skin and eyes I had never seen. She looked at me with what could only be described as a wild emotion. It was something I had never seen before in her face. It was hope. She took a deep breath.

"Dr. Randy, I don't want my baby to grow up to be like me."

That evening I walked in to find kids screaming joyfully through our house. Amy had some neighbor friends over. Their kids were in school with Janie and Reed. "We went up to Dreamy Draw Park," Janie shouted at me as the kids ran by pell-mell, being chased by Ginger. She looked regal in her rust-colored shirt, which brought out her burnished hair. "You won't believe what happened today," I said.

I told her about Sugar. Amy looked at me with wide eyes. "Were you able to get her help?"

"I found her a temporary shelter until she has the baby. Then I called Darlene. She said she would make room at UMOM, even if she had to clear out a broom closet. I'm still worried, though. She has to get through her pregnancy. Anything could happen in the next few months."

Amy gave me a huge, hard hug. "She made the first step," she said. I kissed her. It turned out to be a long kiss.

"Whoa now," her friend said, coming into the room. "I'd like to know your secret." I pulled away. Amy blushed, her cheeks turning red.

"Yeah, really. Tell us all," her friend said. "My husband wants to know your secret."

"Hey!" her husband said.

"Beer?" I asked him, and he accepted a cold Budweiser. We sat at the kitchen counter and chatted. He was already planning a Super Bowl party and insisted that Amy and I join them.

"Maybe" was my answer. I tried to think of the last time I had sat down and watched an entire sports game. The answer had to be since before I started the van. "I'm going to try this year. For sure."

"Definitely," Amy said, giving me a warning look. It was a look that said I needed to make time for a sports game with friends as much as I needed to make time for her. I ate a chip and silently agreed.

Reed raced in. "Hi, Dad! We went to Dreamy Draw! We got lost."

"I'll get the kids in bed tonight," I told Amy as we cleaned up

later that night. "And how about we have waffles tomorrow morning for breakfast."

"Don't tell me you're going to cook."

"Sure I am. Homemade Eggo waffles. Fresh from the box."

She gave me a quick sideways hug, her shoulders shaking with
mirth. "At least you know your limits."

Several months passed. I drove to our new offices. We had recently
moved the offices and the van to new headquarters at UMOM.
HomeBase had fallen on hard times with the recession, and it
looked as if it might be changing hands. We were thankful that
Darlene so kindly offered us office space in her new shelter. Our
new offices were white and clean. We had a tiny kitchen and a
fridge for lunches. The walls smelled fresh with new paint, and
there were no more worries about mold and allergens. Jan, Wendy,
and Michelle were overjoyed with the new space.

I stopped at my own desk. It was crowded with grant applica-
tions. A stack of new brochures waited for approval. They were
small but professionally glossy. Our mission statement was more to
the point: providing health care to homeless youth, the brochure
said.

Already the new shelter seemed like home. I remembered my
initial hesitation at working with Darlene. Darlene clearly was a
force to be reckoned with.

It was early, but the sun was hard and bright as I left the offices and cut across the shelter courtyard. Breakfast smells filled
the air. I caught home fries and bacon and ham and cheese and
fresh homemade flour tortillas. The tortillas smelled so fresh I
could almost taste the bubbles and blackened spots. My stomach
growled, and my mouth watered. While I wasn't doing better at
eating regular meals, I took comfort in the fact I was getting a bit
more sleep.

A toddler on a Big Wheel whizzed by, his big sister merrily chasing him. There was conversational shouting in Spanish and everywhere the smell of beans put on to simmer. Some of the new rooms had kitchens. I was excited to take the van out for the day. New locations needed to be scouted.

I almost walked right past Kim. She was sitting in her nursing scrubs at one of the picnic tables with a mom and her baby.

"You're up early," I told Kim. She gave me a funny smile, and I remembered that she probably got up long before dawn to start her clinic.

Then I did a double take at the woman, who was holding a newborn baby. No, I thought. Yes. It was.

"Hey, Randy," Kim said. "I just met this nice young lady. I've been talking to her about finishing her education so she can join my nursing program."

"Hello. I'm so glad to see you." My voice was low with emotion.

Kim gave me a questioning look. I realized that she hadn't spent enough time on the van to know Sugar. She held her baby almost as a shield. Her curly blond head was lowered so I could see the part. She was acting shy. Out of her element, Sugar didn't know how to act.

"You did it," I said. The overwhelming pride I felt for my patient prevented me from calling her by the name she had had on the streets. Now she wasn't that name anymore. I had promised myself I would never use her street name, and I had not. But I didn't know what to call her now.

There was a long silence as I looked at her. I felt an overwhelming sweep of emotion, and her sudden smile back showed me she felt the same. Kim was looking between the woman and me with concern. The newborn baby on the woman's chest was small with long legs that moved restlessly. He had a narrow head with a coating of light brown hair. The baby was barely a few weeks old. Suddenly Sugar looked up at me. She still had eyes like a crystal white window. They were still so clear and bright. Maybe they would always be that way.

"What should I call you?" I asked.

She put a pacifier in her baby's mouth and stroked his fine hair. "My name, I guess."

I waited for a moment, and she told me her real name. And after so many years with so many visits between us, her name was like a private gift I didn't want to share with anyone.

"That's a nice name." I sat with them for a few minutes. Obviously still confused about how I knew the young woman but too professional to show it, Kim told me about the nursing program.

"I think you'll make a great nurse," I told her.

"You think so?" She looked startled.

"Yes, I do. Really."

She cuddled her baby. I wasn't going to say anything to her about the past. It would be hard enough for her to deal with it. The last thing she would want was a reminder. It was enough that she was safe. The happiness I felt was deep and powerful, like a current that was pulling me to a brand-new place. The woman once called Sugar was finally off the streets.

I got up to leave. "All these smells of breakfast are driving me crazy," I said.

"How's Ginger?" she asked.

"She's doing well," I said warmly. "She really adores our kids."

"Maybe someday I'll have a dog too."

"I'll bet you will."

The van was parked near the tall gates that led to the outside. The blue sides gleamed. The steps were down. Jan was already on board, stocking the van for the day.

"Ready?" she asked.

"Just about." I went to fold up the steps.

"Dr. Randy?"

My old patient once called Sugar was standing at the bottom, as she had so many times before, though now she wouldn't be climbing the steps to receive medical treatment.

"Yes?"

"My sister—do you think we can still find her?"

I saw the baby nestled on her chest. "I think we can," I said.

My mother had continued to struggle with pain following her operation. She was often in the hospital having tests. As before, I felt split in different directions, helping my mother as well as my sister, but I felt I was handling it better now. I also was realizing that I could count on others, like Amy and Stephanie's husband, Curtis, who remained a rock-solid support.

I was in my parents' kitchen in Gilbert, over for Sunday supper, supposedly helping put leftover food away, but really just noshing on the food and hanging out with my mom. She sat on the tall barstool she kept in the middle of the kitchen. She liked to sit there and direct activity. "Stop," she said, leaning forward and lightly smacking my hand away from the baked pasta. "We haven't even had dessert yet."

I started pulling down dessert plates and opened the cupboard drawer for forks. Mom sat on her stool. Beyond her I could see the wide green expanse of watered lawn behind the house; to one side I could see the neighbors' horses. From the other room I could hear Dad playing with the kids. They were running around, laughing. I could also hear Stephanie. She was sitting in front of our parents' computer, talking to Amy. Curtis was someplace out back with their boys. But the happy atmosphere was not to last. My mom had sad news to deliver.

"Randy, you know I had another biopsy. Well, it looks like the cancer is back."

Stunned, I put the forks down.

We had a family meeting that night. Mom smiled for our kids and Stephanie's sons. As always she was gentle and warm with the grandkids. But as soon as they ran to play out back while the sun was setting, she broke down a little. She cried while Dad held her on the couch. "The doctors say I can't handle any more surgery."

"What about more chemo?" Amy asked quietly.

Mom frowned. "I can try, but it doesn't look good."

Dad passed her a tissue. She wiped her face. There was silence in the room. I knew what this meant. My mom was not going to win this war.

Stephanie sat on the couch, holding in her lap a needlepoint pillow that Mom had made. Curtis had his hand on her knee. Amy was sitting on the other couch, absorbing everyone's pain, ready to help. I took a breath. If the colon cancer had returned, the survival rate would be very low even with aggressive treatment. I wondered if my mother knew she would likely die. From outside Reed yelled something at Janie. It had to do with lizards.

Everyone looked at me. For once I didn't want to be the doctor in the family. Was I supposed to speak the truth? Not here, in front of everyone. That was a conversation I would have to have with Mom in private. "We'll do our best, Mom," I said. I looked down and saw I was touching my own wedding ring.

I felt Amy's compassionate gaze. Amy was also a doctor. She knew too.

On the way home from my parents' I had prepared myself for a breakdown once I was alone. But I was OK. Maybe I wasn't meant to break down on a regular basis, I thought. If I did, with my work, I would be breaking down all the time. Maybe I was made for this work after all, I thought. Maybe I was getting stronger. It didn't mean the pain was less. Maybe it just meant I could handle it more.

"Randy?" It was Amy. "You've been sitting in front of your computer for hours. Come to bed."

"I'm sorry. I meant to talk to you, I did."

She came and stroked my head. "Honey, you don't have to talk to me all the time. Some of the time is just fine." She stroked my hair gently, caressing my scalp. When we went to bed, she curled against my back. I still didn't break down. But the peace I felt gave me the same result.

⌐⌐⌐⌐⌐

It doesn't matter how many times you say good-bye. It's never enough. The day after Thanksgiving I stopped by a video rental and got a DVD of *Sleeping Beauty*. I took it to my mom in hospice. When I was small, growing up in the small town of Kremmling, Colorado, children's movies rarely played in the town's only theater. But one day a movie came to town. It was *Sleeping Beauty*. I begged my mom to take me. "It was the first movie you ever took me to see," I told her as we watched it by her white hospital bed. "No wonder I've always believed in happy endings." We both cried a little.

The holidays were coming, but our celebrations felt muted. I spent most of my time with Mom in hospice. On December 16, 2009, she passed away. My dad, Stephanie, and I were by her side at the hospice. She had grown smaller. In her arms, she held some family photos. Two were of her and Dad. The rest were of her grandkids. In one photo Janie and Charlotte and Reed were lying in the grass, laughing. Next to her on the bed stand was an old-fashioned book she had made in my childhood. I opened it. She had taped in every report card, every article about me as an adult. The thick yellow pages felt delicate under my fingers.

I felt we all were doing OK and handling the loss. At least it seemed so to me. Then, in the days following the funeral, I noticed Reed was taking his stuffed turtle with him everywhere he went. I couldn't figure it out. "You didn't take your turtle to school again today, did you?" I asked teasingly one night.

"Yeah," he replied, clutching it tight. "We looked for lizards."

Amy solved the mystery one night. She showed me a poster that Reed had made at school. "Everyone in his class made a poster about themselves," Amy said. Reed had drawn his twin sister and Charlotte. There was a blue van, with me standing next to it. There was Amy with her curly hair. Up in the clouds was his grandma Maria. She had angel wings. At the bottom was a green turtle.

"He told the class his grandma gave him that turtle," Amy said.

□□□□□

Not surprisingly, I was back at work within a few days. If there was anything in life that made me feel normal, I thought, it was doing the job I love. As hard as it was, I found solace in caring for the homeless kids.

Jan and I had had a long day. She hummed as she drove us back to the dock. It was hard to believe she was now sixty. Her teenage kids were now adults. She had recently told me that she wanted to spend her last years before retirement on the van working with the kids. When I thought about her eventually leaving, I felt sad. She and I had started this adventure together, and I couldn't imagine continuing without her.

Jan was telling me about procedures for the new clinic at UMOM. "We're getting it licensed," she remarked.

"You're the expert at licensing," I said in a praising tone. "We always pass inspections thanks to you."

We drove back to the dock in companionable silence. I thought of the dinner I was planning that night with Amy and our children. We were going to grill some hamburgers, and then I was hoping we all could go out together to walk Ginger and look at the stars.

I looked out the window and saw not street corners and alleys but places where homeless kids might be waiting. Around each corner, I thought, were more kids who needed our help. I was eager to find them.

"We've been down a long road together, Jan," I said.

"Don't get all sentimental on me," she said.

"OK."

She tossed me a quick grin. "You're a good friend."

"You too, Jan."

14

BEGINNINGS

The spring sun filled the bedroom, and I woke up thinking, *This is why people live in Arizona.* It's a perfect seventy degrees while other parts of the country are blanketed in snow. It was spring 2010. Then, with a tingle of excitement and wonder, I remembered: It's been ten years since I started the van. A decade.

My schedule quickly played through my mind: volunteer breakfast, then an important phone call at 11:00 A.M., then a meeting with the team, and taking the van out to a new location.

The other day Jan had given me the count. In the last decade, our van had seen close to seven thousand children. It seemed like a miracle. But as much as that was, it still felt like a fraction of the children I wanted to help. There were so many more in Arizona and across the country. *Seven thousand,* and it seemed I could remember them all, in a parade of smiles and souls and hearts. I thought of the ones I had helped and the ones I had never seen again: Mary, who had written from the university; the last card she said she was going for a master's degree. Donald, still married and living in Pastor Richardson's house, having taken over the drywall business. Sugar, moved out of UMOM and doing well on her own with her baby, reunited with her sister, who had grown up in foster care after their mother had been committed. I thought of the ones who had moved on, whom I still longed to hear from. I thought of Nicole with a sharp pang. Part of me still expected to see her in my exam room, waiting for help, still needing help. My grief over her would never fully go away. But of course I couldn't let it stop me from finding the kids like her, the desperate cases that I hoped I would be able to turn around.

I got up and dressed. The face that greeted me in the mirror was forty-three. I thought: Remember when you were thirty-three, starting the van? When you couldn't imagine doing this job for even five years? There were lines worn into my forehead. My once-thick brown hair was mostly gone, and I sported a short, tight haircut, a dramatic change from my younger years, when I wore my hair long. I no longer looked like the bright-eyed young doctor who had marched with determination into his boss's office to say he should be the one to run a brand-new mobile medical clinic. That doctor had been full of passion and zest and sometimes anger. This doctor was a little travel worn, with more humility and an invaluable library of experiences to draw upon.

The cargo pants had been replaced by more serious trousers, the codebooks by a BlackBerry. If I accidentally left it at home, I didn't panic the same way, though I did panic a bit. My attire had become more professional. I wanted to look more serious. It helped the kids understand that I could be trusted to help them. This was something I had learned from Jan: to be comfortable being in charge, because the kids needed that.

Amy, Reed, Janie, and Charlotte tumbled from bed. The tiny smile lines around my wife's mouth gave her grace. She was certainly aging better than I. She barely looked any different now from when we had first met fifteen years before. If anything, Amy at forty-two looked more beautiful than ever.

Reed and Janie were eight now, and Charlotte was six. They brushed their own teeth, chattering quietly in the bathroom. I felt a tug in my heart at how quickly their childhoods were passing. Reed and I had just taken a father-son dune buggying trip out into the nearby mountains. We had gone fishing at Rose Canyon Lake at Mount Lemmon. He caught his first fish, a rainbow trout.

Ginger came wagging into the bedroom. She'd been shaved for the coming summer season, and her soft underbelly fur was much lighter than her head and fluffy tail, giving her a Creamsicle look. There was gray in her muzzle, and her brown eyes were somewhat opaque. Recently she had started losing her hair and had developed one health problem after another. She was getting to be an old dog.

I emerged from the house to a fresh morning. In our driveway was my new hobby, an old Toyota MR2, just like the one my friend Danny and I had dreamed about. I claimed it just needed a lot of work, while Amy had slightly less polite things to say about my rusting heap. The kids called it Daddy's race car, giving Amy endless amusement. I had realized I needed to have a bit of fun and stress relief—or comic relief perhaps—in my life. Working on the car with the kids brought back memories of my own childhood, under the hood with my father. I didn't care if it ever ran.

In my same old truck, I drove to UMOM for the breakfast meeting. It was more of a celebration actually, to welcome new volunteers. Our whole team would be there. Thanks to grants and the support of the community, I had recently been able to hire several new people to supplement the core group. I finally had the solid team I had wanted. The days of having to take the van out alone or with just one or two helpers were over.

Jan was at the door of the conference room as I arrived. Nearby were nurses Julie Watson and Kim Williams, wearing bright yellow scrubs bearing the Crews'n Healthmobile logo. Nora Thibeault, the case manager, and Reece Tovar, the financial specialist, sat together at the far end. Rounding out the crew was Dr. Cody Conklin, our newest addition. No one had been more surprised or pleased than I when the award of funds from the American Idol Gives Back program fulfilled my dream of hiring another doctor for the van. When Dr. Conklin wasn't on the van, she was out riding her horse. I noticed that she was still wearing her riding boots this morning. There was hay on the soles.

In addition to welcoming new volunteers, I was honoring an old one. Up front, I explained to everyone assembling, "Today we are honoring a volunteer who started a few years back as a college student. In part because of his work and dedication to homeless kids, he was just accepted into Tufts Medical School. We know he is going on to be a fine doctor. Alex, will you stand up?"

The room broke into loud applause, as his young face slightly pink, Alex stood up. Then he came up to accept a token of the team's appreciation: a brand-new stethoscope engraved with his name.

I watched the faces of the team and the volunteers, glowing with enthusiasm and a sense of purpose. Over the last ten years, so much had changed. When I started, the concept of universal health care wasn't even on the table. Back then most people didn't seem aware of the devastating effects that a lack of insurance had on the poor, especially homeless children. Now that seemed to be changing, and I was hopeful that someday soon everyone would have easier access to medical care.

The kids certainly deserved it. It wasn't acceptable for them to be forgotten. They were survivors. They were funny, kind, talented, and creative, and they desperately wanted to have happy futures. The societal response had been to ignore them, or put them in jail, or condemn them to marginal lives on the fringes. But after ten years on the van, I felt more strongly than ever that the prevailing treatment of homeless children in the United States was morally wrong. These were children who could be saved. They *deserved* to be saved.

The future of the country, I thought, depends on the next generation, yet I worried that we are failing our children. As the economy had worsened, more kids were hitting the streets. The high rates of depression, suicidal thinking, and anxiety I had been seeing were skyrocketing. The kids weren't being prepared for adulthood, weren't getting the tools and opportunities necessary for successful lives. Instead of jobs and stable families, they got violent video games and reality shows. Girls were taught to care more about their bodies than their minds. Boys were given the weapons to express anger, not the nourishment of character to grow into men.

Children were the same everywhere, I thought. The kids I saw in Arizona were not fundamentally different from the ones in New York or Miami or Louisiana. In many ways the children across our country who were not getting adequate medical care were living in conditions similar to those in an underdeveloped nation. Society didn't want to admit that, but it was true. We are such a rich country, I thought, with so many caring people. It hurts me to think that we let this happen. As much as I loved my country, and as much as I thanked it for all the gifts it had given my family, I still believed we all shared the responsibility for taking care of our children. It was imperative that we ensure their access to medical care and mental health treatment and dental care. It had been talked about enough; now it was time for action.

If I had learned anything on the van, it was to listen to kids. They hungered for adults who truly cared and could offer advice and assistance as they navigated this often frightening new world. And they needed to see role models, to see the adults in their lives helping the homeless, or bringing meals to the elderly, or simply being good neighbors. When adults showed they cared, they strengthened their families and their communities and neighborhoods, and they showed children that life could be lived with passion and hope. I thought about my own kids. Before I knew it, they would be teenagers themselves, growing up, and finding passions in life. I hoped I could inspire them to help others too.

"Randy?" It was Michelle, leaning over my shoulder and interrupting my thoughts. "Don't forget you have that important phone call." She tapped her watch. Michelle had taken over our program director activities from Jan and now controlled my schedule.

"That's right, thanks," I said. I was startled to see it was almost 11:00 A.M. I walked outside, waiting for the call.

My cell rang right when I had expected. It was a nurse-practitioner from the Midwest. She had been working for a hospital that was seriously considering expanding into the community. The area was on economic hard times, and they knew there were many in the community who needed help. So her hospital board had asked her to research a mobile medical unit and then write a proposal. "I did a quick Google search and there you were," she said. "I'll be frank and tell you I know nothing about mobile health care." That sounds like me when I started, I thought. I began taking her through the process. The costs shocked her. "There's gas, insurance, huge maintenance bills, and honestly it combines with the higher overheard of running a small practice," I said. "But a van does have the one advantage that makes it worthwhile. You can take the care where it is needed. There is no other practice that allows you to pick up and drive to where the patients need you."

I spent the next hour pacing outside our offices, taking her on a step-by-step journey through the process of creating a mobile health unit. As we finished, I offered to share with her much of our initial research on the rules and regulations, so she wouldn't have to reinvent the wheel. I wished her luck.

When I returned to the conference room, the table was cleaned and the trash can was overflowing with paper plates. Our offices were nearly empty, meaning the team would be waiting for me on the van, parked outside.

My positive feelings kept me buoyed throughout the afternoon, as I treated a long line of kids. I made sure I stopped for a quick snack of string cheese and an apple. I recognized that nowadays I was happier. It was because of talking to Amy. On the eve of the van's anniversary so many things had been on my mind, and Amy helped me sort them out. Among them was my need to trim my schedule. If I wanted to be the right kind of father and husband, I had told Amy, I had to cut back on all the extras.

So Amy and I had agreed I would train someone to take over my job at the diabetes camp. I had also decided to no longer take the tests to remain certified in adult medicine. From now on it was going to be pediatrics only. But the decision that shocked some other doctors was that I was going to quit "rounding," or visiting hospital patients. For a doctor such rounds were considered important in maintaining a staff position. But I thought I should free my time for what mattered more, which was my family and the van.

My job was now just seeing patients on the Big Blue. What I was giving up in additional job security I was gaining in peace of mind. I knew now exactly what was important to me.

"Everything will work out," Amy had reassured me during one of our marathon talks, when I had worried over finances and the future.

"You always say that," I said.

"As long as we talk," she said.

"We will, always," I told her.

I had help now too. I thought about a recent incident on the van. Dr. Cody was on the van while I was attending to administrative duties at the hospital. She called me in a panic. An extremely sick kid had shown up. She had flown into action, taking a blood oxygen reading. His oxygen stats were dangerously low. She had already called the ambulance, she said, and he was now in emergency care. I told her she had done exactly the right thing. It had hit me later how I was now training other people to carry on the same work. Much of being a healer, I realized now, was not just taking care of patients, but training and encouraging others to do the same.

The afternoon passed quickly, and soon enough I was on my way home. It had been a good day, I thought. A good anniversary. The clock on the dash said it was 6:20 P.M. I had the entire evening free. I could have supper with Amy and the kids, walk the dog, and then help with bathing and bedtime with the kids. There would be time for Amy and me to sit around after the kids were asleep. We could talk, maybe, or watch a movie.

But first, I thought, I'd stop at the ice-cream parlor and pick up some peppermint ice cream for Amy.

FOR MORE INFORMATION AND HOW TO HELP

1. Spend time with your children. Play their video games with them, listen to their music, listen to their stories.

2. Volunteer in your communities. Get involved. Vote.

3. Donate to worthy organizations if you have the means. Here are a few agencies that are mentioned in this story, or are close to my heart:

   www.crcwsnhealthmobile.com
   www.childrenshealthfund.org
   www.umom,org
   www.diabetes.org/adacampazda

ACKNOWLEDGMENTS

Now writing these final words, I feel a sense of accomplishment. But any achievements or goals that have been reached are directly related to the support, advice, and guidance from my family, friends, and mentors. I want to take the opportunity to graciously thank them for helping me along this journey. To my childhood friends, Danny Center, Kim Briamonte, and Greg Davis: you started me out on the path to success. To my high-school friends Tim Sellers, Rob Walsh, and Jeff Thomasson, you made the high-school job meaningful and fun. My college friends and fraternity brothers Glen Mandigo, Jay Ferguson, Mark McLear, John Muehrcke, and Joel Rapp gave me memories to last a lifetime. In addition I want to give a special thanks to Marshall Brennan, who often listened to my ramblings as I tried to piece together the stories and to Ron Couturier, who is the godfather to my children, and that should say enough.

To my medical-school classmates Melissa Smith, Holly Gallivan, and Kimberly Barrie, you made that chaotic time enjoyable. For my colleagues and peers Donna Holland, Sarah Beaumont, Michelle Huddleston, and Jeffrey Weiss, you all set the bar so high for yourselves that I become a better doctor just being around you. To Darlene Newsom at UMOM, thanks for helping out the program when we had no place to go. To my mentors Dr. Jack Copeland and Dr. Irwin Redlener, you both are my heroes and I hope you know how much better the world is just because you cared. The leaders at Phoenix Children's Hospital, CEO Bob Meyer and senior Vice President Steve Schnall, showed me what it meant to truly believe in caring for the community. To Nathaniel Jacks and Richard Pine, my agents at Inkwell Mangement, thanks for believing in the power of these stories. You have never waivered in your commitment to telling the world about homeless children. This story could not have happened without Jenna Ciongoli, my editor at Broadway Books, whose suggestions and comments took the story to the next level. To Rene Denfeld, you were able to able to take my jumbled thoughts and put them to paper with such visual intensity that every time I read the story I am living it. And for my team on the Crews'n Healthmobile, you are the reason for the success of this program. I applaud your dedication and commitment. Each and every one of you has been an asset to our program, and it could not have happened without you: Jan Putnam, Michelle Ray, Wendy Speck, Cody Conklin, Julie Watson, Kim Williams, Reece Tovar, and Nora Thibeault. Lastly I thank my wonderful family, who supported me and picked me up when I thought I couldn't get up any more. Mom, I love you. Dad, I am so proud to be your son. Stephanie, Curtis, Matthew, and Trevor, you all mean so much to me. Amy, you are everything I need and all that I want. You make me a better person every day I am with you. Janie, Reed, and Charlotte: one day you will grow up and read this book. I hope it helps you understand how much I love you, and why it hurts so much to be away from you.

ABOUT THE AUTHORS

RANDY CHRISTENSEN, MD, is a staff physician at Phoenix Children's Hospital. Since 2000, he has been the medical director of Crews'n Healthmobile, a mobile medical clinic that provides primary and comprehensive medical care to homeless children. Dr. Christensen has been the recipient of several awards for his work, including the *CNN* Heroes award and *People* Magazine's "Heroes Among Us." He lives in Phoenix with his wife, Amy, also a pediatrician, and their three children.

RENE DENFELD is the author of three books, including the international bestseller *The New Victorians* (1995) and has written for *The New York Times Magazine,* the *Philadelphia Inquirer,* and the *Oregonian.* A passionate advocate for the adoption of foster children, she lives in Portland, Oregon, with her three children, all adopted from foster care.